AMERICAN
COLLEGE
REGALIA

AMERICAN COLLEGE REGALIA

A Handbook

Compiled by
Linda Sparks
and
Bruce Emerton

Greenwood Press
New York • Westport, Connecticut • London

Library of Congress Cataloging-in-Publication Data

Sparks, Linda.
    American college regalia.

    Includes index.
    1. Universities and colleges—United States—
Insignia—Handbooks, manuals, etc. I. Emerton, Bruce.
II. Title.
LB3630.S64   1988   378.73   88-188
ISBN 0-313-26266-7 (lib. bdg. : alk. paper)

British Library Cataloguing in Publication Data is available.

Library of Congress Catalog Card Number: 88-188
ISBN: 0-313-26266-7

First published in 1988

Greenwood Press, Inc.
88 Post Road West, Westport, Connecticut 06881

Printed in the United States of America

∞

The paper used in this book complies with the
Permanent Paper Standard issued by the National
Information Standards Organization (Z39.48-1984).

10 9 8 7 6 5 4 3 2 1

CONTENTS

PREFACE

As reference librarians at the University of Florida we often receive questions requesting various facts about colleges and universities, which we refer to as college regalia. Occasionally school histories furnish part of the information as do several reference books but nowhere is it located in a single, easy to use source. We hope this book will fill a basic reference need for school, academic, and public libraries.

Because we perceived a need for this information, we began researching and compiling data in the Fall of 1986. American College Regalia was conceived as a comprehensive source for such information as nickname, mascot, school newspaper, school colors, school yearbook, fight song and alma mater for American colleges and universities with enrollment of 2,500 or above.

Letters requesting information were sent to Offices of Information and Publicity and/or the president of each institution. The completeness of institutional information was dependent on the extent of material received from each. In some cases fight songs and alma maters could not be included because of copyright restrictions. In several cases, copyright permission for songs was received too late for inclusion. Many institutions were included for which all material was not available. After several requests, if no response was received, the institution had to be omitted. 469 schools are included. We have attempted to be as accurate as possible. A draft was sent to each institution for approval and editing. Any errors are unintentional.

Acknowledgement and appreciation is expressed to the many individuals who participated in the compiling of the information included. Without their cooperation this book would not be possible. Our colleagues in the University of Florida Libraries, especially in the Systems Department, have helped in many ways. We would also like to thank the staff of the Faculty Support Center for their technical assistance.

ALABAMA

Alabama State University
915 S. Jackson St.
P.O. Box 271
Montgomery, AL 36195-0301

School Nickname: *ASU*

School Colors: *Old Black and Gold*

School Mascot: *Hornet*

School Newspaper: *ASU Today (official) Hornet Tribune (student paper)*

School Yearbook: *The Hornet*

Alma Mater: *University Hymn*

> Alabama State, O Mother Dear
> Again we come to thee
> Our pains and sorrows we forget
> When e'er thy face we see,
> O happy harbor, blessed place
> O sweet and pleasant soil,
> In thee we hope, in thee we trust
> For thee we pray and toil

Thy Sons and Daughters love thy halls,
Aglow with truth and light
And every heart beats true to thee,
In whom there is no night.
O Alma Mater, fair and dear,
We proudly hail thy name
Which far and near is known and loved
And crowned with glowing fame.

Thy campus flowers and shady walks
Bring thoughts of Marion Green
Before thy trials in Beulah Vale,
Which God from us did screen.
But now we stand on College Heights
Content with God's decree
For all He does is right and good
And makes for liberty.
                  McCall, '00

Fight Song: *Hail Alabama Fight Song*

Hail, Alabama State University
How we love your name.
Your spacious halls respond with knowledge
Deeds extol your fame.
Hurrah, hurrah for the Black and Gold!
Hurrah, hurrah for heroes bold!
Dear Alma Mater, we will adore you,
In one loud acclaim.

        Chorus
Alabama! Alabama!
Hail, hail, hail, hail college so dear
Alabama! Alabama!
'tis for you we'll cheer
All hail the men who fight on the field
All hail your glory that can't be repealed;
So hail, hail, hail Alabama!
Hail, hail, hail!

        Trio
To the Black and Gold
Let our giant echoes roll
In the breeze, on the air,
Let our banner wave so fair,
Sing Hurrah, sing Hurrah,
Sing Hurrah, rah-rah-rah-rah
Hey!
            (Back to Chorus)

Auburn University
Auburn, AL 36849

School Nickname: *Tigers*

School Colors: *Orange and Blue*

School Mascot: *Eagle (golden eagle)* Name: *Tiger*

School Newspaper: *The Auburn Plainsman*

School Yearbook: *The Glomerata*

Alma Mater: *The Alma Mater*

On the rolling plains of Dixie
'Neath its sun-kissed sky,
Proudly stands, our Alma Mater
Banners Higʰ

To thy name we'll sing thy praise,
From hearts that love so true,
And pledge to thee our
Loyalty the ages through.

We hail thee, Auburn, and we vow
To work for thy just fame,
And hold in memory as we do now
Thy cherished name.

Hear thy students voices swelling.
Echoes strong and clear,
Adding laurels to thy fame
Enshrined so dear.

From thy hallowed halls we'll part,
And bid thee sad adieu;
Thy sacred trust we'll bear with us
The ages through.

We hail thee, Auburn, and we vow
To work for thy just fame.
And hold in memory as we do now
Thy cherished name.
                    Bill Wood, '24
                    Word revision, '60

Fight Song: *War Eagle*

>War...Eagle, fly down the field, Ever to conquer, never to yield.
>War...Eagle fearless and true. Fight on, you orange and blue.
>Go! Go! Go!
>On to Vic'try, strike up the band, Give'em hell, Give'em hell.
>Stand up and yell, Hey! War...Eagle, win for Auburn,
>Power of Dixie Land.

Jacksonville State University
Jacksonville, AL 36265

School Colors: *Red and Gray*

School Mascot: *Gamecock*

School Newspaper: *Chanticleer*

School Yearbook: *Mimosa*

Samford University
800 Lakeshore Dr.
Birmingham, AL 35229

School Colors: *Red and Blue*

School Mascot: *Bulldog*

School Newspaper: *Samford Crimson*

School Yearbook: *Entre Nous*

Alma Mater: *Alma Mater*

>Oh Samford Alma Mater true
>Her halls shall ever ring,
>With sounding glories of the past
>With plans and future dreams.
>On knowledge that we seek, O Lord,
>We pray thy blessings true.
>With pride we pledge our hearts
>and minds,
>To the Samford Red and Blue.

Fight Song: *Fight Song*

> Fight, Fight, Fight, for Samford Bulldogs going
> onward to victory.
> Oh, we'll wear the red and blue,
> Samford we're all for you ... and we love you too!
> Fight, Fight, Fight, for Samford Bulldogs go
> onward to victory.
> Oh, we'll give a cheer or two,
> Samford we're all for you ... Fight! Fight! Fight!

Troy State University
Troy, AL 36082

School Nickname: *Trojans*

School Colors: *Red and Black*

School Mascot: *T-Roy*

School Newspaper: *The Tropolitan*

School Yearbook: *The Palladium*

Alma Mater: *T.S.U. Alma Mater*

> Our vow of love, our vows of faith dear school we've said to thee.
> Each strong man, each gentle maid will ever loyal be.
> Not for a day, not for a year shall we each other greet.
> As fellow students fellow friends but till in heav'n we meet.
> So, hail, Alma Mater, dear school we all love thee.
> So, hail, Alma Mater, We'll aye be true to thee.
> So when in days that are to come fond mem'ries we recall.
> The mem'ries of dear Troy State, We'll cherish most of all.
> Your stately portals spacious halls in dreams we will enjoy.
> And hearts again will sadly yearn for you, and days at Troy.

Fight Song: *Trojans, One and All*

> Here's to the school we love,
> We are Trojans, one & all.
> We will always cheer for victory,
> And you'll never let us fall--
> GO! GO! GO!
> Cheers to old Troy State;
> We are with you all the way,
> So get out there team
> And FIGHT! FIGHT! FIGHT!
> And win today!

Tuskegee University
Tuskegee, AL 36088

School Nickname: *Skegee*

School Colors: *Crimson and Gold*

School Mascot: *Tiger*

School Newspaper: *Campus Digest*

School Yearbook: *Tuskeana*

Alma Mater: *The Tuskegee Song*

> Tuskegee, thou pride of the swift growing South.
> We pay thee our homage today.
> For the worth of thy teaching, the joy of thy care;
> And the good we have known 'neath thy sway.
> Oh, long-striving mother of diligent sons.
> And daughters, whose strength is their pride.
> We will love thee forever, and ever shall walk
> Thro' the oncoming years at thy side.
>
> Thy hand we have held up the difficult steeps.
> When painful and slow was the pace.
> And onward and upward we've labored with thee
> For the glory of God and our race.
> The fields smile to greet us, the forests are glad.
> The ring of the anvil and hoe
> Have a music as thrilling and sweet as a harp
> Which thou taught us to hear and to know.
>
> Oh, mother Tuskegee, thou shinest today
> As a gem in the fairest of lands;
> Thou gavest the heaven 'n-blessed power to see
> The worth of our minds and our hands.
> We thank thee, we bless thee, we pray for thee years
> Imploring with grateful accord,
> Full fruit for thy striving, time longer to strive.
> Sweet love and true labor's reward.
> > *Words by Paul Laurence Dunbar*
> > *Music by N. Clark Smith*

University of Alabama
Tuscaloosa, AL 35487

School Nickname: *Crimson Tide* *

School Colors: *Crimson and White*

School Mascot: *Big Al* *

School Newspaper: *The Crimson and White*

School Yearbook: *Corolla*

Alma Mater: *Alma Mater*

> Alabama, listen Mother
> To our vows of love,
> To thyself and each other
> Faithful friends we'll prove.
> > *Chorus:*
> Faithful, loyal, firm and true
> Heart bound to heart will beat
> Year by year the ages through
> Until in heaven we meet.
>
> College days are swiftly fleeting.
> Soon we'll leave thy halls,
> Ne'er to join another meeting
> 'Neath thy hallowed walls.
> > *Chorus*
> So, farewell, dear Alma Mater,
> May thy name, we pray,
> Be reverenced, pure and stainless
> As it is today.

Fight Song: *Yea Alabama!!*

> Yea Alabama
> Crimson Tide!
> Every 'Bama man's behind you
> Hit your stride.
> Go teach the Bulldogs to behave
> Send the Yellow Jackets to a watery grave.
> And if a man starts to weaken
> That's a shame.
> For 'Bama's pluck and grit have
> Writ her name in Crimson flame.
> Fight on, fight on, fight on men
> Remember the Rose Bowl, we'll win then.
> So roll on to victory
> Hit your stride.
> You're Dixie's football pride
> Crimson Tide, Roll Tide, Roll Tide!!!

*Registered trademarks of the Board of Trustees of The University of Alabama. These items cannot be reprinted or reproduced without permission from the University.

University of Alabama at Birmingham
University Station
Birmingham, AL 35294

School Nickname: *UAB Blazers*

School Colors: *Green and Gold*

School Mascot: *Beauregard T. Rooster*

School Newspaper: *Kaleidoscope*

School Yearbook: *Phoenix*

Fight Song: *UAB Blazer Fight Song*

> At UAB in Birmingham
> All hail our players bold.
> They are the mighty Blazers
> Who wear the green and gold,
> Tonight let's fire their golden blaze,
> The flame of victory.
> Go Blazers!
> Go Blazers!
> Win for UAB.
> *Joel Hearn*

University of Alabama in Huntsville
Huntsville, AL 35899

School Nickname: *Chargers*

School Colors: *Blue and White*

School Mascot: *Charger Blue*

School Newspaper: *Exponent*

University of Montevallo
Montevallo, AL 35115

School Nickname: *Falcons*

School Colors: *Purple and Gold*

School Newspaper: *The Alabamian*

School Yearbook: *The Montage*

Alma Mater: *Alma Mater*

> "Alma Mater ever glorious,
> Seeking Right and Freedom's way,
> Raise a beacon high to guide us;
> Shed thy light afar, we pray.
>
> Sons and daughters sing thy praises;
> Steadfast virtues win thee fame,
> May the years be rich and fruitful,
> Truth and Honor crown thy name."
> *Virginia Powell Figh*
> *Lucy L. Underwood*

University of North Alabama
Florence, AL 35632-0001

School Nickname: *Lions*

School Colors: *Purple and Gold*

School Mascot: *Lion* Name: *Leo (a live, 500-lb. lion)*

School Newspaper: *The Flor-Ala*

School Yearbook: *Diorama*

Alma Mater: *Alma Mater*

> In the Sunny heart of Dixie,
> On the Tennessee,
> Stands the school we owe all honor,
> Love and Loyalty.
>
> Happy days within thy portals
> Bless our memory;
> Friendships dear and truths immortal,
> We have found in thee.
>
> Through the future generations
> Honored by thy name;
> May thy sons and daughters bring thee
> Everlasting fame.

Chorus
Alma Mater, Alma Mater;
Bring we homage due;
Pledge we here our heart's devotion
To our colors true.

University of South Alabama
307 University Blvd.
Mobile, AL 36688

School Nickname: *Jaguars*

School Colors: *Red, White and Blue*

School Mascot: *Southpaw*

School Newspaper: *The Vanguard*

School Yearbook: *Nexus*

ALASKA

University of Alaska-Fairbanks
Fairbanks, AK 99775

School Nickname: *UAF*

School Colors: *Blue and Gold*

School Mascot: *Nanook (means polar bear in the language of the Eskimos)*

School Newspaper: *SunStar*

School Yearbook: *Denoli*

ARIZONA

Arizona State University
Tempe, AZ

School Nickname: *ASU - The Sun Devils*

School Colors: *Maroon and Gold*

School Mascot: *Sun Devil*   Name: *Sparky*

School Newspaper: *State Press*

School Yearbook: *Sun Devil Spark*

Alma Mater: *Alma Mater*

> Where the bold saguaros
> Raise their arms on high,
> Praying strength for brave tomorrows
> From the western sky;
> Where eternal mountains
> Kneel at sunset's gate,
> Here we hail thee, Alma Mater,
> Arizona State.
> > *Ernest Hopkins*
> > *Miles Dresskell*

Fight Song: *Maroon and Gold*

> Fight team on down the field,
> Fight with your might 'til victory is ours;
> Long may your colors wave o'er all others,
> Sing it to the tune of Hoorah Maroon and Gold;
> So cheer, cheer for A. S. U.
> Cheer for the varsity;
> For it's hail! hail! the gang's all here,
> As we march on to victory.
> > *Felix E. McKernan*

Northern Arizona University
Flagstaff, AZ 86011

School Nickname: *NAU*

School Colors: *Blue and Gold*

School Mascot: *Lumberjack*

University of Arizona
Tucson, AZ 85721

School Nickname: *Wildcats*

School Colors: *Cardinal Red and Navy Blue*

School Mascot: *Wilbur Wildcat*

School Newspaper: *Arizona Daily Wildcat*

School Yearbook: *Desert*

Fight Song: *Fight! Wildcats! Fight!*

> Fight! Wildcats! Fight for Arizona,
> We're with you ever staunch and true,--
> This day we hear you and we cheer you,--
> They can't defeat the Red and Blue.--
> Circle the ends and crash through center,--
> Hit hard and gain on ev'ry play ...
> Fight! Wildcats! Fight! Fight! Fight!
> We'll win today!
> > *Words by Doug Holsclaw, '25*
> > *Music Doug Holsclaw and T. W. Allen*

ARKANSAS

Arkansas State University
State University, AR 72467

School Nickname: *A-State*

School Colors: *Black and Red*

School Mascot: *Indians*

School Newspaper: *The Herald*

School Yearbook: *Indian*

Alma Mater: *Hail A.S.U.*

> Our Alma Mater A.S.U. Your hallowed halls shall
> ring with praise by daughter and noble son who proudly stand and
> sing. Mem'ries of your stirring glory and of youthful friends we
> knew--The Red and Black shall Ever wave on high for A.S.U.

Fight Song: *A.S.U. Loyalty Song*

> On, on, on to victory.
> Brave team you're second to none.
> Let make this game history--Along with the others you've won.
> Fight, Fight, Fight with all your might--
> So that the world may see that I-N-D-I-A-N-S means victory!

University of Arkansas
Fayetteville, AR 72701

School Colors: *Cardinal and White*

School Mascot: *Razorback*

School Newspaper: *The Arkansas Traveler*

School Yearbook: *The Razorback*

University of Arkansas at Little Rock
Little Rock, AR 72204

School Colors: *Maroon and White*

School Mascot: *Trojan*

School Newspaper: *Forum*

University of Central Arkansas
Conway, AR 72032

School Nickname: *UCA*

School Colors: *Purple and Gray*

School Mascot: *UCA Bear "Huggy"*

School Newspaper: *The Echo*

School Yearbook: *The Scroll*

Alma Mater: *Alma Mater*

> From the hills and from the lowlands,
> Comes the song of praise anew,
> Sung by thousands of thy children,
> Alma Mater, we sing to you,
> Then we'll unfurl our colors,
> the Purple and the Gray,
> In the breezes see them ever proudly sway;
> They lead us upward; they lead us onward;
> they lead to victory.
> Then let us gather 'round with loyal hearts and true,
> Our Alma Mater's call obey,
> Our dear old colors, they live forever,
> The royal Purple and the Gray.

CALIFORNIA

California Polytechnic State University, San Luis Obispo
San Luis Obispo, CA 93407

School Nickname: *Mustangs (Cal Poly)*

School Colors: *Green and Gold*

School Mascot: *Mustang*

School Newspaper: *Mustang Daily*

Alma Mater: *All Hail, Green and Gold*

> All Hail, Green and Gold,
> May your praises e'er be told
> Of friendship and of courage
> And stalwart sons of old!
> All Hail, Green and Gold,
> In your name we shall prevail,
> So to California Polytechnic,
> Hail! Hail! Hail!
> *Harold P. Davidson*

Fight Song: Ride High, You Mustangs

Ride high, you Mustangs,
Kick the frost out, burn the breeze.
Ride high, you Mustangs,
Those bow-wows we'll knock to their knees.
Ride high, you Mustangs,
Chin the moon and do it right.
Ride high and cut a rusty,
Fight, Fight, Fight.

California State College, Bakersfield
9001 Stockdale Hwy.
Bakersfield, CA 93311-1099

School Colors: *Blue and Gold*

School Mascot: *Roadrunner*

School Newspaper: *Runner*

California State Polytechnic University, Pomona
3801 W. Temple Ave.
Pomona, CA 91768

School Nickname: *Broncos*

School Colors: *Green and Gold*

School Mascot: *"Special K" Arabian Horse*

School Newspaper: *Poly Post*

School Yearbook: *Tangent*

California State University, Dominguez Hills
1000 E. Victoria St.
Carson, CA 90746

School Nickname: *Toros*

School Colors: *Maroon and Gold*

School Mascot: *Bull*

School Newspaper: *Dominguez Weekly*

School Yearbook: *Landscapes*

Alma Mater: *Alma Mater*

> O give us wings to fly, to spurn our night;
> Where, Earthbound, we aspired to don the wings of joyous flight,
> Let friendships soar in human harmony!
> *Chorus*
> With lifted voice, uplifted voice, we dedicate to thee,
> Dominguez Hills, Dominguez Hills, Our love and loyalty.
>
> Inspire the hearts of all who value truth,
> Let knowledge grow, let purpose bloom in lives of love and peace;
> Let ever human dignity increase.
> *Chorus*
> Dominguez Hills, Dominguez Hills, our University.
> WE sing your name for all to hear, Our alma mater dear.

California State University, Fresno
Fresno, CA 93740

School Nickname: *Fresno State*

School Colors: *Cardinal Red and Royal Blue*

School Mascot: *Bulldog*

School Newspaper: *The Daily Collegian (daily) Insight (weekly)*

Alma Mater: *Alma Mater*

> Let us, in song, our voices raise
> In cloister'd courts to sound thy praise,
> Each voice and heart that sings is true to thee,
> Oh Cardinal and Blue.
> For thee our hopes and memories
> For thee our hearts and loyalties
> Thy sons and daughters hail thee great,
> Our Alma Mater Fresno State.
> *Charles Dana Gibson, '27*

Fight Song: *Fight! Varsity!*

> Fight! Varsity
> On your toes dig in and hit that line!
> We're all pulling hard for you
> So fight and give the best there is in you

Fight! Varsity
On your toes dig in and hit that line!
We'll fight on to victory
For ever and ever Fresno State.
Words by Chet Enos
Music by Cuyler H. Leonard

California State University, Fullerton
Fullerton, CA 92634

School Nickname: *Titans*

School Colors: *Royal Blue and White plus Orange on athletic gear*

School Mascot: *Tuffy Titan*

School Newspaper: *Daily Titan*

Alma Mater: *CSUF Alma Mater*

Where the mountains and the oceans lie nearby on either side,
Fair and gleaming tall in sunlight stands the Titans' Home and Pride.

Ev'ry color creed, persuasion finds a welcome in these halls,
Never languishing unheeded 'till the love of Learning palls.

Summer hills like tawny lions, Winter mountains cloaked in snow,
Land of stately eucalyptus where the mind and spirit grow.
Refrain
Fair and gleaming tall in sunlight stands the Titans' Home and Pride!
Words by the Class of English 304, Fall 1984
Music by the Class of Music 422a, Fall 1984

California State University, Hayward
Hayward, CA 94542

School Nickname: *Pioneers*

School Colors: *Red, White and Black*

School Mascot: *Pioneer Pete*

School Newspaper: *The Pioneer*

School Yearbook: *The Elan*

Alma Mater: *Alma Mater*

Up from the restful bay
Stretch Hayward's Hills a-way
Into the Eastern sky,
Mounting their watch on high.
Bounds fade and views expand,
Up with the mounting land,
'Til on these rolling hills,
Visions broad greet the eye.
Visions broad greet--the eye.
So may our spirits find these ageless hills a teacher,
And so may lonely truth reward their flights to reach her
Hearts and minds which seek the heights!
                    Fry
                    Kjelson

Fight Song: *Pioneer Fight Song*

The Pioneers are blasting off
the countdown has begun,
No matter how tough the foe we meet
we'll have them on the run,
The spirit of our college fair
is one that can't be beat,
And when the starting whistle blows
we'll just turn on the heat.

The colors of our college fair--
the Red, the White, the Black,
Will carry us onward into space
and keep us on the track,
And when the final chips are down
for everyone to see,
We'll FIGHT! FIGHT! FIGHT! FIGHT!
on to victory.
                    Cory

California State University, Los Angeles
5151 State University Dr.
Los Angeles, CA 90032

School Nickname: *Cal State L. A.*

School Colors: *Black and Gold*

School Mascot: *Eagle*

School Newspaper: *University Times*

School Yearbook: *Aerie*

Alma Mater: *University Hymn*

All hail to thee, our alma mater dear!
We sing with faith and pride
Thy praises far and near.
We dedicate our lives
To truth and peace and right,
To give the world
The torch of freedom's light.
Hail All Hail!
            Marian Crowell Bessette, '49

California State University, Northridge
18000 Nordhoff St.
Northridge, CA 91330

School Nickname: *CSUN (C-sun)*

School Colors: *Red and White*

School Mascot: *Matador (used by athletic teams)*

School Newspaper: *Sundial*

School Yearbook: *Sunburst*

California State University, Long Beach
1250 Bellflower Blvd.
Long Beach, CA 90840

School Nickname: *Forty-niners*

School Colors: *Brown and Gold*

School Mascot: *Prospectin' Pete*

School Newspaper: *Daily Forty-Niner*

School Yearbook: *Prospector*

California State University, Sacramento
6000 J St.
Sacramento, CA 95819

School Nickname: *CSUS*

School Colors: *Green and Gold*

School Mascot: *Herk the Hornet*

School Newspaper: *State Hornet*

School Yearbook: *Statesman, 1948-1985; Capital Collegian, 1986-*

Alma Mater: *CSUS Alma Mater*

> The lofty Sierra watch over you as you teach from your chair of gold,
> and we who have heard your inspiring word are the heirs to wealth untold.
> We pledge our eternal loyalty. Our devotion shall never abate.
> Oh, Mother of Truth, wise mentor of youth, all hail SACRAMENTO STATE.
> *Words and Music by Don J. McDonald*
> *Class of '49*

Fight Song: *CSUS Fight Song*

> Fight on, Sacramento State, Fight on to victory. The Hornet is on the
> wing.
> The foe will know that we can show them we're meant for fame and glory.
> All the World will know the Hornet's <u>NEST</u> is <u>BEST</u> in the <u>WEST</u> by
> <u>TEST!</u>
> Sacramento State, <u>LET'S GO!!!</u>
> *Words and Music by Don J. McDonald*
> *Class of '49*

California State University, San Bernardino
5500 University Parkway
San Bernardino, CA 92407

School Nickname: *Cal State*

School Colors: *Blue and Brown*

School Mascot: *Coyote*

School Newspaper: *The Chronicle*

California State University, Stanislaus
801 W. Monte Vista Ave.
Turlock, CA 95380

School Colors: *Red and Gold*

School Mascot: *Indian (The Warriors: Athletic teams)*

School Newspaper: *The Signal*

School Yearbook: *The Legend*

Chapman College
333 North Glassell St.
Orange, CA 92666

School Colors: *Cardinal and Gray*

School Mascot: *Panther*

School Newspaper: *The Panther*

School Yearbook: *The Ceer*

Humboldt State University
Arcata, CA 95521

School Nickname: *Humboldt State or HSU*

School Colors: *Green and Gold*

School Mascot: *Lumberjack*

School Newspaper: *Lumberjack*

National University
University Park
San Diego, CA 92108

School Colors: *Blue and Gold*

School Mascot: *Eagle*

School Newspaper: *NU Weekly*

San Diego State University
5300 Campanile Dr.
San Diego, CA 92182

School Nickname: *Aztecs*

School Colors: *Red and Black*

School Mascot: *Montezuma, King of the Aztecs*

School Newspaper: *Daily Aztec*

Alma Mater: *Alma Mater*

> Hail, Montezuma
> We with loyal hearts our homage pay;
> Proud working and glorying,
> In the Spirit of the Aztec name.
> To thee, San Diego
> And the fond traditions, old and new.
> A tribute raise of lasting praise and steadfast faith,
> Hail, Montezuma.
>
> Hail, Montezuma
> We salute thy glorious destiny;
> Far seeing in coming days.
> Men and women strong who live in truth.
> To thee, San Diego
> And the black and scarlet we'll be true.
> An echo comes from Aztec drums through all the years,
> Hail, Montezuma.

Fight Song: *Fight Song*

> Fight on, fight on, ye Aztec men.
> Sons of Montezuma we must win again.
> Keep your spirits high, never bow a knee,
> Smashing, crashing, always dashing through that line.
> Fight, fight, fight on, fight on ye Aztec men.
> Red and Black will never yield,
> And we will take our trophies,
> Honors to our home in San Diego Town.

San Francisco State University

1600 Holloway Ave.
San Francisco, CA 94132

School Nickname: *SF State or State*

School Colors: *Purple and Gold*

School Mascot: *The Gator*

School Newspaper: *The Golden Gater*

School Yearbook: *The Franciscan*

Alma Mater: *Hail To San Francisco State*

Hail to San Francisco State
sing we now our song to thee
College by the Golden Gate
Alpha and Omega be
In the purple and the gold
Let thy history be told
San Francisco San Francisco
On to Victory.
Words and Music by Clarence Kaull

Fight Song: *State Victory Song*

Golden tide is rising we're out to meet the foe
Fighting ever on to victory
For San Francisco 'neath our Golden Banner
We'll win today for State
Our Colors o'er us they go before us
We're coming thru the Golden Gate.
Words by Dorothy Williamson
Music by Mildred Roof

San Jose State University
San Jose, CA 95192-0001

School Nickname: *San Jose State*

School Colors: *Gold (Old), White and Blue (Royal)*

School Mascot: *Spartans*

School Newspaper: *Daily Spartan*

School Yearbook: *LaTorre (ceased publication)*

Alma Mater: *Hail! Spartans Hail!!!*

Hail, Spartans, Hail Hail, Gold, Blue and White! ---
We pledge our hearts and hands to keep thy colors ever bright-
Forward we go! We will not fail!
Sing to our Alma Mater, Hail! Hail! Hail!
Hail, Spartans, Hail! All hail to thee, ---
Hail to thy cloister'd halls and tower standing straight and
free ---
Thy Gold, Blue and White, Long May they sail!
For thee we sing forever, Hail! Hail! --- Hail!

Fight Songs: *Spartan Fight Song*

> Fight on for dear old San Jose State:
> Fight on for victory! --
> We are with you in every way.
> No matter what the price may be! --
> On-ward for Sparta noble and true.
> Fight hard in everything you do!
> And so we'll Fight! (Rah!) Win! (Rah!)
> March onward down the field and we will win the day!

Down From Under

> Down from under rum-bles the thunder
> Spartans upon the field of play.
> Let's all shout --- so there is no doubt ---
> that our hearts are with them all the way. ---
> Spartan shields down the field ---
> fighting for victory and for fame.
> Go team!! Fight team!!!
> Let's sweep the field clean!
> Show them how to win the game -----

Santa Clara University
Santa Clara, CA 95053

School Nickname: *Broncos*

School Colors: *Cardinal and White*

School Newspaper: *The Santa Clara*

School Yearbook: *The Redwood*

Sonoma State University
1801 E. Cotati Ave.
Rohnert Park, CA 94928

School Nickname: *Cossacks (Teams)*

School Colors: *Dark Blue, Light Blue and White*

School Newspaper: *Sonoma State Star*

School Yearbook: *Sonoman (irregular)*

Stanford University
Stanford, CA 94305

School Nickname: *The Farm*

School Colors: *Cardinal*

School Newspaper: *The Stanford Daily*

School Yearbook: *The Quad*

Alma Mater: *Hail, Stanford Hail!*

Where the rolling foothills rise
Up t'wards mountains higher,
Where at eve the Coast Range lies,
In the sunset fire,
Flushing deep and paling;
Here we raise our voices hailing
Thee, our Alma Mater.

Tender vistas ever new
Thru' the arches meet the eyes,
Where the red roofs rim the blue
Of the sun-steep'd skies,
Fleck'd with cloud-lets sailing,
Here we raise our voices hailing
Thee our Alma Mater.

When the moon light bathed arcade
Stands in evening calms,
When the light wind half afraid
Whispers in the palms,
Far off swelling failing,
Student voices glad are hailing
Thee our Alma Mater.
        Refrain
From the foot hills to the bay,
It shall ring
As we sing;
It shall ring and float alway;
Hail, Stanford hail!
Hail, Stanford hail!
        Words by A. W. S.
        Music by M.R. C. '93

Fight Song: *Come Join The Band*

Come join the band
And give a cheer for Stanford red
Through out the land
Our banner waving over head
Stanford for you
Each loyal comrade brave and true
With might and main sings this refrain,
Forever and forever Stanford red.

After the game
When Stanford red has won the day
Praising her name
Down to the field we'll force our way
And on the green
Each man who joins the serpentine
With might and main sings this refrain
Forever and forever Stanford red.

Words by Aurania Ellerbeck
Music by R. B. Hall

University of California, Berkeley
Berkeley, CA 94720

School Nickname: *Cal*

School Colors: *Blue and Gold*

School Mascot: *Oski*

School Newspaper: *The Daily Californian*

School Yearbook: *Blue and Gold*

Alma Mater: *All Hail! Blue and Gold*

All hail! Blue and Gold,
Thy colors unfold,
O'er loyal Californians,
Whose hearts are strong and bold.
All hail! Blue and Gold,
Thy strength ne'er shall fail;
For thee we'll die!
All hail! All hail!

All hail! Blue and Gold,
To thee we shall cling;
O'er golden fields of poppies,
Thy praises we will sing.

All hail! Blue and Gold,
On breezes ye sail;
Thy sight we love!
All hail! All hail!
Words and Music by Harold W. Bingham, '06

Fight Song: *Fight for California*

Our sturdy Golden Bear,
Is watching from the skies,
Looks down upon our colors fair,
And guards us from his lair.
Our banner gold and blue,
The symbol on it too,
Means FIGHT for California,
For California through and through!

Stalwarts girded for the fray,
Will strive for victory,
Their all at Mater's feet will lay,
That brain and brawn will win the day.
Our mighty sons and true,
Will strive for us anew,
And FIGHT for California,
For California through and through!
Words by Robert N. Fitch '09

University of California, Davis
Davis, CA 95616

School Nickname: *The Aggies*

School Colors: *Royal Blue and Bright Gold*

School Mascot: *Ollie the Mustang*

School Newspaper: *The California Aggie*

Alma Mater: *Hail To California*

Hail to California,
Alma Mater dear--
Sing the joyful chorus,
Sound it far and near,
Rallying 'round her banner--
We will never fail;
California, Alma Mater,
Hail! Hail! Hail!

Hail to California,
Queen in whom we're blest,
Spreading light and goodness
Over the west.
Fighting 'neath her standard,
We shall sure prevail;
California, Alma Mater,
Hail! Hail! Hail!

Fight Song: *Aggie Fight Song*

Lift up your voices, now's the time to sing
This is the day the Victory Bell will ring
Loyal Aggies, all for one
Never stopping, 'till we've won
Because the Mustang will show our team the way to fight,
Charging the enemy with all his might
Let's go, Let's win, today's the day
The Aggies will Fight, Fight, Fight!

University of California, Irvine
Irvine, CA 92717

School Nickname: *UCI*

School Colors: *Blue and Gold*

School Mascot: *Anteater*

School Newspaper: *New University*

School Yearbook: *The Anteater*

University of California, Los Angeles
405 Hilgard Ave.
Los Angeles, CA 90024

School Nickname: *Bruins*

School Colors: *Blue and Gold*

School Mascot: *Joe and Josephine Bruin*

School Newspaper: *Daily Bruin*

School Yearbook: *Bruin Life*

University of California, Riverside
Riverside, CA 92521-0144

School Nickname: *Highlanders*

School Colors: *Blue and Gold*

School Mascot: *Highland Bear*

School Newspaper: *The Highlander*

School Yearbook: *The Scotsman*

University of California, San Diego
La Jolla, CA 92093

School Nickname: *Tritons*

School Colors: *Blue and Gold*

School Mascot: *Triton*

School Newspaper: *Daily Guardian*

School Yearbook: *UCSD Yearbook*

University of California, Santa Barbara
Santa Barbara, CA 93106

School Colors: *Blue and Gold*

School Mascot: *Gauchos*

School Newspaper: *Daily Nexus*

School Yearbook: *La Cumbre*

University of California, Santa Cruz
Santa Cruz, CA 95064

School Colors: *Blue and Gold*

School Mascot: *Banana Slug*

University of San Francisco
Ignatian Heights
San Francisco, CA 94117

School Nickname: *USF*

School Colors: *Green and Gold*

School Mascot: *Dons*

School Newspaper: *Foghorn*

School Yearbook: *USF Don*

Alma Mater: *Hail San Francisco*

> Hail San Francisco! Hail to thee,
> Enthroned beside the western sea,
> Thy storied past shall ever be
> Our theme of loving song!
> Unfurl thy banners Green and Gold,
> As echoes ev'ry hill and vale,
> The homage of our grateful hearts,
> All hail to thee all hail!
>
> Hail San Francisco! Hail to thee,
> We pledge our lasting loyalty,
> E'er true and steadfast we will be
> To thee our Mother Blest!
> Thru endless days thy sons shall strive
> To make thy name and fame prevail,
> Oh, Alma Mater glorious,
> All hail to thee all hail!
>   *By F. J. Colligan*

Fight Song: *Victory Song*

> Alma Mater loyal and true
> All our hearts we pledge to you
> Send forth your sons gloriously onward on to victory
> On to victory
> We're out to win today here's why
> For the green and gold
> The Dons are going in to do or die
> Win or lose today we're gonna try and try the same old way
> And with all our might
> We're gonna fight, fight, fight, fight, fight, fight
> On to victory.

Onward U. S. F.
Our college here beside the sea
All together now
We're going onward on to victory
Let the Dons roll
And keep them rolling, rolling across their goal
And with all our might
We're gonna fight, fight, fight, fight, fight, fight
On to victory.
                    Words and Music by Bud Smith

University of Southern California
Los Angeles, CA 90089-0018

School Nickname: *Trojans*

School Colors: *Cardinal and Gold*

School Newspaper: *Daily Trojan*

School Yearbook: *El Rodeo*

Alma Mater: *Alma Mater*

> All Hail to Alma Mater
> To thy glory we sing.
> All Hail to Southern California
> Loud let thy praises ring.
> Where Western sky meets Western sea
> Our college stands in majesty
> Sing our love to Alma Mater,
> Hail all Hail to thee.

Fight Song: *Fight On*

> Fight on for ol' SC
> Our men fight on to victory
> Our Alma Mater dear,
> Looks up to you
> Fight on and win
> For ol' SC
> Fight on to victory
> Fight on!

University of the Pacific
Stockton, CA 95211

School Nickname: *UOP*

School Colors: *Orange and Black*

School Mascot: *Tiger*

School Newspaper: *The Pacifican*

School Yearbook: *EPOCH*

Alma Mater: *Pacific, Hail!*

> From o're the rugged mountains
> standing high:
> From out the broad low valleys,
> 'Neath the sky;
> Our Alma Mater calls,
> We cannot fail,
> Our voices blend in praise
> Pacific Hail! Pacific Hail!
>
> Long may her flaming torch
> Give out its light:
> Long may her spirit guide us
> In the right;
> To her we pledge our hearts,
> We dare not fail;
> To her we raise our song
> Pacific Hail! Pacific Hail!
> *Lois Warner Winston, ex '23, '58*

COLORADO

Colorado State University
Fort Collins, CO 80523

School Nickname: *Colorado State*

School Colors: *Green and Gold*

School Mascot: *Ram*

School Newspaper: *Rocky Mountain Collegian*

School Yearbook: *Silver Spruce*

Fort Lewis College
Durango, CO 81301

School Colors: *Blue and Gold*

School Newspaper: *The Independent*

School Yearbook: *FLC Katzima (Discontinued in 1979)*

Mesa College
Grand Junction, CO 81502

School Nickname: *Mavericks*

School Colors: *Red and White*

School Newspaper: *Criterion*

School Yearbook: *Maverick (currently not published)*

Alma Mater: *Our Alma Mater*

Mesa College, Alma Mater,
This is my pledge to thee:
Maroon and White will
E'er be right,
And lead to victory.

Mesa College, Alma Mater,
Queen of memory.
Through life's short span,
Till death I stand,
In faith and love to thee.

Metropolitan State College
Denver, Co 80204

School Nickname: *Metro*

School Colors: *Midnight Blue and Light Blue*

School Mascot: *Roadrunner*

School Newspaper: *Metropolitan*

United States Air Force Academy
Colorado Springs, CO 80840

School Nickname: *Academy (Falcons)*

School Colors: *Blue and Silver*

School Mascot: *Falcons*

School Newspaper: *Falcon Flyer*

School Yearbook: *The Polaris*

University of Colorado, Boulder
Campus Box 17
Boulder, CO 80309

School Nickname: *CU Buffs*

School Colors: *Silver and Gold (symbolic of the minerals in Colorado)*

School Mascot: *Buffalo* Name: *Ralphie*

School Newspaper: *The Colorado Daily*

School Yearbook: *The Coloradan*

Alma Mater: *Alma Mater*

> Hail, all Hail our Alma Mater!
> Ever will our hearts be true;
> You will live with us forever,
> Loyal we will be to you.
> We will sing forever your praises,
> Ever more our love renew,
> Pledge our whole devotion to you.
> Dear old C.U.!

Fight Song: *Fight Song*

> Glory, glory Colorado
> Glory, glory Colorado
> Glory, glory Colorado
> Hurrah for the Silver and Gold

University of Colorado at Denver
1100 14th St.
Denver, CO 80202

School Nickname: *CU-Denver*

School Colors: *Silver and Gold*

School Newspaper: *The Advocate*

Alma Mater: *Alma Mater*

> Hail, all Hail our Alma Mater!
> Ever will our hearts be true;
> You will live with us forever,
> Loyal we will be to you.

We will sing forever your praises,
Ever more our love renew,
Pledge our whole devotion to you.
Dear old C.U.!

University of Denver
University Park
Denver, CO 80208

School Nickname: *DU*

School Colors: *Crimson and Gold*

School Mascot: *Boone*

School Newspaper: *Clarion*

School Yearbook: *Kynwisbok (K-Book)*

University of Northern Colorado
Greeley, CO 80639

School Nickname: *Northern Colorado*

School Colors: *Blue and Gold*

School Mascot: *Bear*

School Newspaper: *Mirror*

School Yearbook: *Cache La Poudre*

Fight Song: *UNC Fight Song*

On down the field we go to victory
The colors navy blue and gold
And to our fighting team
We hold our courage bold.
The mighty Golden Bears are we.
Fight, fight to win each battle fairly.
The only way we e're shall be.
We shout out the name
To keep the fame and fight
of old UNC.

University of Southern Colorado
2200 Bonforte Blvd.
Pueblo, CO 82002-4901

School Nickname: *USC and Indians*

School Colors: *Scarlet Red and Columbia Blue*

School Mascot: *Indians*

School Newspaper: *USC Today*

Alma Mater: *Alma Mater*

> To our dear old Alma Mater,
> Heart and voice are raised to thee.
> May our footsteps never falter
> From the paths of loyalty.
> We will pledge ourselves to thee;
> And when we have all departed,
> We'll stay true to USC.

CONNECTICUT

Central Connecticut State University
1615 Stanley St.
New Britain, CT   06050

School Nickname: *Blue Devils*

School Colors: *Blue and White*

School Mascot: *Blue Devil*

School Newspaper: *The Central Recorder*

School Yearbook: *The Dial*

Alma Mater: *Alma Mater*

> Alma Mater, Alma Mater
> We thy praises sing
> Of thy triumph and thy glory
> Let our voices ring
> Serving, loving only thee
> Pledged unto eternity
> Alma Mater, Alma Mater
> We thy children sing
> Alma Mater, Alma Mater
> May thy fame increase

Guardian of all earthly widsom
Vigil never cease
Till the searching minds of youth
Come to know thy right, thy truth
Alma Mater, Alma Mater
Hear us as we sing.
Julie Ritch '39

Fight Song: *C. C. S. U. Victory*

We're starting out for victory today
We're going to win because there's no other way
We're starting out for victory today
We're going to win for CCS, for CCS.
The boys of CCS are we
The boys of CCS are we
Starting out on a stormy sea,
We're starting out for victory today
We're going to win because there's no other way
We're starting out for victory today
We're going to win for CCS, for CCS.

Fairfield University
North Benson Rd.
Fairfield, CT 06430-7524

School Nickname: *The Stags*

School Colors: *Cardinal Red and White*

School Mascot: *Stag*

School Newspaper: *The Mirror*

School Yearbook: *The Manor*

Alma Mater: *Alma Mater*

Fairfield see the stag with cross of gold
Rears once more it's undefeated head
Fair our field as any field of old
Bids our banners like our blood be red
Through faith unto total truth
Our cry swells from sea to spire and sky
Hear Alma Mater! hear Fairfield hail!
Lyrics by John L. Bonn, S.J.

Fight Song: *When The Stags Come Marching In*

Oh, when the stags come marching in,
When the stags come marching in,
Oh, I want to be in that number,
When the stags come marching in.

Quinnipiac College
Mt. Carmel Ave.
Hamden, CT 06518

School Nickname: *Braves*

School Colors: *Blue and Gold*

School Mascot: *The Brave*

School Newspaper: *The Chronicle*

School Yearbook: *Brave*

Alma Mater: *Quinnipiac Alma Mater*

Quinnipiac, thy light shines about us fair
We see thy guiding light here and everywhere.
Thy guidance in the past, in the future dwells
Onward we go our way, word of life to tell.
Alma Mater, all hail to thee Quinnipiac,
We praise with a song
May we lift our voices loud and strong.
Words and Music by Frank V. Bigelow '30

Southern Connecticut State University
501 Crescent St.
New Haven, CT 06515

School Nickname: *Southern*

School Mascot: *Owl*

School Newspaper: *Southern News*

School Yearbook: *Laurel*

Alma Mater: *Alma Mater*

A moment of reflection, of gratitude, and pride,
A feeling of affection as we stand here side by side!
We honor truth and know-ledge,
And pledge that while they last,
Thro' the future that's be-fore us,
We will not for-get the past,
From your humble beginnings on a city street,
To the spacious campus where your students meet,
You've led us on our way,
To you we sing today,
And loyalty we proudly pay to Southern University!

University of Bridgeport
Bridgeport, CT 06601

School Nickname: *U B*

School Colors: *Purple and White*

School Mascot: *Purple Knight (offical) Shmoo (unoffical)*

School Newspaper: *Scribe*

School Yearbook: *Wistarian*

Alma Mater: *Alma Mater*

> Alma Mater a toast to thee
> Pledge our honor and loyalty
> From the ocean far across the land,
> Our noble college will proudly stand
> Golden memories of days serene
> Golden seasons familiar scenes
> Bonds will keep us forever true
> Alma Mater "Bridgeport U"

University of Connecticut
Storrs, CT 06268

School Nickname: *UConn (pronounced Yukon)*
            Football team is called the Huskies

School Colors: *Blue and White*

School Mascot: *Husky dog* Name: *Jonathan*

School Newspaper: *The Daily Campus*

School Yearbook: *The Nutmeg*

University of Hartford
West Hartford, CT 06117

School Colors: *Crimson and White*

School Mascot: *The Hawk*

School Newspaper: *The Informer*

School Yearbook: *Primus*

Alma Mater: *Alma Mater*

> University of Hartford
> Now and ever strong and true,
> Inspiration of the future,
> Vision of a stalwart few;
> Ever onward to new glories,
> Ready for the tasks at hand,
> Sending forth the light of knowledge
> Into dark uncharted lands.
> Thanks to you, dear Alma Mater,
> Young in heart and wise in truth,
>
> Open wide your doors of learning
> For our eager, searching youth.
>
> Harbinger of paths untrodden
> Anchor of old glories won,
> Raise your sights to worlds unconquered,
> Toiling still with tasks undone.
> Forward, onward Alma Mater
> Ours is an unswerving band
> Reaching towards a great fulfillment,
> Done with His enduring hand.
> *Joseph Soifer*
> *March 19, '61*

Fight Song: *Hartford On To Victory*

> The red and the white are set for victory,
> The Hawks are the best that can be;
> Oh Hartford has spirit that is next to none,
> For sure we are NUMBER 1!

We'll win every battle with a shout and cheer,
Our message is really very clear;
On red and white,
Go out and win the fight,
Go Hartford CHARGE to victory!

University of New Haven
300 Orange Ave.
West Haven, CT 06516

School Nickname: *UNH*

School Colors: *Blue and Gold*

School Mascot: *Charlie the Charger*

School Newspaper: *The News*

School Yearbook: *The Chariot*

Yale University
New Haven, CT 06520

School Nickname: *Eli; Elis when referring to football team*

School Colors: *Yale Blue and White*

School Mascot: *Bulldog* Name: *Handsome Dan*

School Newspaper: *Yale Daily News*

School Yearbook: *The Yale Banner*

DELAWARE

University of Delaware
Newark, DE 19716

School Colors: *Blue and Gold*

School Mascot: *Fightin' Blue Hens*

School Newspaper: *The Review*

School Yearbook: *The Blue Hen*

Alma Mater: *University of Delaware Alma Mater*

    Hail to thee proud
Delaware,
In loyalty we stand.
We give thee thanks for glorious days
Beneath thy guiding hand.
Full often will we praise thy name,
Thy colors proudly bear;
We lift our voices now to sing
All hail to Delaware.
           Robert Currie
           A. J. Loudis

Fight Song: *University of Delaware Fight Song*

And then we'll fight! fight! fight! for Delaware,
Fight for the Blue and Gold,
And when we hit that line,
Our team is there with a daring spirit bold.
And when we strike with might
Let foes beware
Our glorious name we'll uphold,
And then we'll fight! fight! fight! for Delaware,
Fight for the Blue and Gold.
Delaware will shine tonight,
Delaware will shine.
When the sun goes down and the moon comes up,
Delaware will shine.

Music and Lyrics by
George F. Kelly '15

DISTRICT OF COLUMBIA

The Catholic University of America
Washington, DC 20064

School Nickname: *CUA*

School Colors: *Red and Black (sporting colors)*
Gold and White (official papal colors)

School Mascot: *The Cardinal*

School Newspaper: *The Tower*

School Yearbook: *The Cardinal Yearbook*

Alma Mater: *Alma Mater*

> Alma Mater, thee we hail;
> Guardian of truth.
> Ours the love that cannot fail,
> Sunshine of youth.
> Raise thy towers to the skies.
> Gifted from above;
> By the light that never dies,
> Haven of love.
> *Refrain*
> Alma Mater, we behold thee;
> Sons and daughters true;
> Days of sunshine e'er enfold thee, C.U., C.U.

Georgetown University
Washington, DC 20057

School Nickme: *Hoyas*

School Colors: *Blue and Gray*

School Mascot: *Jack the Bulldog*

School Newspaper: *The Hoya, The Voice*

School Yearbook: *Ye Domesday Booke*

Alma Mater: *Alma Mater*

> Hail, oh Georgetown, Alma Mater
> Swift Potomac's lovely daughter,
> Ever watching by the water
> Smile on us today;
>
> Now her children gather 'round her
> Lo, with garlands they have crowned her
> Reverent hands and fond enwound her
> With the Blue and Gray.
> *Chorus*
> Wave her colors ever,
> Furl her standard never,
> But raise it high,
> And proudly cry,
> May Georgetown live forever.
> Where Potomac's tide is streaming
> From her spires and steeples beaming
> See the grand old banner gleaming
> Georgetown's Blue and Gray.
>
> Throned on hills beside the river,
> Georgetown sees it flow forever,
> Sees the ripples shine and shiver,
> Watching night and day.
> And each tender breeze upspringing,
> Rarest woodland perfumes bringing,
> All its fold to fullness flinging,
> Flaunts the Blue and Gray.
> *Robert Collier, '94*

Fight Song: *Georgetown Fight Song*

> It's been so long since last we met,
> Lie down forever, lie down;
> Oh have you any money to bet,

Lie down forever, lie down!
There goes old Georgetown,
Straight for a touchdown,
See how they gain ground--
Lie down forever, lie down,
Lie down forever, lie down.

Rah, rah, rah! Hurrah for Gorgetown!
Cheer for victory today!
Ere the sun has sunk to rest
In the cradle of the West,
In the clouds will proudly float the Blue and Gray.

We've heard those loyal fellows up at Yale
Brag and boast about their Boola-boola,
We've heard the Navy yell,
We've listened to Cornell,
We've heard the sons of Harvard tell how Crimson
lines could hold them.
Choo, choo! Rah, rah! dear to Holy Cross
The proud old Princeton tiger is never at a loss,
But the yell of all the yells--
The yell that wins the day--
is the HOYA! HOYA! SAXA!
For the dear old Blue and Gray.

Howard University
Washington, DC 20059

School Nickname: *H-U*

School Colors: *Royal Blue and White*

School Mascot: *The Bison*

School Newspaper: *The Hilltop*

School Yearbook: *Howard University Bison*

Alma Mater: *Alma Mater*

Reared against the eastern sky
Proudly there on hilltop high
Far above the lake so blue
Stands old Howard firm and true.
There she stands for truth and right,
Sending forth her rays of light,
Clad in robes of majesty;
O Howard, we sing of thee.

Be thou our guide and stay,
Leading us from day to day;
Make us true and leal and strong,
Ever bold to battle wrong.
When from thee we've gone away,
May we strive for thee each day
As we sail life's rugged sea,
O Howard, we'll sing of thee.

Words, J. H. Brooks, '16
Music, F. D. Malone, '16

University of the District of Columbia
4200 Connecticut Ave., N. W.
Washington, DC 20008

School Colors: *Red and Gold*

School Mascot: *Firebird*

School Newspaper: *The Trilogy*

School Yearbook: *Firebird (changes yearly)*

FLORIDA

Embry-Riddle Aeronautical University
Regional Airport
Daytona Beach, FL 32014

School Nickname: *Riddle*

School Colors: *Blue and Gold*

School Mascot: *Eagle*

School Newspaper: *Avion*

School Yearbook: *Phoenix*

Florida Agricultural and Mechanical University
Tallahassee, FL 32307

School Nickname: *FAMU*

School Colors: *Orange and Green*

School Mascot: *Rattlers (for the Rattlesnake)*

School Newspaper: *The FAMUan*

School Yearbook: *The Rattler*

Alma Mater: *Alma Mater*

> College of love and charity
> We gather 'round thy noble shrine;
> We lift our voice in praise to thee,
> And ask a blessing all divine.
> > *Chorus*
> FAM-U! FAM-U! I love thee!
> I'll fight and win what'er the battle be.
> The Orange and the Green thy Sons shall e'er defend
> And loyal to thy voice of love attend
> FAM-U! FAM-U! FAM-U! I love thee!
>
> On gridiron, diamond, track and field,
> Thy sons the vict'ry never yield,--
> And while they tread a broader life
> Thy Love shall stay them in the strife.
> > *Chorus*
> God ever keep us true to thee;
> Thy faith that truth shall make men free,
> Shall guide thy loyal sons aright
> And fend them thru' the skeptic night.
> > *Chorus*

Fight Song *Our Florida*

> Dear old Florida we are yearning, we will fight for you;
> while our loyal hearts are burning, we'll be ever true.
> Florida, Florida, bless her name, Orange and Green we'll proudly wave;
> we will honor and protect your sons and daughters brave.

Florida Atlantic University
P. O. Box 3991
Boca Raton, FL 33431-0991

School Colors: *French Blue and Silver*

School Mascot: *Owl*

Alma Mater: *Alma Mater*

> With the Gulf stream breezes blowing
> The search for truth goes on.
> Seeking, learning, sharing knowledge.
> Finding the meaning of the past that is gone.
> Where nature beams with pleasant weather.

We strive to learn to work together
Florida Atlantic, We praise and hail thy name.
Words and Music by Clark Bell
Copyright 1977, Florida Atlantic University

Florida International University
University Park
Miami, FL 33199

North Miami Campus
North Miami, FL 33181

School Nickname: *FIU*

School Colors: *Blue and Gold*

School Mascot: *Golden Panthers*

School Newspaper: *The Sunblazer*

School Yearbook: *Flashback*

Alma Mater: *Alma Mater*

> Hail to Thee, dear FIU
> With voices true we pledge to thee
> All our love and deep devotion,
> Humble faith and loyalty
>
> We will strive for understanding
> And for peace and unity
> We will search for truth and wisdom
> We will always honor thee.

Florida Institute of Technology
150 W. University Blvd.
Melbourne, FL 32901

School Nickname: *F.I.T. -- Florida Tech*

School Colors: *Crimson and Silver*

School Mascot: *Panther*

School Newspaper: *Crimson*

School Yearbook: *Ad Astra*

Florida Southern College
Lakeland, FL 33802

School Nickname: *The Mocs or Frank Lloyd Wright's "Child of the Sun"*

School Colors: *Red and White*

School Mascot: *Water Moccasin*

School Newspaper: *The Southern*

School Yearbook: *The Interlachen*

Alma Mater: *Alma Mater*

> Orange groves o'erspread her campus;
> Chimes her hymns intone.
> India greets across the garden
> Southern's mystic throne.
> *Chorus*
> Florida Southern, thee we love,
> Thee we'll never fail.
> Hail to thee our alma mater,
> Hail to Southern, Hail!
> Stately walls alone can never
> Compass learning's goal.
> Heart to heart must pass the token,
> Soul in spirit soul.

Florida State University
Tallahassee, FL 32306

School Nickname: *Seminoles*

School Colors: *Garnet and Gold*

School Mascot: *Renegade (Appaloosa horse mascot)*

School Newspaper: *The Florida Flambeau (independent)*

School Yearbook: *Artifacts*

Alma Mater: *Alma Mater*

> High o'er the towering pines our voices swell,
> Praising those Gothic spires we love so well,
> Here sons and daughters stand, faithful and true,
> Hailing our ALMA MATER, FSU.
> *Words and Music by Johnny Lawrence*

Fight Song: *F.S.U. Fight Song*

> You got to fight, fight, fight, for F. S. U.
> You got to scalp 'em, Seminoles
> You got to win, win, win, win,
> Win this game and roll on down to make those goals.
> For F. S. U. is on the war path now,
> And at the battle's end she's great;
> So fight, fight, fight, fight, to victory,
> Our Seminoles from Florida State!
> *Words by Doug Alley*
> *Music by Thomas Wright*

Nova University
3301 College Ave.
Ft. Lauderdale, FL 33314

School Colors: *Blue and Silver*

School Mascot: *Knight*

School Newspaper: *The Nova Knight*

School Yearbook: *The Palladin*

Saint Leo College
Saint Leo, FL 33574

School Colors: *Green and Gold*

School Mascot: *The Monarchs*

School Newspaper: *The Monarch*

School Yearbook: *The Golden Legend*

Alma Mater: *Saint Leo Alma Mater*

> Loyal friends assembled here
> Praise our Alma Mater Dear
> Stir those memories deeply felt
> Throughout the years
>
> Loyal lions true and bold
> For Saint Leo's Green and Gold
> Work and pray that
> Through the years, love endures

Honored deeds as yet untold
Fill our hallowed halls of old
Let us lift our gaze beyond
To truth and God
Saint Leo, Saint Leo, Saint Leo
Zaitz and Salvatore

Stetson University
DeLand, FL 32720

School Nickname: *Hatters*

School Colors: *Green and White*

School Mascot: *The Little Hatter (He resembles the Mad Hatter from
Alice in Wonderland)*

School Newspaper: *The Reporter (Oldest collegiate newspaper in Florida)*

School Yearbook: *The Hatter*

Alma Mater: *Alma Mater*

Dear Alma Mater, smile upon thy children,
Gladly we greet thee, altogether lovely;
Peace be within thy classic halls and temples,
Hail Alma Mater dear!

Hail to the heroes who have gone before us,
Young men and maidens filled with true devotion
Bright is their glory, fadeless and undying.
Hail to our heroes gone!

Hail to our classmates, bound by ties ne'er broken,
Here once again we pledge our vows of friendship;
Brave hearts and true hearts sound aloud the chorus:
Long live our comrades dear.

Dear Alma Mater, tenderly thy children
Gather and bring to thee gracious salutations;
Comrades, your voices lift once again in chorus:
Hail Alma Mater dear!

University of Central Florida
Orlando, FL 32816

School Nickname: *Fighting Knights*

School Colors: *Gold and Black*

School Mascot: *Knight*

School Newspaper: *The Central Florida Future*

Alma Mater: *Alma Mater*

> Sing Praise to Alma Mater
> Our Voices ringing clear
> The joy and love for college days
> Will echo through the years.
>
> Wherever we may journey
> Be it near or be it far
> Devotion will inspire us
> As we strive to reach the stars.
>
> With honor and affection
> Our friendship will renew
> We sing of thee an Alma Mater
> Ever true.
>
> All hail to Alma Mater
> Whose banner black and gold
> Will wave in fame and splendor
> As the passing years unfold.
>
> May loyalty and friendship
> Within our hearts unite
> And light the star to guide us
> Ever upward in our flight.
>
> With honor and affection
> Our friendship will renew
> We sing of thee an Alma Mater
> Ever true.
> *Words and Music by Burt Szabo*

Fight Song: *Fight Song*

> UCF charge onto the field,
> With our spirit we'll never yield.
> We're singing,
> Black and Gold charge right thru the line
> Victory is our only cry
> V I C T O R Y
> Tonight our Knights will shine!!

University of Florida
Gainesville, FL 32611

School Nickname: *Gators*

School Colors: *Orange and Blue*

School Mascot: *Alligator*   Name: *Albert*

School Newspaper: *The Independent Florida Alligator (published off campus)*

School Yearbook: *Tower*

Alma Mater: *Alma Mater*

> Florida, our Alma Mater
> Thy glorious name we praise;
> All thy loyal sons and daughters
> A joyous song shall raise.
> Where palm and pine are blowing,
> Where southern seas are flowing,
> Shine forth thy noble Gothic walls,
> Thy lovely vine-clad halls.
> 'Neath the Orange and Blue victorious
> Our love shall never fail.
> There's no other name so glorious--
> All Hail, Florida, Hail!
> *Milton L. Yeats*

Fight Song: *We Are The Boys*

> We are the boys from Old Florida,
> F-L-O-R-I-D-A
> Where the girls are the fairest,
> The boys are the squarest,
> Of all the great states down our way.
> We are all strong for old Florida,
> Down where the old Gators play.
> In fair or foul weather
> We all stick together
> For F-L-O-R-I-D-A.
> *Words and Music by Robert M. Swanson*
> *and John E. Icenhour*

University of Miami
P. O. Box 248105
Coral Gables, FL 33124

School Colors: *Orange and Green*

School Mascot: *Sebastian - Ibis*

School Newspaper: *The Hurricane*

School Yearbook: *Ibis*

Alma Mater: *Alma Mater*

Southern suns and sky -
blue water
Smile upon you, Alma
Mater;
Mistress of this fruitful
land,
With all knowledge at your
hand,
Always just, to honor true,
All our love we pledge to
you.
Alma Mater, stand forever,
On Biscayne's wondrous
Shore.
Words by William Lampe

Fight Song: *Miami Fight*

Miami fight down the field,
Fight for the Orange, Green and White,
Miami fight, Make them yield,
Fight for the score with all your might,
Then give a cheer for our team,
Our Hurricanes in white and green,
Rah, Rah, Miami, Fight, fight, Miami,
Let our banners fly supreme.
Used with permission of the Univ. of Miami

University of North Florida
4567 St. Johns Bluff Rd., South
Jacksonville, FL 32216

School Nickname: *UNF*

School Colors: *Light Blue and White*

School Mascot: *Osprey*

School Newspaper: *Spinnaker*

School Yearbook: *Northstar*

University of South Florida
Tampa, FL 33620

School Nickname: *Golden Brahmans or Bulls*

School Colors: *Green and Gold*

School Mascot: *The Golden Brahman (a Brahma bull)*

School Newspaper: *The Oracle*

School Yearbook: *20th Century*

Alma Mater: *University of South Florida Alma Mater*

> Hail to thee, our Alma Mater, may thy name be told,
> Where above thy gleaming splendor, waves the Green and Gold.
> Thou our guide in quest for knowledge where all men are free,
> UNIVERSITY OF SOUTH FLORIDA, ALMA MATER, Hail to Thee!
>
> Be our guide to truth and wisdom, as we onward go,
> May thy glory, fame and honor never cease to grow.
> May our thoughts and pray'rs be with thee through eternity,
> UNIVERSITY OF SOUTH FLORIDA, ALMA MATER, Hail to Thee!
> *R. Wayne Hugoboom*

The University of Tampa
401 W. Kennedy Blvd.
Tampa, FL 33606-1490

School Nickname: *The Spartans*

School Colors: *Red, Gold and Black*

School Mascot: *Spartan*

The University of West Florida
Pensacola, FL 32514

School Nickname: *UWF*

School Colors: *Blue and Green*

School Mascot: *Argonaut*

School Newspaper: *Voyager*

GEORGIA

Atlanta University
223 James P. Brawley Dr.
Atlanta, GA 30314

School Colors: *Crimson and Gray*

Alma Mater: *Alma Mater*

> Hail to thee, our Alma Mater,
> Guardian of the right,
> Love and truth and sacred honor,
> Lead us toward the light.
> > *Chorus*
> Atlanta, Atlanta, school we love,
> Deeply graven on each heart,
> We, thy faithful sons and daughters,
> Pledge to thee our part.
>
> Where our graduates may gather,
> Striving every day,
> Thoughtful of their Alma Mater,
> God will make a way.
>
> When the crimson and gray banner
> Waves its victory,
> True and loyal sons Atlanta,
> We'll come back to thee.

Augusta College
2500 Walton Way
Augusta, GA 30910

School Colors: *Blue and White*

School Mascot: *Jaguar*

School Newspaper: *Bell Ringer*

School Yearbook: *White Columns*

Alma Mater: *Alma Mater*

> Where sentinels once guarded
> Thy armaments of yore,
> Now aged oaks sublimely
> Bespeak a lofty lore.
> *Chorus*
> Thy sword is now a plowshare,
> And peace enshrines thy name;
> The flag unfurled above thee
> Adds glory to thy fame.
> *Chorus*
> And we, thy sons and daughters,
> Who pass thy portals through,
> Will keep thy inspiration
> With honor high and true.
> *Chorus*
> All hail, Augusta College
> Our voices now we raise
> To give thee, Alma Mater,
> Our fervent love and praise.

Columbus College
Algonquin Dr.
Columbus, GA 31907

School Colors: *Red, White and Blue*

School Mascot: *Cougars*

School Newspaper: *The Saber*

Emory University
Atlanta, GA 30322

School Colors: *Blue and Gold*

School Mascot: *Eagle*   Name: *Swoop*

School Newspaper: *The Wheel and The Voice*

School Yearbook: *The Campus*

Alma Mater: *Alma Mater*

> In the heart of dear old Dixie
> Where the sun doth shine
> That is where my heart is turning
> Round old Emory's shrine.
> *Chorus*
> We will ever sing thy praises
> Sons and Daughters true
> Hail thee now our Alma Mater
> Hail the gold and blue.
>
> Though the years around us gather
> Filled with love and cheer
> Still the memory of old Emory,
> Grows to us more dear.
> *Chorus*

Georgia Institute of Technology
225 North Ave., N. W.
Atlanta, GA 30332

School Nickname: *Georgia Tech; Yellow Jackets*

School Colors: *White and Gold*

School Mascot: *Buzz*

School Newspaper: *Technique*

School Yearbook: *Blueprint*

Alma Mater: *Alma Mater*

Oh sons of Tech arise behold
The banner as it reigns supreme
For from on high the White and Gold
Waves in its triumphant gleam
The spirit of the cheering throng
Resounds with joy revealing
A Brotherhood in praise and song
In the mem'ry of the days gone by.
Oh Scion of the Southland
In our hearts you shall forever fly!

We cherish thoughts so dear for thee
Oh Alma Mater in our prayer
We plead for you in victory
And then in victory we share,
But when the battle seems in vain
Our spirits never falters
We're ever one in joy and pain
And our union is a lasting bond;
Oh may we be united
Till the victory of life is won!
Words, Ivan Granath
Music, Frank Roman

Fight Song: *Rambling Wreck From Georgia Tech*

Oh, if I had a daughter, sir, I'd dress her in White and Gold,
And put her on the campus, to cheer the brave and bold.
But if I had a son, sir, I'll tell you what he'd do.
He would yell, "To Hell with Georgia," like his daddy used to do.
Chorus
I'm a Ramblin' Wreck from Georgia Tech and a hell of an engineer,
A hell of a, hell of a, hell of a, hell of a, hell of an engineer,
Like all the good jolly fellows, I drink my whiskey clear,
I'm a Ramblin' Wreck form Georgia Tech and a hell of an engineer.

Oh, I wish I had a barrel of rum and sugar three thousand punds,
A college bell to put it in and a clapper to stir it round.
I'd drink to all good fellows who come from far and near.
I'm a ramblin', gamblin', hell of an engineer.
Frank Roman

Georgia Southern College
Statesboro, GA 30460

School Colors: *Blue and White*

School Mascot: *Eagles*

School Newspaper: *The George-Anne*

School Yearbook: *Reflector*

Alma Mater: *Alma Mater*

> Down among the murmuring pine trees
> Where old nature smiles,
> GSC holds up a standard
> Known for miles and miles.
>
> Lift the chorus, speed it onward
> Ne'er her standard fail,
> Hail to thee, our Alma Mater,
> GSC, all hail.
>
> From the blue and broad Atlantic
> Balmy breezes blow.
> Wafting far GSC's spirit
> May she ever grow.
>
> Lift the chorus, speed it onward,
> Ne'er her standard fail,
> Hail to thee, our Alma Mater,
> GSC, all hail.

Georgia State University
University Plaza
Atlanta, GA 30303

School Nickname: *GSU*

School Colors: *Red and Gray*

School Mascot: *Crimson Panthers*

School Newspaper: *Signal*

School Yearbook: *Rampway*

Alma Mater: *Alma Mater*

> Alma Mater, we are loyal
> to the name of Georgia State
> Love and honor we accord thee
> and devotion from our hearts.

In respect and veneration
we shall always hold thy name.
Nurturer of light and knowledge,
we shall ever tell thy fame.

Happy are thy sons and daughters
spread abroad throughout the land
knowing that we are forever part
of thine own faithful band.

Where the paths of life are crowded
we have known thy pleasant bond.
And the love of Alma Mater
we shall never pass beyond.

University of Georgia
Athens, GA 30602

School Colors: *Red and Black*

School Mascot: *Bulldog*   Name: *Uga IV (Ugh-ah 4)*

School Newspaper: *Red and Black (Independent)*

School Yearbook: *Pandora*

Alma Mater: *Alma Mater*

From the hills of Georgia's northland
Beams thy noble brow,
And the sons of Georgia rising
Pledge with sacred vow.
         Chorus
Alma Mater, thee we'll honor
True and loyal be,
Ever crowned with praise and glory,
Georgia, hail to thee.

'Neath the pine trees' stately shadow
Spread thy riches rare,
And thy sons, dear Alma Mater,
Will thy treasures share.

Through the ages, Alma Mater,
Men will look to thee;
Through the fairest of the Southland,
Georgia's Varsity.
         J. B. Wright, Jr., '12

FightSong: *Fight Song*

> Glory, glory to old Georgia
> Glory, glory to old Georgia
> Glory, glory to old Georgia
> G-E-O-R-G-I-A

Valdosta State College
Valdosta, GA 31698

School Nickname: *Blazers*

School Colors: *Red and Black*

School Mascot: *The Blaze (A person dressed up in flame costume)*

School Newspaper: *Spectator*

School Yearbook: *Milestones*

Alma Mater: *Alma Mater*

> 'Mong the stately pines of Georgia
> Glorious to the view
> Stands our noble Alma Mater
> Basking 'neath the blue.
>
> Alma Mater, thee we honor
> Praises never fail,
> For thy fame shall never perish,
> Red and Black--all hail!
>
> Alma Mater's sons and daughters
> We will ever be,
> Always to thy heart returning,
> Dear old VS.C.
>
> Alma Mater, thee we honor
> Praises never fail,
> For thy fame shall never perish,
> Red and Black--all hail!
> > *Words by Helen Allen Thomas, '21*
> > *and Evelyn Brown, '24*
> > *Music by Dr. John Huxford, '85*

West Georgia College
Carrollton, GA 30118

School Nickname: *WGC*

School Colors: *Red and Blue*

School Mascot: *Braves*

School Newspaper: *The West Georgian*

Alma Mater: *West Georgia Alma Mater*

> In the western pines of Georgia standing strong and true,
> Our wise Alma Mater beckons to the Red and Blue,
> Though you be in learning founded youthful yet you be,
> While thus guided by tradition yet you still breath free,
> Dear West Georgia Dear West Georgia standing strong and true,
> Our wise Alma Mater beckons to the Red and the Blue.
> > *Felton Dunn*
> > *Bruce Borton*

HAWAII

University of Hawaii
Honolulu, HI 96822

School Nickname: *Rainbows*

School Colors: *Green and White*

School Newspaper: *Ka Leo O Hawaii*

Alma Mater: *University Alma Mater*

In green Manoa Valley our Alma Mater stands
Where mountain winds and showers refresh her fertile lands;
The flag of freedom beckons above her shining walls,
To larger truth and service our Alma Mater calls.

Hawaii, we have gathered within thy wide flung doors,
As sons and daughters claiming thy freely offered stores;
Our loyal praise we tender, and pledge to hold thy aim,
Till ocean's far horizons shall hear thy honored name.

Ha'aheo 'o Hawai'i i kona Kulanui
Hawai'i is proud of its University
Ho'ohilu 'ia nei e ka ua Tuahine
Graced and distinguished by the Tuahine rain

Its flag beckons above in the gentle winds of Manoa
E 'imi i ka pono o ka maiamalama
Seek out the excellence of enlightenment
Komo mai e na kini i na hale e ku nei
Enter, o multitude, into these buildings
A huli i ka nani o ka ho'ona'auao
And find the beauty of learning
Pai a'e i ke aho a puka i ke ao
Lift up your aims and go forth into the world
Lanakila kou inoa, Kulanui o Hawai'i
Victorious is your name, University of Hawai'i.
*Hawaiian language version
composed by Larry L. Kimura*

University of Hawaii at Hilo
1400 Kapiolani St.
Hilo, HI 96720-4091

School Nickname: *Vulcans*

School Colors: *Red and White*

School Newspaper: *Vulcan News*

School Yearbook: *Kani O Hilo (no longer published)*

Alma Mater: *Alma Mater*

In verdant hills of Hilo
Our Alma Mater stands
Where mountain winds and showers
Refresh her fertile land
The flag of freedom beckons
Above her shining walls
To larger truth and service
Our Alma Mater calls.

IDAHO

Idaho State University
Pocatello, ID 83209-0009

School Nickname: *Bengals*

School Colors: *Orange and Black*

School Mascot: *Bengal Tiger*

School Newspaper: *Bengal*

Alma Mater: *Idaho State University Alma Mater Hymn*

> Hail to thee, our Alma Mater; Glorious is thy name
> Evermore thy sons and daughters carry on thy fame.
> May thy student e'er be loyal to thy mem'ry true,
> Hail to thee, our Alma Mater; Hail to I.S.U.
> *Wesley M. Harris*

Fight Song: *Growl, Bengals, Growl!*

> Growl, Bengals, Growl!
> Fight, Bengals, Fight!
> Gnash your teeth and bare your claws
> And fight with all your might!

March onto the field;
They will surely yield!
Bring a victory home to us
You Bengals of Idaho State!

University of Idaho
Moscow, ID 83843

School Nickname: *Vandals*

School Colors: *Silver and Gold*

School Mascot: *Vandal*

School Newspaper: *The Argonaut*

School Yearbook: *The Gem*

Alma Mater: *Here We Have Idaho*

Alma Mater, the hope of a pioneer race;
You're fashioned of dreams and of toil,
Your walls and your towers by stouthearted men
Were raised from the rock and the soil.
Chorus
And here we have Idaho
Winning her way to fame
Silver and Gold in the sunlight blaze,
And romance lies in her name;
Singing, we're singing of you,
ah, proudly too;
All our lives through
We'll go singing, singing of you
Alma Mater, our Idaho.

Now ours is the heritage, rich and so full,
The gain of their toil and their tears;
And ours is the fruit, and the harvest is ours,
Oh, Idaho, gift of the years.
Chorus

Fight Song: *Go, Vandals, Go*

Came a tribe from the North brave and bold,
Bearing banners of Silver and Gold;
Tried and true to subdue all their foes!
Vandals! Vandals! Go, Vandals, go,

Fight on with hearts true and bold
Foes will fall before your Silver and your Gold
The victory cannot be withheld from thee;
So all bear down for Idaho,
Come on, you Vandals, go!

ILLINOIS

Bradley University
Peoria, IL 61625

School Nickname: *Bradley Braves*

School Colors: *Red and White*

School Newspaper: *The Bradley Scout*

School Yearbook: *Anaga*

Alma Mater: *Hail, Red and White*

> Lift up your hearts and sing!
> Lift up thy light!
> Let all your voices ring!
> Hail, Red and White!
>
> Red for courage, strength, and right,
> White for Purity,
> Shining as a beacon light,
> For the University!
>
> Go onward, ever onward!
> Let courage and truth prevail!
> To Bradley University
> All hail, hail, hail!
> *F. Thompson*

Fight Song: *Bradley Loyalty Song*

Here's our pledge to Bradley,
Loyal hearts and hands,
Loudly sing your praises,
In a mighty band,
Ever forward Bradley,
We'll praise you to the sky,
Ever keep your banners flying while you hear our cry!
Charge on, Charge on, Bradley,
March right down the field,
Foes may press you,
Foes may even stress you,
But we'll never yield,
Fight for Alma Mater,
Plunge right thru to victory,
Fight on, Fight on, Bradley, And fight for varsity!
Words by John Fritz and
Fred'k Siebert

College of St. Francis
500 Wilcox St.
Joliet, IL 60435

School Colors: *Brown and Gold*

School Mascot: *Fighting Saints*

School Newspaper: *The Encounter*

Alma Mater: *Alma Mater*

Engraven in the history of Joilet's bright years,
There's traced a College story wrought by daring pioneers.
St. Francis Alma Mater in grateful love of Thee,
Thy students raise in chorus a hymn of loyalty.
We cherish every memory linked with thy fair name
And ever laud the brown and gold which herald wide thy name.

DePaul University
Lincoln Park Campus
2323 North Seminary Ave.
Chicago, IL 60614

Loop Campus
25 East Jackson Blvd.
Chicago, IL 60604

School Colors: *Scarlet and Blue*

School Mascot: *Blue Demon*

School Newspaper: *DePaulia*

Alma Mater: *Victory Song*

> We will gather, neath the banner,
> Neath the scarlet and the blue.
> While in song we, tell your praises,
> Praises for old De Paul 'U'.
> Let the battle, wage and threaten,
> your's the victory to claim.
> For we fight beneath your standard proud,
> Exulting in your name.
> > *Words by J. Leo Sullivan*
> > *Music by Arthur C. Becker*
> > *Copyright 1930 by DePaul University*

Eastern Illinois University
Charleston, IL 61920

School Nickname: *Panthers*

School Colors: *Blue and Gray*

School Mascot: *Panther*

School Newspaper: *Daily Eastern News*

School Yearbook: *Warbler*

Alma Mater: *Alma Mater*

> For us arose thy walls and towers;
> Their beauty, strength, and grace are ours.
> The hills and prairies at thy feet
> For us in lovely landscape meet
> So must our hearts remember thee,
> So may our lives, our tribute be;
> Strong, true, and beautiful, and brave, and free.
> So shall our hearts, our hearts, remember thee.

Fight Song: *Eastern's Loyalty*

We are loyal EIU
We're loyal and true;
Though the odds be great or small,
We'll still be cheering you;
Rah! Rah! Rah!
Fight you Panthers for the glory
Of our dear name;
Fight on for Eastern,
Come on you Panthers, win the game.

Elmhurst College

190 Prospect
Elmhurst, IL 60126

School Colors: *Blue and White*

School Mascot: *Bluejays*

School Newspaper: *Leader*

School Yearbook: *Elms*

Alma Mater: *Alma Mater*

Where the elms in stately glory
Spreading branches raise,
There our cherished Alma Mater
Hears our song of praise. (Refrain)

Student days will soon be over
For our happy throng
Still we hold thy memory precious
Ever dear and strong. (Refrain)

When life's closing days draw nearer,
Sad the heart may be,
Still shall dreams of youth and glory
Linger long o'er thee. (Refrain)
   Refrain
School we love, Elmhurst, live for aye,
God shed His grace on thee;
Loyal be thy sons and daughters
To thy memory.

Governors State University

Governors Highway & University Parkway
University Park, IL 60466

School Colors: *Black and White*

School Newspaper: *The Innovator*

Illinois Institute of Technology
IIT Center
Chicago, IL 60616-3793

School Nickname: *IIT*

School Colors: *Scarlet and Gray*

School Mascot: *Scarlet Hawk*

School Newspaper: *Technology News*

Illinois State University
Normal, IL 61761

School Nickname: *Redbirds*

School Colors: *Red and White*

School Mascot: *Reggie Redbird*

School Newspaper: *Daily Vidette*

Loyola University of Chicago
820 No. Michigan Ave.
Chicago, IL 60611

School Nickname: *LU*

School Colors: *Maroon and Gold*

School Mascot: *Bo, the Rambler Hobo*

School Newspaper: *Phoenix*

School Yearbook: *Loyolan*

Alma Mater: *Alma Mater*

> True to the beauty of wisdom and learning
> And eager as sons of tradition and fame,

We gather our prowess and loyalty turning
To honor a beautiful name.
On the field we fight for that line
To bring our colors through!
Loyal, inspired, we pledge to Loyola
Our spirit, our courage anew.

Fight Song: *Fight Song*

Go Loyola push on and win that game!
Go Loyola to Alma Mater fame!
Go Loyola fighting for all to see!
Give them a fight and do it with might,
And Ramble on to VICTORY!

Northeastern Illinois University
5500 North St. Louis Ave.
Chicago, IL 60625

School Nickname: *UNI - Golden Eagles*

School Colors: *Gold and Brown*

School Newspaper: *The Print*

School Yearbook: *UNI*

Alma Mater: *Northeastern Illinois University Alma Mater*

All Hail to thee UNI,
We sing your praises true
We'll always hold thine honor high,
Our faith in thee renew.

Thou art our Alma Mater Dear,
Let it by all be known
That we will hold within our minds,
The love that thou hast shown.

In years to come we may forget,
We might not oft recall
The joys we've shared within thy rooms
And Peace in every hall.
        Refrain
Then sing out loud and sing out clear,
Oh, may we be heard far and near
Ring out the song NORTHEASTERN.

Fight Song: *Go Golden Eagles*

> When those Golden Eagles fall in line
> We're going to win that game another time
> We'll give those Gold'n' Brown Boys a cheer
> That can be heard around the world by every ear.
>
> We're going to FIGHT, FIGHT, FIGHT, with all our might
> We're going to put that other team up tight
> With a V I C T O R Y, our victory cry
> For UNI.

Northern Illinois University
DeKalb, IL 60115

School Nickname: *Northern*

School Colors: *Cardinal Red and Black*

School Mascot: *Huskie*

School Newspaper: *Northern Star*

Alma Mater: *Alma Mater*

> Alma Mater fair 'mid opening buds of Springtime.
> When the meadow lark is piping first his lay;
> When the lake o'erflown reflects thy towers and turrets;
> When the moon sends down its softest, purest ray;
> When the air is sweet with balmy breezes laden;
> Oh 'tis then I sit and dream and think of thee;
> How majestic and how grand,
> Meadow and prairie in command,
> School of mine I dream of thee.
> > *Chorus*
> Dreaming, Dreaming, Dreaming,
> Dreaming of the good old school days,
> When hearts were light from care and burden free
> Hours of work and hours of play
> Made our life a holiday
> I am dreaming Alma Mater still of thee.
>
> Alma Mater 'lone in frost and snow of winter,
> When the meadow lark has stilled his lilting song;
> When the lake iced o'er, reflects no more thy beauty;
> When the moon shines cold through nights so dear and long;
> When the air is filled with joyous happy laughter,
> And the click of skates on ice bound lake rings free,

Home majestic and how grand,
Snowbound meadow in command
School of mine I dream of thee.
Words and Music by A. N. Annas

Fight Song: *Fight Song*

Huskies, come on you Huskies
and make a score or two
Huskies, you're Northern Huskies
the team to pull us through
Forward, together forward
there's victory in view
Come on you Huskies, Fight on you
Huskies and win for N.I.U.
Words and Music by A. Neil Annas

Northwestern University
Evanston, IL 60201

School Nickname: *Wildcats*

School Colors: *Purple and White*

School Mascot: *Willie the Wildcat*

School Newspaper: *The Daily Northwestern*

School Yearbook: *Syllabus*

Alma Mater: *Alma Mater*

Hail to Alma Mater, we will sing thy praise forever.
All thy sons and daughters pledge thee victory and honor.
Alma Mater praise be thine, may thy name forever shine.
Hail to purple, hail to white. Hail to thee Northwestern.

Fight Song: *Fight Song*

Go U Northwestern, break right through that line.
With our colors flying, we will cheer you all the time.
U RAH RAH! Go U Northwestern, fight for victory.
Spread far the fame of our fair name.
Go Northwestern win that game.
Go Northwestern go! Go Northwestern go!
Hit 'em hard, hit 'em low! Go Northwestern go!

Roosevelt University
430 So. Michigan Ave.
Chicago, IL 60615

School Colors: *Green*

School Newspaper: *Torch*

Southern Illinois University at Carbondale
Carbondale, IL 62901

School Colors: *Maroon and White*

School Mascot: *Saluki*

School Newspaper: *Daily Egyptian*

School Yearbook: *Obelisk*

Alma Mater: *Southern Alma Mater*

> Hail Alma Mater Southern to thee
> Strong thru the years you stand triumphantly
> Beacon to guide us over life's sea
> Light that can never fail us Hail, hail to thee.
> *Clarke Morgan*

Fight Song: *Go! Southern Go!*

> Go! Southern Go!
> Fight on the victory!
> Go! Southern Go!
> March on triumphantly!
> Come on and show,
> Southern, Show,
> For all the world to know
> Nothing's gonna stop you now
> Hit that line and show them how to go!
> Southern Go! Go!
> *Words amd Music by*
> *Grover Clarke Morgan*

Southern Illinois University at Edwardsville
Edwardsville, IL 62026

School Colors: *Red and White*

School Mascot: *Kenya the Cougar*

School Newspaper: *Alestle*

University of Chicago
5801 S. Ellis Ave.
Chicago, IL 60637

School Nickname: *Maroons*

School Colors: *Maroon and White*

School Newspaper: *The Chicago Maroon*

School Yearbook: *The Cap and Gown*

Alma Mater: *Alma Mater*

> Today we gladly sing the praise
> Of her whose daughters and whose sons
> Now loyal voices proudly raise,
> To bless her with our benisons.
> Of all fair mothers, fairest she,
> Most wise of all the wisest be,
> Most true of all the true, say we,
> Is our dear Alma Mater.
> Her mighty learning we would tell,
> Tho life is something more than lore,
> She could not love her children well,
> Loved she not truth and honor more.
> We praise her breadth of charity,
> Her faith that truth shall make us free.
> That right shall live eternally,
> We praise our Alma Mater.

University of Illinois at Chicago
P. O. Box 4348
Chicago, IL 60680

School Nickname: *The Flames*

School Colors: *Flame (red/orange) and Indigo (blue/black)*

School Mascot: *Dragon*

School Newspaper: *Chicago Illini*

University of Illinois at Urbana-Champaign
Urbana, IL 61801

School Nickname: *Fighting Illini*

School Colors: *Orange and Blue*

School Mascot: *Chief Illiniwek*

School Newspaper: *Daily Illini*

School Yearbook: *Illio*

Alma Mater: *Hail To The Orange*

> Hail to the Orange,
> Hail to the Blue,
> Hail Alma Mater,
> Ever so true.
>
> We love no other,
> So let our motto be
> Victory, Illinois
> Varsity.

Fight Song: *Oskee - Wow - Wow*

> Old Princeton yells her tiger,
> Wisconsin her varsity,
> And they give the same old Rah! Rah! Rah!
> At each University,
> But that yell that always thrills me,
> And fills my heart with joy,
> Is the good old Os-kee-wow-wow,
> That they yell at Illinois.
> *Chorus*
> Os-kee-wow-wow, Illinois
> Our eyes are all on you,
> Os-kee-wow-wow, Illinois,
> Wave your Orange and your Blue, Rah! Rah!
> When the team trots our before you,
> Ev'ry man stand up and yell,
> Back the team to gain a victory,
> Os-kee-wow-wow, Illinois.

Western Illinois University
Macomb, IL 61455

School Nickname: *Fighting Leathernecks*

School Colors: *Purple and Gold*

School Mascot: *Rocky*

School Newspaper: *Courier*

School Yearbook: *Sequel*

Alma Mater: *Western Loyalty*

1. Western's sons and daughters gather as a band to sing her praise
2. Western's deeds and actions give her rank a-breast the brave and strong;
3. Western's sons and daughters greet her as the author of their dreams.
4. Western sounds her cry of battle as her teams grid for the fray.

She did rear us' die we'd rather as we chant our heartfelt lays.
She will strive and never waiver; she will win her battles long.
She has made our lives completer; she has brought us sunshine's beams.
"Be not like dumb driven cattle"; courage, we will win the day.
Than to suffer should she falter, just one moment in despair.
Join us then ye sturdy foe-men--yield to us what is our due.
In her glory flows our life blood; in her frame we have a part.
Purple, gold, our colors flying, must on high float first and last.
Lo! we place upon her altar all our love for her so fair.
Yes, we lift our heads as freemen; e'er to her we will be true.
We do crown her with true knighthood; we would strengthen her brave heart.
Hurrah, Western! Still defying. All together one loud blast.
Chorus
Hail to Western, Alma Mater, may we honor thy fair name;
(4th stanza) Hail to Western, Alma Mater, you have honored your fair name;
Hail to Western, ever greater, on to conquest and to fame.
Hail to Western, ever greater, you have won unsung fame.
Words by Walter P. Morgan
Music by Harold F. Schory

Fight Song: *We're Marching On*

> We are marching on 'neath the Purple and Gold;
> We are singing a song that will never grow old.
> All the Sons and Daughters of Western today,
> Go marching on.
> W-E-S-T-E-R-N Yea Western.
> Hail to Western, true and loyal,
> We are here to win this day.
> When you see those conqu'ring heroes
> Marching down the way (Rah Rah Rah!)
> Ev'ry heart and voice will sing this melody of Vict'ry song:
> Fling out the Purple and Gold,
> We're Marching On.

INDIANA

Ball State University
Muncie, IN 47306

School Nickname: *Cardinals*

School Colors: *Cardinal Red and White*

School Mascot: *Charlie Cardinal*

School Newspaper: *Daily News*

School Yearbook: *Orient*

Alma Mater: *Ball State University Alma Mater*

> Dear Alma Mater, hear our vow
> of faith and trust in thee!
> Thy spirit hovers near us now
> and through eternity.
> Thy colors true of red and white
> shall e're exhalted be.
> We'll honor thee both day and night
> Dear Alma Mater, we love thee!

Dear Alma Mater, hear our cry
of laud and praise to thee!
To bring thee honor e'er we'll try
No matter where we be.
Fond memories we e'er shall hold
of Ball State U. so dear.
Though years may pass and we grow old
May Alma Mater still be near!

Fight Song: *Ball State University Fight Song*

Fight team fight, for Ball State;
We must win this game;
Onward, now you Cardinals,
Bring glory to your name!
Rah! Rah! Rah!
Here's to both our colors-
Cardinal and white,
Praying for a victory--
So fight, fight, fight!

Butler University
4600 Sunset Ave.
Indianapolis, IN 46208

School Nickname: *Bulldogs*

School Colors: *Blue and White*

School Newspaper: *Collegian*

School Yearbook: *Carillon*

Alma Mater: *Gallery of Memories*

In the gallery of memories
There are pictures bright and fair,
And I find that dear old Butler
Is the brightest one that's there.
Alma Mater, how we love thee,
With a love that ne'er shall fade.
And we feel we owe a debt to thee
That never can be paid.
                    Fred W. Wolfe
                    Class of '16

Fight Song: *Butler War Song*

We'll sing the Butler war song,
We'll give a fighting cry;
We'll fight the Butler battle--
...Bulldogs ever do or die.
And in the glow of the victory firelight,
Hist'ry cannot deny
To add a page or two
For Butler's fighting crew
Beneath the Hoosier sky.
John Heiney
Class of '23

Indiana State University
Terre Haute, IN 47809

School Nickname: *The Sycamores*

School Colors: *Blue and White*

School Mascot: *Chief Ouabachi and the Indian Princess*

School Newspaper: *Indiana Statesman*

School Yearbook: *Sycamore*

Alma Mater: *Alma Mater*

Out upon the swelling breezes, let our voices ring
As to thee, our Alma Mater, heartfelt praise we sing
Though the years to come may part us,
Friends and comrades true,
ISU, our Alma Mater, here's our pledge to you.

Fight Song: *March On! Sycamores*

March on! March on, you fighting Sycamores, Sycamores,
March on, you Statesmen tried and true.
March on! March on, to glorious vic-tor-y.
Raise that flag of Royal Blue!
March on! March on, you fighting Sycamores, Sycamores,
Shout out the vic-t'ry song!
Onward, ever onward to the goal, as you march, on and on!
Used with permission of Indiana State University

Indiana University
Bloomington, IN 47405

School Nickname: *Hurryin' Hoosiers or Hoosiers*

School Colors: *Cream and Crimson*

School Newspaper: *Indiana Daily Student (IDS)*

School Yearbook: *Indiana University Arbutus*

Alma Mater: *Hail to Old I. U.*

> Come and join in song together,
> Shout with might and main;
> Our beloved Alma Mater,
> Sound her praise again.
> *Chorus*
> Gloriana, Frangipana,
> E'er to her be true;
> She's the pride of Indiana,
> Hail to old I.U.!
> *Joe T. Giles, '94*

Fight Song: *Indiana, Our Indiana*

> Indiana, our Indiana
> Indiana, we're all for you.
> We will fight for the Cream and Crimson,
> For the glory of old I.U.
> Never daunted, we cannot falter,
> In the battle, we're tried and true.
> Oh, Indiana, our Indiana
> Indiana, we're all for you.

Indiana University at South Bend
1700 Mishawaka Ave.
South Bend, IN 46634

School Nickname: *Titans*

School Colors: *Blue and White*

School Newspaper: *The Preface*

Alma Mater: *Hail to Old I.U.*

> Come and join in song together,
> Shout with might and main;
> Our beloved Alma Mater,
> Sound her praise again.

Chorus
Gloriana, Frangipana,
E'er to her be true;
She's the pride of Indiana,
Hail to old I.U.!
Joe T. Giles, '94

Indiana University Northwest
3400 Broadway
Gary, IN 46408

School Colors: *Red and White*

School Newspaper: *The Phoenix*

Indiana University-Purdue University at Fort Wayne
2101 Coliseum Blvd. East
Fort Wayne, IN 46805

School Nickname: *IPFW*

School Colors: *Red and Gold*

School Mascot: *Mastodons*

School Newspaper: *The Communicator*

Indiana University-Purdue University at Indianapolis
1100 West Michigan St.
Indianapolis, IN 46202

School Nickname: *IUPUI Metros*

School Colors: *No official colors. Metros use Red and Orange*

School Newspaper: *The Sagamore*

Indiana University Southeast
4201 Grant Line Rd.
New Albany, IN 47150

School Nickname: *IUS*

School Colors: *Red, White and Blue*

School Mascot: *Grenadier*

School Newspaper: *The Southeast Horizon*

Alma Mater: *Hail to Old I.U.*

> Come and join in song together,
> Shout with might and main;
> Our beloved Alma Mater,
> Sound her praise again.
> *Chorus*
> Gloriana, Frangipana,
> E'er to her be true;
> She's the pride of Indiana,
> Hail to old I.U.!
> *Joe T. Giles, '94*

Purdue University
West Lafayette, IN 47907

School Nickname: *Boilermakers*

School Colors: *Old Gold and Black*

School Mascot: *Boilermaker Special III and Boilermaker Extra Special*

School Newspaper: *Purdue Exponent*

School Yearbook: *Debris*

Alma Mater: *The Purdue Hymn*

> Close by the Wabash, in famed Hoosier land
> Stands Old Purdue serene, and -- grand!
> Cherished in mem'ry by all her sons and daughters true.
> Fair Alma Mater, All Hail Purdue.
> Fairest in all the land, our own Purdue.
> Fairest in all the land, our own Purdue.

Fight Song: *Hail Purdue*

> To your call once more we rally,
> Alma Mater, hear our praise;

Where the Wabash spreads its valley,
Filled with joy our voices raise.
From the skies in swelling echoes
Come the cheers that tell the tale,
Of your vict'ries and your heroes,
Hail Purdue! We sing all hail!
> *Chorus*
Hail, Hail to old Purdue!
All hail to our old gold and black!
Hail, Hail to old Purdue!
Our friendship may she never lack,
Ever grateful ever true,
Thus we raise our song anew,
Of the days we've spent with you,
All hail our own Purdue.

When in after years we're turning,
Alma Mater, back to you,
May our hearts with love be yearning,
For the scenes of old Purdue.
Back among your pathways winding
Let us seek what lies before,
Fondest hopes and aims e'er finding,
While we sing of days of yore.
> *Words by J. Morrison '15*
> *Music by E. J. Wotawa, '12*

University of Evansville
800 Lincoln Ave.
Evansville, IN 47722

School Nickname: *UE*

School Colors: *Purple and White*

School Mascot: *Ace Purple*

School Newspaper: *The Crescent*

School Yearbook: *Linc*

Alma Mater: *Alma Mater*

School of our fathers known of old
Our Alma Mater we revere.
We give thee loyalty untold;
We love thee more and more each year;

And when sweet memories of thee return
Of lessons learned, of friendships made;
We face the future unafraid.

Fight Song: *Fight Song*

Evansville, all hail to thee.
True and loyal we will be,
We'll fight, fight, fight
With all our might,
Cheering with pep and vim for
white and purple
And with every victory
Our hearts with praise will fill.
So we'll back you with a
Rah! Rah! Rah!
All hail to our Evansville.

University of Notre Dame
Notre Dame, IN 46556

School Nickname: *Fighting Irish*

School Colors: *Blue and Gold*

School Mascot: *Leprechaun* (*A student chosen by competition each year.*)

School Newspaper: *Observer*

School Yearbook: *Dome*

Alma Mater: *Notre Dame, Our Mother*

Notre Dame, our Mother,
Tender, strong and true.
Proudly in the heavens,
Gleams the gold and blue,
Glory's mantle cloaks thee,
Golden is thy fame,
And our hearts forever,
Praise thee, Notre Dame.
And our hearts forever,
Love thee, Notre Dame.

Fight Song: *Notre Dame Victory March*

Rally sons of Notre Dame
Sing her glory and sound her fame,

Raise her Gold and Blue
And cheer with voices true;
Rah, rah, for Notre Dame.
We will fight in ev-ry game,
Strong of heart and true to her name
We will ne'er forget her
And will cheer her ever
Loyal to Notre Dame.
Chorus
Cheer, cheer for old Notre Dame,
Wake up the echoes cheering her name,
Send a volley cheer on high,
Shake down the thunder from the sky.
What though the odds be great or small
Old Notre Dame will win over all,
While her loyal sons are marching
Onward to victory.

University of Southern Indiana
8600 University Blvd.
Evansville, IN 47712

School Nickname: *USI*

School Colors: *Red, White and Blue*

School Mascot: *Screaming Eagles*

School Newspaper: *The Shield*

School Yearbook: *Transitions*

Valparaiso University
Valparaiso, IN 46383

School Nickname: *Valpo*

School Colors *Brown and Gold*

School Mascot: *Crusader*

School Newspaper: *Torch*

School Yearbook: *The Beacon*

IOWA

Drake University
25th and University
Des Moines, IA 50311

School Nickname: *Drake Bulldogs*

School Colors: *Blue and White*

School Mascot: *Spike and Spice*

School Newspaper: *Times-Delphic*

School Yearbook: *Quax*

Iowa State University
Ames, IA 50011

School Nickname: *Cyclones*

School Colors: *Cardinal and Gold*

School Mascot: *Cy*

School Newspaper: *Iowa State Daily*

School Yearbook: *BOMB*

Alma Mater: *Bells of Iowa State*

> Green Hills for thy throne,
> and for crown a golden melody
> Ringing in the hearts of all who bring
> thee love and loyalty;
> Dear Alma Mater, make our spirits
> great, true and valiant like
> the Bells of Iowa State.

Fight Song: *Iowa State Fight Song*

> O we will fight, fight, fight, for Iowa State
> And may her colors ever fly
> Yes, we will fight with might for Iowa State
> With a will to do or die, Rah! Rah! Rah!
> Loyal sons forever true
> And we will fight the battle through
> And when we hit that line we'll hit it hard
> Every yard for I-S-U.

University of Iowa
Iowa City, IA 52242

School Nickname: *Hawkeyes*

School Colors: *Old Gold and Black*

School Mascot: *Herky the Hawk*

School Newspaper: *The Daily Iowan*

School Yearbook: *Hawkeye*

Alma Mater: *Old Gold*

> O, Iowa, calm and secure on thy hill,
> Looking down on the river below,
> With a dignity born of the dominant will
> Of the men who have lived long ago.
> O, heir of the glory of pioneer days,
> Let thy spirit be proud as of old,
> For thou shalt find blessing, and honor and praise
> In the daughters and sons of Old Gold.

II

We shall sing and be glad with the days as they fly
In the time that we spend in thy halls,
And in sadness we'll part when the days have gone by,
And our paths turn away from thy walls.
Till the waters no more in thy river shall run,
Till the stars in the heavens grow cold,
We shall sing of the glory and fame thou has won,
And the love that we bear for Old Gold.

Fight Song: *Iowa Fight Song*

What's the Word? Fight! Fight! Fight!
The word is "Fight! Fight! Fight! for Iowa",
Let every loyal Iowan sing;
The word is "Fight! Fight! Fight! for Iowa".
Until the walls and rafters ring;
Rah! Rah!
Come on and cheer, cheer, cheer, for Iowa.
Come on and cheer until you hear the final gun,
The word is "Fight! Fight! Fight! for Iowa".
Until the game is won.

University of Northern Iowa
Cedar Falls, IA 50614

School Nickname: *UNI*

School Colors: *Purple and Gold*

School Mascot: *Panther*

School Newspaper: *Northern Iowan*

School Yearbook: *Old Gold*

KANSAS

Emporia State University
1200 Commercial St.
Emporia, KS 66801

School Nickname: *Hornets*

School Colors: *Black and Gold*

School Mascot: *Corky*

School Newspaper: *Bulletin*

School Yearbook: *Sunflower*

Alma Mater: *Alma Mater*

Let us exalt our University
True to our forbears and posterity
Our finest efforts we shall yield
In classroom, concert, lab and field
And cheers for ESU
And cheers for ESU.

Let us remember in our future years
Bold shouts of victory or sentimental tears
Then shall the memories abound;
We made these hallowed halls resound
With cheers for ESU, With cheers for ESU.

Fort Hays State University

600 Park St.
Hays, KS 67601-4099

School Colors: *Black and Gold*

School Mascot: *Tiger*

School Newspaper: *University Leader*

School Yearbook: *Reveille*

Alma Mater: *University Anthem*

On the plains of Western Kansas
Stands a school we all love well.
'Twas built by the toil of our fathers;
To its glory our voices swell.
　　Chorus
Hail to old Fort Hays State!
Let your voices ring.
Praise for the Black and Gold
We will ever sing.

Long may our valor last
Through the future days,
Hon'ring and praising
Dear Fort Hays.

In the years that lie before us
We foresee our land's many needs.
Through the efforts of new generations
We'll go on to more noble deeds.
　　Jack Juergens

Pittsburg State University

1701 S. Broadway
Pittsburg, KS 66762

School Nickname: *Pitt State*

School Colors: *Crimson and Gold*

School Mascot: *Gorilla (Gus and Gussie)*

School Newspaper: *Collegio*

School Yearbook: *KANZA*

Alma Mater: *My Alma Mater*

There's a country I love best, of the north, south, east, and west;
'Tis America, the homeland of the free.
In fair Kansas is a spot that can never be forgot
For the crimson and gold are dear to me.

Pittsburg State, how I love you, all the earth, sky above you:
First in education, inspiration, recreation, too.
How proud I am of you, Pittsburg State.
My Alma Mater, P.S.U.!

Though your sons and daughters stray to lands near or far away,
Deep within each heart your precepts they revere.
Truth and honor will prevail as your loyal children hail
"A new world on your horizon" loud and clear.

Pittsburg State, how I love you, all the earth, sky above you:
First in education, inspiration, recreation, too.
How proud I am of you, Pittsburg State. My Alma Mater, P.S.U.!
Written by Eva Jessye, '78

Fight Song: *On To Victory*

Pittsburg State team--fight for your college--
Come and join the fray.
Pass that ball around for a touchdown
And we'll win this game today,
Fight! Fight! Fight! for glory and fame
Because our spirit is so great,
And when this game is over
We'll shout the whole world over
"Pittsburg State!"
Written by Willanora Pratt Heinrich, '53

Kansas State University
Manhattan, KS 66506

School Nickname: *Wildcats; K-State*

School Colors: *Purple and White*

School Mascot: *Wildcat*

School Newspaper: *Kansas State Collegian*

School Yearbook: *Royal Purple*

Alma Mater: *Alma Mater*

> I know a spot that I love full well,
> 'Tis not in forest nor yet in dell,
> Ever it holds me with magic spell,
> I think of thee, Alma Mater.
>
> KSU, we'll carry the banner high,
> KSU, long, long may the colors fly.
> Loyal to thee thy children will swell
> the cry.
> Hail, hail, hail, Alma Mater.

The University of Kansas
Lawrence, KS 66045

School Nickname: *KU*

School Colors: *Crimson and Blue*

School Mascot: *Jayhawk*

School Newspaper: *The University Daily Kansan*

School Yearbook: *Jayhawker*

Alma Mater: *Crimson and The Blue*

> Far above the golden valley
> Glorious to view
> Stands our noble Alma Mater,
> Towering toward the blue.
> > *Chorus*
> Lift the chorus ever onward,
> Crimson and the blue,
> Hail to thee our Alma Mater,
> Hail to old KU.
>
> Far above the distant humming
> Of the busy town,
> Reared against the dome of heaven,
> Looks she proudly down.
>
> Greet we then our foster mother,
> Noble friend so true,
> We will ever sing her praises,
> Hail to old KU.
> > *By George "Dumpy" Bowles (rev. '58)*

Fight Song: *I'm A Jayhawk*

> Talk about the Sooners,
> The Cowboys and the Buffs,
> Talk about the Tiger and his tail,
> Talk about the Wildcats,
> And those Cornhuskin' boys,
> But I'm the bird to make 'em weep
> and wail.
> > *Chorus*
> 'Cause I'm a Jay, Jay, Jay, Jay, Jayhawk
> Up at Lawrence on the Kaw.
> 'Cause I'm a Jay, Jay, Jay, Jay, Jayhawk
> With a sis boom, hip hoorah!
> Got a bill that's big enough to
> Twist that Tiger's tail;
> Husk some corn and listen to the
> Cornhusker's wail;
> 'Cause I'm a Jay, Jay, Jay, Jay, Jayhawk
> Riding on a Kansas Gale.
>
> Looking down the valley
> The lord of all he views
> Jayhawk sees some tombstones in the
> vale.
> The Tigers and the Sooners,
> The Huskers and the Buffs,
> And he's the bird that made them
> Kick the pail.

Washburn University of Topeka
1700 College
Topeka, KS 66621

School Nickname: *The Ichabods*

School Colors: *Royal Blue, Gold and White*

School Mascot: *Ichabod*

School Newspaper: *Washburn Review*

School Yearbook: *The KAW*

The Wichita State University
Wichita, KS 6708-1595

School Nickname: *WSU*

School Colors: *Yellow and Black*

School Mascot: *A Wheatshock* Name: *WuShock*

School Newspaper: *The Sunflower*

School Yearbook: *Parnassus*

Alma Mater: *Alma Mater*

> Our Alma Mater, Wichita,
> Stands proudly on the hill
> Our sons and daughters bow to thee
> Our hearts with praise we fill.
> Then hail our Alma Mater
> Hail thee, grand and true
> Long wave the yellow and the black
> O Wichita, here's to you.
> > *W. H. Mikesell*
> > *J. Bert Graham*

Fight Song: *Hail Wichita*

> All Hail! Hail! Wichita
> U Rah! Rah! Rah for Wichita
> March onward, banners high
> With courage, force that can never die.
> Rah! We'll fight for Wichita
> Brave spirits never fail
> To Wichita all loyalty
> Hail! Our varsity, triumphantly hail!
> > *Samual A. Wofsy*
> > *Thurlow Lieurance*

KENTUCKY

Eastern Kentucky University
Lancaster Ave.
Richmond, KY 40475-0931

School Nickname: *The Colonels*

School Colors: *Maroon and White*

School Mascot: *Colonel*

School Newspaper: *The Eastern Progress*

School Yearbook: *Milestone*

Alma Mater: *Alma Mater*

> Hail to thee, our Alma Mater,
> Faithful guide of youth,
> Holding high amid the darkness
> Duty, light and truth;
> Still above, the skies attend thee;
> Still thy stately columns stand;
> Still thy sons and daughters love thee,
> Sing thy praises o'er the land.

All the earth's resplendent beauty,
Nature gathered here,
Rolling lawns and trees and grasses
On thy hillsides fair;
Happy days within thy shadow,
Friends and comrades we have won,
Fill our hearts with exaltation
For thy work so nobly done.

When, beloved Alma Mater,
Memory recalls
Other days of youth and laughter
In thy gracious halls;
When thy sons and daughters scattered
Turn again to thee,
Still thy lamp is brightly lighting
Us afar that we may see.
> Nancy Evans
> Jane Campbell

Fight Songs: *Hail, Hail Eastern Maroons!*

Hail, Hail, Eastern Maroons
You're the pride of dear old Alma Mater,
Hail, Hail, Eastern Maroons,
For thee we'll give three rousing cheers,
Rah! Rah! Rah!
Hail! Hail, Eastern Maroons,
Loyal to thee we stand
Ever fight for the right,
We'll make our school the best in the land.
> Frank Wilcox
> Henri Schnabl

Yea, Eastern!

Yea, Eastern let's win this fight
Rally Maroon and White
We've got the spirit; you've got the speed.
These two with grit are all that we need
So carry and pass that ball;
Show them our boys beat all
Show them we're right with main and might;
The way to win is fight, fight, fight!
> Mary Katherine Burns
> Helen Hull Lutes

Morehead State University
Morehead, KY 40351

School Nickname: *The Eagles*

School Colors: *Royal Blue and Gold*

School Mascot: *The Eagle*

School Newspaper: *The Trail Blazer*

School Yearbook: *The Raconteur*

Alma Mater: *Alma Mater*

> Far above the rolling campus resting in the dale,
> Stands the dear old Alma Mater we will always hail.
> Shout in chorus, raise your voices Blue and Gold praise you
> Winning through to fame and glory, Dear old M- S- U.
>> *Words by Elwood Kozee, '53*
>> *Music by Betty Jo Whitt, '52*

Fight Song: *Fight Song*

> Fight, Fight, Fight for Morehead.
> Fight on, varsity.
> Ever onward marching
> To our victory.
> We're gonna Fight, Fight, Fight for Morehead.
> Colors gold and blue.
> Our hopes on you we're pinning whether losing or winning.
> Go, you Eagles and fight, fight, fight.

Murray State University
Murray, KY 42071

School Colors: *Blue and Gold*

School Mascot: *Dunker* *(appears with cheerleaders at athletic events)*
Racers *(athletic teams)*

School Newspaper: *The Murray State News*

School Yearbook: *The Shield*

Alma Mater: *Murray State University*

> In the heart of Jackson's Purchase

'Neath the sun's warm glow,
Is the home of Murray State,
Finest place we know.
    Chorus
May we cherish thy traditions,
Hold thy banner high.
Ever guard thy name and glory,
Live and do or die.

Though we leave thy halls forever
Many miles go hence,
May our love for alma mater
Only have commenced.
                Words by A. B. Austin

Northern Kentucky University
Highland Heights, KY 41076

School Nickname: *Northern or NKU*

School Colors: *Gold, White and Black*

School Mascot: *Norseman*

School Newspaper: *Northerner*

School Yearbook: *Polaris*

Alma Mater: *Northern Kentucky State College*

Northern let your standard lead us, hearts of men from hearts of youth,
Days will have their golden moments, years will blend them, hold them true,
Help us seek the higher virtues, guide us to the greater truth,
Make us sturdy, make us worthy, of the trust we have in you;
Northern, Northern, Alma Mater, may our lives enrich your name,
Northern, Northern, build within us precepts of the nobler mind,
And in time leave us, your children, better far than when we came.
Be the light that stirs us outward for the good of human kind.

Fight Song: *Fight Song*

Onward ye Norsemen win that game for the Gold and the White we cheer!
We will win over all shouting our mighty call that the victory is near!
So, onward ye Norsemen, get that ball, now our glory is near at hand,
For when the mighty all fall down still the Norse----Men Stand!

University of Kentucky
Lexington, KY 40506

School Colors: *Blue and White*

School Mascot: *Wildcat*

School Newspaper: *Kentucky Kernel*

School Yearbook: *Kentuckian*

Alma Mater: *U.K. Alma Mater*

Hail Kentucky, Alma Mater!
Loyal sons and daughters sing;
Sound her praise with voice united;
To the breeze her colors fling.
To the blue and white be true;
Badge triumphant age on age;
Blue, the sky that o'er us bends;
While Kentucky's stainless page.

Hail Kentucky, Alma Mater!
'Neath thy arching trees we roam;
Thru thy halls our voices echo
Alma Mater second home.
For the blue and white we strive,
Fight we ever for its fame
Daring any fate to bring
Glory to Kentucky's name.

Hail Kentucky, Alma Mater!
Distant lands thy children claim;
Still Kentucky's soil is dearest,
Dearest still Kentucky's name.
To the blue and white we're true;
True, Kentucky, unto thee.
Teach each generation new
Ne'er to fail in loyalty.

Hail thee ever, old Kentucky!
Glorious is thy heritage;
Proud thy name and thy traditions;
Proud thy place on history's page!
May we ne'er forget fame
Mother of the great and free;
May we e'er uphold thy name,
Old Kentucky, hail to thee.
Words by Josephine Funkhouser
Music by C. A. Lampert

Fight Song: *On, On, U. of K.*

> On, on, U. of K. we are right for the fight today.
> Hold that ball and hit that line;
> Ev'ry wild cat star will shine;
> We'll fight, fight, fight, for the blue and white,
> As we roll to that goal, Varsity,
> And we'll kick pass and run till the battle is won,
> And we'll bring home the victory.
> > *Words by Troy Perkins*
> > *Music by C. A. Lampert*

University of Louisville
Louisville, KY 40292

School Nickname: *Cardinals*

School Colors: *Cardinal and Black*

School Mascot: *Cardinals*

School Newspaper: *The Cardinal*

School Yearbook: *Minerva*

Alma Mater: *Alma Mater*

> We thy loyal sons now stand,
> To sing thy highest praise,
> With deepest reverence in our hearts
> For these college days.
> Thy honor true we all defend,
> 'Tis known we love thee well.
> Our thoughts for years to come will be
> Of thee our U. of L.
> > *Words by John N. Young*
> > *Music by James Powell*

Fight Song: *Fight! U of L*

> FIGHT! now for vict'ry and show them how we sure will win this game
> FIGHT! on you Card'nals and prove to them that we deserve our fame.
> Roll up the score now and beat the foe so we can give a Yell with a
> FIGHT! give them all you've got for we are with you U of L!
> > *Words and Music by R. B. Griffith*

Western Kentucky University
Bowling Green, KY 42101

School Nickname: *Hilltoppers (athletic teams)*

School Colors: *Red and White*

School Mascot: *Big Red*

School Newspaper: *The College Heights Herald*

School Yearbook: *The Talisman*

Alma Mater: *College Heights*

> College Heights, on hilltop fair,
> With beauty all thine own,
> Lovely jewel for more rare
> Than graces any throne!
>
> College Heights, with living soul
> And purpose strong and true,
> Service ever is thy goal,
> Thy spirit ever new.
>
> College Heights, thy noble life
> Shall e'er our pattern be,
> Teaching us through joy and strife
> to love humanity.
> *Chorus*
> College Heights, we hail thee;
> We shall never fail thee.
> Falter never--live forever,
> Hail! Hail! Hail!

Fight Song: *Stand Up and Cheer*

> Stand up and cheer.
> Cheer loud and strong for
> dear old Western
> For today we raise the Red
> and Grey above the rest
> Our boys are fighting and are
> bound to win the fray.
> We've got the team, Rah! Rah!
> We've got the steam, Rah! Rah!
> This is dear old Western's day.
> Rah! Rah! Rah!
> *By Dr. D. W. Richard*

LOUISIANA

Grambling State University
Grambling, LA 71245

School Colors: *Black and Gold*

School Mascot: *Tiger*

School Newspaper: *Gramblinite*

School Yearbook: *Tiger*

Louisiana State University
Baton Rouge, LA 70803

School Nickname: *Tigers*

School Colors: *Purple and Gold*

School Mascot: *Bengal Tiger*   Name: *Mike*

School Newspaper: *Daily Reveille*

School Yearbook: *Gumbo*

Alma Mater: *Alma Mater*

>Where stately oaks and broad magnolias shade inspiring halls,
>There stands our dear old Alma Mater who to us recalls
>Fond memories that waken in our hearts a tender glow
>And make us happy for the love that we have learned to know.
>All praise to thee, our Alma Mater, moulder of mankind,
>May greater glory, love unending, be forever thine.
>Our worth in life will be thy worth, we pray to keep it true,
>And may thy spirit live in us forever, LSU.
>>*Downey - Funchess*

Fight Song: *Hey, Fightin' Tigers!*

>Hey, Fightin' Tigers! Fight all the way!
>Play, Fightin' Tigers, win the game today.
>You've got the know-how; you're doing fine.
>Hang on to the ball as you hit the wall
>And smash right through the line.
>You gotta go for a touchdown, run up the score.
>Make Mike, the Tiger, stand right up and roar.
>Give it all of your might as you fight tonight,
>And keep the goal in view: Victory for LSU.
>>*Lyrics by Gene Quaw*

Louisiana State University in Shreveport
8515 Youree Dr.
Shreveport, LA 71115

School Nickname: *The Pilots*

School Colors: *Blue and Gold*

School Newspaper: *The Almagest*

School Yearbook *The Manifest*

Louisiana Tech University
Ruston, LA 71272

School Nickname: *Tech*

School Colors: *Red and Blue*

School Mascot: *Bulldog*

School Newspaper: *Tech Talk*

School Yearbook: *Lagniappe*

Alma Mater: *Alma Mater*

> O Tech, thy halls so beautiful,
> Thy pleasant walks, thy noble trees,
> That charmed me in my college days,
> Are ever dear to me.
> Louisiana Tech I love thee
> My Alma Mater, my Alma Mater;
> I will ever loyal be
> To thee my Alma Mater.
>
> Those old Tech days, those joyful days,
> So cherished in my memory,
> Though days of toil, in many ways
> Were happy days and free.
> Louisiana Tech I love thee
> My Alma Mater, my Alma Mater;
> I will ever loyal be
> To thee my Alma Mater.
> *John P. Graham*

Fight Song: *Fight Song*

> Fight! Fight! Fight! for old Red and Blue;
> Show your might and we'll root for you.
> Get on your toes when you meet your foes
> And don't let them go through.
>
> TECH! TECH! TECH!
>
> Hit those lines like good old Canines;
> Break through for a touchdown or two.
> Hold up your chin and let's all go in
> To win for our Red and Blue.
> *James A. Smith*

Loyola University, New Orleans
6363 St. Charles Ave.
New Orleans, La 70118

School Colors: *Maroon and Gold*

School Mascot: *Wolf*

School Newspaper: *The Maroon*

School Yearbook: *Wolf*

Alma Mater: *Loyola Alma Mater*

> Hail Alma Mater Loyola all hail
> Tower of strength and a beacon of truth
> Thine is the courage that never shall fail
> Courage imparted to men and to youth.
>
> Youthful in years in traditions and fame
> Thou, as descendant of shield without taint
> Reach through the centuries blessed by thy name
> Name of a student a soldier and saint.
> *Chorus*
> Bearing thy standard of Maroon and Gold
> We shall be true to our heritage old.
> Loyal to God to country and thee
> Loyal Loyola with thy loyalty.

Fight Song: *Loyola Fight Song*

> Here's to the spirit of Loyola,
> Here's to her fame and glory;
> Drink to her future victories,
> Drink to her sacred memories.
> Here's to her loyal sons and daughters,
> Here's to her warriors true;
> Drink to the friends of Alma Mater,
> Loyola U.
> *Chorus*
> Fight! Fight! Fight! You men of the South!
> We hail your courage born of old,
> Fight! Fight! Fight! You men of the South!
> Loyola's honor to uphold;
> You men who fight and grin,
> and squarely play the game,
> We know that you go in,
> a victory to claim;
> So, Fight! Fight! Fight! You men of the South!
> For the Old Maroon and Gold.
> Make a Gold. RAH! toast!
> Make a boast! to Loyola's warriors bold!
> Cheer again! For the men!

Who defend Maroon and Gold!
So cheer them right, with all your might!
RAH! RAH! RAH! RAH!
Milo B. Williams
Raymond McNamara
Charles C. Chapman

McNeese State University
Ryan St.
Lake Charles, LA 70609

School Nickname: *Cowboys*

School Colors: *Blue and Gold*

School Newspaper: *Contraband*

School Yearbook: *Log*

Alma Mater: *Alma Mater*

We hail our Alma Mater
with hearts full of gratitude;
Where knowledge dwells with friendship,
and all that is right and true.
Our mem'ries here will linger,
with faith in all you do;
McNeese, McNeese, may glory reign here, too -
All hail! All hail! McNeese,
we are proud of you.
Kenneth L. Gaburo

Nicholls State University
Thibodaux, LA 70310

School Nickname: *The Colonels*

School Colors: *Red and Grey*

School Mascot: *The Colonel*

School Newspaper: *The Nicholls Worth*

School Yearbook: *La Pirogue*

Northeast Louisiana University
700 University Ave.
Monroe, LA 71209

School Nickname: *Indians*

School Colors: *Maroon and Gold*

School Mascot: *Chief Brave Spirit*

School Newspaper: *Pow Wow*

School Yearbook: *Chacahoula*

Alma Mater: *Alma Mater Northeast Louisiana University*

Near the bayou's tranquil water
And the highway's ceaseless flow,
Proudly stands our alma mater
Through the years that swiftly go.
Our loyalty to you we pledge,
And true to you we'll ever be.
We'll lift the tribal banner high
For all the world to see.
Faithful we will be and true,
Ever loyal N-L-U.

Where magnolias shed their fragrance
Graceful pine trees touch the breeze,
And tender memories linger
In the shadow of the trees.
Our loyalty to you we pledge,
And true to you we'll ever be.
We'll lift the tribal banner high
For all the world to see.
Faithful we will be and true,
Ever loyal N-L-U.

Fight Song: *NLU Fight Song*

Cheer for Northeast Indians,
With their fighting spirit bold.
We will keep our banners waving
The old maroon and gold.
Our battle cry rings to the sky
Our goal is victory.
But win or lose
We'll stand by you
And ever loyal we will be.

Northwestern State University of Louisiana

College Station
Natchitoches, LA 71457

School Nickname: *NSU*

School Colors: *Purple and White*

School Mascot: *Demon*

School Newspaper: *Current Sauce*

School Yearbook: *Potpourri*

Alma Mater: *Alma Mater*

> Oh Alma Mater here today,
> We for thy lasting blessings pray,
> We know not where our paths may go,
> But thou'lt uphold us still we know.
> Unchanging thou 'mid changes vast,
> Unswerved from ideals of the past,
> Steadfast and true, our watchword e'er shall be -
> To thee our Alma Mater, Loyalty!
>
> Thy trees their solemn chorus bend,
> About thee, flowers their censers blend.
> Our voices swell their murmuring strain,
> Our hearts repeat the old refrain,
> Thy purpose high to carry on
> Northwestern, thou has honor won!
> Steadfast and true, our watchword e'er shall be -
> To thee, our Alma Mater, Loyalty!
>
> In after years, when far away,
> Thy presence strong will near us stay;
> And as the echo of our song
> Will, with new courage, lead us on;
> And to our eager vision then
> Each subtle memory meaning lend,
> Steadfast and true, our watchword e'er shall be -
> To thee, our Alma Mater, Loyalty!
> > *By Isabel Williamson*
> > *(Mrs. S. J. Cumming)*

Fight Song: *Fight Song*

> GO, ye Demons take the field

Northwestern Demons never yield
Fight, Demons, win tonight
A victory is on our side
GO, FIGHT, WIN!
Purple and white shall ever reign
Filling the air with battle strain
So, Demons forever stand, and
Fight for Dear old Demonland.

Southeastern Louisiana University
Hammond, LA 70402

School Nickname: *SLU and Southeastern*

School Colors: *Green and Gold*

School Mascot: *Lion* Name: *Roomie*

School Newspaper: *Lion's Roar*

School Yearbook: *Le Souvenir*

Alma Mater: *Alma Mater Southeastern Louisiana College*

Down in dear old Louisiana stands our college home,
Its whisp'ring pines and mighty oaks are swaying in the gloam,
How can we pay thee tribute who guides us all so well?
We lift our voices once again thy praises proud to tell
We hail Thee now Southeastern, For Thee we'll always stand;
Thy eager sons and daughters form one united band.
We'll sing Thy praises ever from sea to shining sea,
And love Thee Alma Mater, Thru all eternity.
> *Ruth Smith*
> *Arr. Ralph R. Pottle*

Fight Song: *Green and Gold*

Cheer on the Green and Gold of SLU,
Cheer our team on to victory.
We've got to play this game to win today,
We've got to play hard,
Get in there and make it pay.
It's time to fight on to a victory;
Stand up and roar with all your might.
Go! Go! Lions Go
Get out and fight! fight! fight! Hey!
> *Words and Music by James M. Stafford*
> *Arr. by Grier Williams*

Southern University A & M College
Southern Branch Post Office
Baton Rouge, LA 70813

School Colors: *Columbian Blue and Gold*

School Mascot: *Jaguar*

School Newspaper: *The Digest*

School Yearbook: *Jaguar*

Alma Mater: *Dear Southern*

> O Southern, Dear Southern, Thy praises we shall sing
> Until all the heavens and echoes loudly ring,
> The Winds of the Sky as they pass us by
> Will adoration bring.
>
> O Southern, Dear Southern, we owe our all to Thee
> In down-fall or victory, we'll always loyal be
> Thy Sons and Daughters as they work,
> Will be inspired by Thee.
>
> O Southern, Dear Southern, Thy name will ever be
> As mighty as the river that flows on to the sea.
> As pure and true as the Gold and Blue,
> That stand out bold for Thee.

Fight Song: *Fight Song*

> Southern University defenders of the Gold and Blue
> We will always loyal be and sing a cheer for you
> All for one and one for all we've got the will to win for thee
> So we're fight, fight, fight, fight til we win the victory.

The Tulane University of Louisiana
New Orleans, LA 70118-5698

School Nickname: *Tulane*

School Colors: *Olive Green and Powder Blue*

School Mascot: *Green Wave*

School Newspaper: *The Hullabaloo*

School Yearbook: *The Jambalaya*

Alma Mater: *Alma Mater*

> We praise thee for thy past, O Alma Mater!
> Thy hand hath done its work full faithfully.
> The incense of thy spirit has ascended
> And filled America from sea to sea!
>
> Olive Green and Blue! we love thee!
> Pledge we now our fealty true
> Where the trees are ever greenest,
> Where the skies are purest blue.
> Hear us now, O Tulane, hear us,
> As we proudly sing to thee!
> Take from us our heart's devotion,
> Thine we are and thine shall be!
> > *Words and Music by*
> > *William and Ruebush*
> > *May not be reproduced without*
> > *Tulane's written consent*

University of New Orleans
Lakefront
New Orleans, LA 70148

School Nickname: *UNO*

School Colors: *Silver and Blue*

School Mascot: *Alligators* Names: *Lafitte and Dominique*

School Newspaper: *Driftwood*

Alma Mater: *UNO, Our Alma Mater*

> UNO, our Alma Mater
> Proud we stand to sing your fame,
> UNO
> We honor your dear name.
>
> Mem'ries will linger on
> When our years with you have gone
> And keep us true
> To the Silver and Blue.
> > *Music, Beethoven's "Consecration of the House"*
> > *Overture, Opus 124*
> > *Lyrics, Deborah H. Crosby*

Fight Song: *Let's Hear It For UNO*

> Let's give a cheer for old UNO,
> Fling out her banner forward we go,
> Come on U-N-O-! let's carry her colors silver and blue,
> Shout out her praises true. U-N-O!
> Our Privateers will march on to fame,
> New Orleans glory they will proclaim,
> So let that U-N-O spirit frighten our foe,
> let's hear it for U--N------O!
> > *Music and Lyrics by*
> > *Lois D. Ostrolenk*

University of Southwestern Louisiana
East University Ave.
Lafayette, LA 70504

School Nickname: *USL*

School Colors: *Vermillion (Red) and White*

School Mascot: *Ragin' Cajuns*

School Newspaper: *The Vermillion*

School Yearbook: *L'Acadien*

Alma Mater: *The University of Southwestern Louisiana Alma Mater*

> Alma Mater, beloved old Southwestern,
> Pride of our Southland so fair!
> Oaks and pines and sweet magnolia's beauty,
> Show forth thy charms so rare,
> Alma Mater, for honor, truth and wisdom
> Thy halls for aye shall stand,
> Loyal sons and daughters sing proclaiming
> Here's my heart and hand.

Fight Song: *Ragin' Cajun Fight Song*

> Fight on, Cajuns, fight on to victory
> For the Red and White,
> We will sing of triumph and glory
> For our team tonight,
> You will hear the rage of the Cajuns,
> So let's give a yell,
> Hustle up and bustle up and
> Fight on to victory--U.S.L.

MAINE

University of Maine
Orono, ME 04469

School Colors: *Blue (pale) and White*

School Mascot: *Black Bear* Name: *Bananas*

School Newspaper: *The Daily Maine Campus*

School Yearbook: *Prism*

Alma Mater: *Stein Song*

Fill the steins to dear old Maine!
Fill as the rafters ring!
Stand and drink the toast once again!
Let ev'ry loyal Maine man sing,
Drink to all the happy hours,
Drink to the careless days!
Drink to Maine, our Alma Mater
The college of our hearts always.
To the trees To the sky
To the Spring in its glorious happiness!
To the youth To the fire
To the life that is moving and calling us!

To the Gods To the Fates
To the Rulers of men and their destinies!
To the lips To the eyes
To the girls who will love us some day!

Fill the steins to dear old Maine!
Fill as the rafters ring!
Stand and drink the toast once again!
Let ev'ry loyal Maine man sing,
Drink to all the happy hours,
Drink to the careless days!
Drink to Maine, our Alma Mater
The college of our hearts always.
Words by Lincoln Colcord
Music by E. A. Fenstad

University of Southern Maine
96 Falmouth St.
Portland, ME 04103

School Nickname: *Huskies*

School Colors: *Navy, Crimson and White*

School Mascot: *Husky*

School Newspaper: *Free Press*

MARYLAND

Frostburg State University
Frostburg, MD 21532

School Colors: *Red and White*

School Mascot: *Bobcat*

School Newspaper: *The Bottom Line*

School Yearbook: *Nemacolin*

Alma Mater: *Alma Mater*

Our Alma Mater, Mother of Knowledge,
We sing of thy glory, and thy honored name.
Founded for learning, of minds that are yearning
We treasure, we treasure our years at Frostburg State.

Our Alma Mater, Guide us still nearer,
As striving for truth, we follow in thy light.
Grant us thy grace, that our minds may embrace
The wisdom, the wisdom ours here at Frostburg State.
Lyrics by the Class of 1966
Music by Thomas Green
Phi Mu Alpha

The Johns Hopkins University
3400 North Charles St.
Baltimore, MD 21218

School Nickname: *The Hop*

School Colors: *Old Gold and Sable (Black and Blue for undergraduates
and sports teams)*

School Mascot: *Blue Jay*

School Newspaper: *The Johns Hopkins News-Letter*

School Yearbook: *The Hullabaloo*

Alma Mater: *The Johns Hopkins Ode (Veritas Vos Liberabit)*

> Truth guide our University,
> And from all error keep her free!
> Let wisdom yield her choicest treasure,
> And freedom reach her fullest measure;
> O let her watchword ever be:
> The truth of God will make you free,
> Will make you free!
>
> Let knowledge grow from more to more,
> And scholars versed in deepest lore,
> Their souls for light forever burning,
> Send forth their fire, unlock their learning;
> And let their faithful teaching be:
> The truth alone can make us free,
> Can make us free!
>
> The truth shall crown her sons with fame,
> Their lives inspire with noble aim,
> Their names make known throughout our borders,
> As learning's guide and wisdom's warders;
> Then let their watchword ever be:
> The truth for aye shall keep us free,
> Shall keep us free!
> > *Wm.Levering Devries, '88, '92*
> > *Elizabeth E. Starr*
> > *Arr. by D. Coulter, '21*

Loyola College in Maryland
4501 N. Charles St.
Baltimore, MD 21210

School Nickname: *Loyola*

School Colors: *Green and Grey*

School Mascot: *Greyhound*

School Newspaper: *Greyhound*

School Yearbook: *Green and Grey*

Alma Mater: *Alma Mater*

> To Loyola we raise our voices loud in your praise;
> In days of youth you have steadied our gaze
> On compassion and wisdom and honor and truth,
> Over power and pleasure we treasure your ways.
> This is your legacy:
> Strong truths, well lived.
> Strong truths, well lived.
> We can never forget we are deep in your debt;
> You have taught us to grow and wherever we go.
>
> For the good of every neighbor we will labor.
> And give heart and hands to what conscience commands,
> Tho' we meet hardship and pain, Loyal we will remain.
> For we, your sons and daughters, pledge that all you give
> Will live in us--Gratitude never will cease.
> We'll repay you working for justice, faith and peace,
> Serving justice, faith and peace.
> > *Words by William Davish*
> > *Arr. by Betsie Devenny*

Morgan State University
Coldspring Lane and Hillen Rd.
Baltimore, MD 21239

School Nickname: *MSU*

School Colors: *Blue and Orange*

School Mascot: *Bear*

School Newspaper: *The Spokesman*

School Yearbook: *The Promethean*

Alma Mater: *"Fair Morgan"*

Fair Morgan, we love thee, so
Tried and so true
Our Hearts at thy name
Thrill with pride;
We owe thee allegiance, we
Pledge thee our faith
A faith which shall ever
Abide.
Chorus
We pledge thee our love, we
Pledge thee our faith
Whatever the future may
Bring
And thus our devotion,
Fidelity too.
And homage we pay as we sing.

Fair Morgan, as onward the
Years quickly fly,
And thou livest in memory
Sweet,
We bring thee our laurels
Whatever they be,
And lay them with joy at thy
Feet.

Salisbury State College
Salisbury, MD 21801

School Nickname: *Sea Gulls*

School Colors: *Maroon and Gold*

School Mascot: *Sea Gull* Name: *Sammy*

School Newspaper: *The Flyer*

School Yearbook: *Evergreen*

Alma Mater: *Alma Mater*

O Alma Mater, standing wise and stately,
We dedicate our song to thee--
A song of praise, a song of deep devotion,
A song of love and endless loyalty.
Salisbury College, school of gracious beauty,
Thy portals stand, an open door
Through which we enter lives of deeper wisdom,
Oh, we shall love thy name forever more.

Towson State University
Towson, MD 21204

School Nickname: *The Tigers*

School Colors: *Gold, Black and White*

School Mascot: *The Tiger*

School Newspaper: *Towerlight*

School Yearbook: *Tower Echoes*

Alma Mater: *Alma Mater*

> Alma Mater, Alma Mater,
> We will ever faithful be,
> In our hearts thy beauty lingers.
> Though we've gone from thee,
> Now thy praises we are chanting,
> Now our voices rise in tune,
> Sing thy beauty, Alma Mater,
> And our love so true.
>
> Sparkling in the morning brightness,
> Rosy in the sunset light,
> Stately rising on the hilltop,
> Ever our delight.
> Now thy praises we are chanting,
> Now our voices rise in tune,
> Sing thy beauty, Alma Mater,
> And our love so true.

United States Naval Academy
Annapolis, MD 21402

School Nickname: *USNA*

School Colors: *Blue and Gold*

School Mascot: *Bill the Goat*

School Yearbook: *Lucky Bag*

Alma Mater: *Navy Blue and Gold*

> Now, college men from sea to sea

May sing of colors true;
But who has better right than we
To hoist a symbol hue?

For sailor men in battle fair,
Since fighting days of old,
Have proved the sailor's right to wear
The Navy Blue and Gold.

So hoist our colors, hoist them high,
And vow allegiance true,
So long as sunset gilds the sky
Above the ocean blue,
Unlowered shall those colors be
Whatever fate they meet,
So glorious in victory,
Triumphant in defeat.

Four years together by the bay
Where Severn joins the tide,
Then by the Service called away,
We've scattered far and wide;
But still when two or three shall meet,
And old tales be retold,
From low to highest in the fleet
Will pledge the Blue and Gold.

Words by Cdr. Roy DeS. Horn, USN (Ret)
Music by J. W. Crosley

The University of Baltimore

1420 North Charles St.
Baltimore, MD 21201-5779

School Nickname: *UofB*

School Colors: *White and Maroon*

School Newspaper: *UBIQUE*

University of Maryland Baltimore County

Cantonsville, MD 21228

School Nickname: *UMBC*

School Colors: *Black, Gold and White*

School Mascot: *Chesapeake Bay Retriever*

School Newspaper: *The Retriever*

School Yearbook: *The Golden Retriever*

The University of Maryland College Park
College Park, MD 20742

School Colors: *Red, Black, Gold and White*

School Mascot: *Diamondback Terrapin (athletic teams nicknamed "TERPS")*

School Newspaper: *The Diamondback*

School Yearbook: *Terrapin*

Alma Mater: *The Alma Mater*

> HAIL! ALMA MATER!
> Hail to thee, Maryland!
> Steadfast in loyalty
> For thee we stand.
> Love for the Black and Gold,
> Deep in our hearts we hold,
> Singing, thy praise forever,
> Throughout the land.

Fight Song: *Maryland Victory Song*

> Maryland we're all behind you
> Wave high the Black and Gold
> For there is nothing half so
> glorious
> As to see our men victorious.
> We've got the team, boys
> We've got the steam, boys
> So keep on fighting, don't
> give in M-A-R-Y-L-A-N-D
> Maryland will win.

MASSACHUSETTS

Boston University
Boston,MA 02215

School Nickname: *Terriers*

School Colors: *Scarlet and White*

School Mascot: *Terrier*   Name: *Rhett*

School Newspaper: *Daily Free Press (Independent)*
Boston University Today

School Yearbook: *Bostonian*

Alma Mater: *The Alma Mater*

> O glorious thy name and fame,
> Resplendent from thy youth!
> O radiant the holy flame that lights thy lamp of truth!
> O Boston University,
> O Alma Mater dear,
> We'll cherish, love and honor thee,
> And thy great name revere;
> We'll cherish, love and honor thee,
> And thy great name revere.

O wonderful thy Charter's aim--
High learning's perfect flower
And virtue's fruit. Let these proclaim
Thy nurture and thy power.
O Boston University,
O Alma Mater true:
We'll strive to make the future free,
And thus thy goal pursue.

O beautiful thy colors' gleam,
The scarlet and the white,
When love and life mean all they seem,
Courageous for the right!
O Boston University,
O Alma Mater brave:
We'll boldly stand for purity
Where'er thy banners wave.

O meaningful thy coat of arms--
The shield with cross and crown--
Inspiring us with Oxford's charms,
Reflecting Boston Town.
O Boston University,
O Alma Mater fair:
Crusading for true piety,
Thine arms we'll proudly wear.

O Vision splendid! Thine the art
To make all visions real:
The call to serve with all the heart
Is blazoned on thy seal.
O Boston University,
O Alma Mater fine:
We'll live to give reality
To thine ideals divine.
                    Daniel L. Marsh

Fight Song: *Go B.U.!*

Go B.U., Go B.U.
Sing her praises loud and true
We'll fight for our Alma Mater
On to sure victory.

Go B. U., Go B.U.
Down the field to score anew
Our hearts are with you as you meet the foe,
We hail you old B.U.
                    Randy Weeks, '29

Fitchburg State College
160 Pearl St.
Fitchburg, MA 01420

School Nickname: *Falcons*

School Colors: *Yellow, White and Green*

School Newspaper: *The Strobe*

School Yearbook: *Saxifrage*

Alma Mater: *In Old Wachusett's Shadow*

> In old Wachusett's shadow our Alma Mater stands.
> Her proud New England banner she holds aloft to all the land.
> Hail to Alma Mater! O Raise her name!
> Always may her sons and daughters justify her fame!
> *Priscilla Taylor, '63*

Framingham State College
Box 2000
Framingham, MA 01701

School Colors: *Black and Gold*

School Mascot: *Ram*

School Newspaper: *Gatepost*

School Yearbook: *Dial*

Alma Mater: *Alma Mater Hymn*

> Dear Framingham, thy children round thee gather;
> Our vows of love to thee we pledge anew.
> Unfailing font of hope and joy forever,
> We shall proclaim our homage to you.
> Through countless years to all a fostering mother,
> Thy bounteous blessings poured on age and youth;
> Our suppliant prayer til time our chain shall sever
> Will ever be "Live to the truth".
> *Words: Martin F. O'Connor*
> *Tune: "Finlandia" - J. Sibelius*

Harvard University
Cambridge, MA 02138

School Colors: *Crimson and White*

School Newspaper: *The Harvard Crimson and The Harvard Independent*

School Yearbook: *Class Album*

Alma Mater: *Fair Harvard*

> Fair Harvard! thy sons to thy jubilee throng,
> And with blessings surrender thee o'er,
> By these festival rites, from the age that is past
> To the age that is waiting before.
> O relic and type of our ancestors' worth
> That has long kept their memory warm,
> First flower of the wilderness! star of their night!
> Calm rising through change and through storm!
> S. Gilman, '11

Fight Song: *Ten Thousand Men of Harvard*

> Ten thousand men of Harvard want vict'ry today
> For they know that o'er old Eli
> Fair Harvard holds sway;
> So then we'll conquer old Eli's men,
> And when the game ends we'll sing again;
> Ten thousand men of Harvard gained vict'ry today.
> A. Putnam, '18

The Massachusetts Institute of Technology
77 Massachusetts Ave.
Cambridge, MA 02139

School Nickname: *Tech; The Engineers*

School Colors: *Cardinal and Gray*

School Mascot: *The Beaver (nature's engineer)*

School Newspaper: *The Tech*

School Yearbook: *Technique*

Alma Mater: *In Praise of M.I.T.*

> Arise! All ye of M.I.T.

In loyal fellowship,
The future beckons unto thee
and life is full and rich,
Arise and raise your glass on high
tonight shall ever be
A memory that will never die,
For ye of M.I.T.

Thy sons and daughters, M.I.T.,
Return from far and wide,
And gather here once more to be
renourished by thy side,
And as we raise our glasses high
to pledge our love for thee,
We join all those of days gone by
in praise of M.I.T.
Lyrics revised 1985
by Alvin Kahn

Merrimack College
North Andover, MA 01845

School Nickname: *The Warriors*

School Colors: *Blue and Gold*

School Newspaper: *Warrior*

School Yearbook: *Merrimacken*

Alma Mater: *Merrimack College Alma Mater*

Merrimack, your honored name
Enchains our hearts to thee.
Reverently we rise to claim
Respect and loyalty.
Inspirations,
Mould of nations,
Abound within your walls.
Children proud, we cherish having
Known your hallowed halls.

May you grow in truth and wisdom,
Educative shrine,
Reaping from the highest kingdom
Recompense divine.
Inspirations,
Mould of nations,

Abound within your walls.
Children proud, we cherish having
Known your hallowed halls.

Merrimack, in song we'll arise your
Earthly Majesty.
Reign eternally.
Alma Mater,
Alma Mater,
Merrimack we pray,
Loyalty to God and thee
Your truth shall light our way.
Words: Lawrence Farrell, '60
Music: Rev. Thomas F. Walsh, O.S.A.

Northeastern University
360 Huntington Ave.
Boston, MA 02115

School Colors: *Red and Black*

School Mascot: *Husky*

School Newspaper: *Northeastern News*

School Yearbook: *Cauldron*

Alma Mater: *Alma Mater*

Oh Alma Mater, here we throng
And sing your praises strong.
Your children gather far and near
And seek your blessings dear.
Fair memories we cherish now
And will forevermore.
Come, let us raise our voices strong.
Northeastern, we adore.
Music by Louis J. Bertolami, '60E
Lyrics by Joseph Spear

Fight Song: *All Hail Northeastern*

All Hail, Northeastern,
We sing in jubilee,
All Hail, Northeastern
March proudly, ever free;
All Hail, Northeastern,
We give salute to thee,

Through the years,
We ever will acclaim
Thy glorious destiny.
Music and lyrics by
C. A. Pethybridge, '32

Southeastern Massachusetts University
Old Westport Rd.
North Dartmouth, MA 02747

School Nickname: *S.M.U.*

School Colors: *Blue, White and Gold*

School Mascot: *The Corsair*

School Newspaper: *The Torch*

School Yearbook: *Scrimshaw*

Tufts University
Medford, MA 02155

School Nickname: *Jumbos*

School Colors: *Brown and Blue*

School Mascot: *Jumbo*

School Newspaper: *Tufts Observer (weekly) Daily (daily)*

School Yearbook: *Jumbo*

Alma Mater: *Dear Alma Mater*

We con beside thy knee,
Dear Alma Mater,
Earth's book of mystery,
Dear Alma Mater;
We track the storied past,
Dear Alma Mater,
Over plains of learning vast,
Dear Alma Mater, With thee.

Yet more to thee is due,
Dear Alma Mater,
Truth lov'd because 'tis true,

Dear Alma Mater!
Handclasp of friendship fair,
Dear Alma Mater,
Strength to fight as heroes dare,
Dear Alma Mater, Life through.

Speed on thy sunlit way,
Dear Alma Mater!
We vow new faith today,
Dear Alma Mater!
May glory light thy name,
Dear Alma Mater,
All thy children sing thy fame,
Dear Alma Mater, For aye!
Music by L. R. Lewis, '87
Text by D. L. Maulsby, '87

University of Lowell
One University Ave.
Lowell, MA 01854-9985

School Nickname: *Chiefs*

School Colors: *Red, White and Blue*

School Newspaper: *Connector*

School Yearbook: *Sojurn*

University of Massachusetts at Amherst
Amherst, MA 01003

School Nickname: *UMASS*

School Colors: *Maroon and White*

School Mascot: *Indian*   Name: *Metawampe*

School Newspaper: *Massachusetts Daily Collegian*

School Yearbook: *Index*

University of Massachusetts at Boston
Harbor Campus
Boston, MA 02125

School Nickname: *Beacons (after a lighthouse beacon)*

School Colors: *Blue and White*

School Newspaper: *Mass Media*

School Yearbook: *Yearbook*

Western New England College
1215 Wilbraham Rd.
Springfield, MA 01119

School Nickname: *The Golden Bears*

School Colors: *Royal Blue and Gold*

School Mascot: *The Kodiak Bear*

School Newspaper: *The Westerner*

School Yearbook: *Cupola*

Alma Mater: *College Hymn*

> Hail, Alma Mater wisdom's light,
> Beacon of truth and loyalty bright!
> Grant us ideals which win our hearts;
> From the true path we'll never depart.
> Western New England mem'ries warm
> Keep us in faith through calm and storm.
> Science and service on thy seal
> Call us to work with steadfast zeal.
> Challenge to youth and flow'r of the past
> We shall be true while life doth last.
> Western New England mem'ries warm
> Keep us in faith through calm and storm.
> B. A. Herman

Westfield State College
Western Ave.
Westfield, MA 01086

School Colors: *Royal Blue and White*

School Mascot: *Owl*

School Newspaper: *The Owl*

School Yearbook: *Tekoa*

Alma Mater: *Alma Mater*

> Westfield! Alma Mater.
> We salute and honor thee.
> Thy loved name instills in us
> Thoughts of hope and victory.
> Through the years that are before us
> May we keep within our hearts
> Memories inspirational
> That thy proud name imparts.
> Westfield, we are loyal to thee,
> Westfield! Alma Mater.
> > *M. Ruth Reavey, '35*
> > *Louise Hagen Lane, '33*

Worcester Polytechnic Institute
100 Institute Rd.
Worcester, MA 01609

School Nickname: *The Engineers*

School Colors: *Crimson and Gray*

School Newspaper: *WPI Newspeak*

School Yearbook: *The Peddler*

Alma Mater: *Alma Mater W P I*

> Dear Worcester Tech, our Worcester Tech; our praises ring to thee,
> To Alma Mater, good and true, We pledge our loyalty.
> Long have we felt thy guiding hand,
> Thy teachings broad and free,
> With praises loud in every land,
> We'll show our love for Thee.
> > *Refrain*
> Then here's to good old Worcester Tech,
> Come fellows join in our refrain,
> Wave high the colors, Crimson and Grey,
> For good old Worcester Tech.

As years roll on, and changes bring
To all things great and small,
We still will thee with reverence hold,
We'll greet thee, one and all,
In accents which no one may doubt,
In terms so strong and bold,
The world will know thy worth to us
Increases many fold.
Willard Hedlund, '10

Worcester State College
486 Chandler St.
Worcester, MA 01602-2597

School Nickname: *WSC*

School Colors: *Blue and Gold*

School Mascot: *A Lancer*

School Newspaper: *The Student Voice*

School Yearbook: *Transitions (1986)*

Fight Song: *Proud Lancers*

We are the Lancers, very proud and true
Blue and Gold forever, that's our motto too
We fight, fight, fight, with all our might (to make thing right)
Win or lose, we keep shining bright
For, we are the Lancers, very proud and true.
Refrain (Slow)
Our college with its song, makes us happy we belong
Looking at the future now, leads us on with courage strong.

For, we are the Lancers, very proud and true
Worcester State forever, always serving you (serving just for you).
Lyrics and Music
Bernie Guarini

MICHIGAN

Calvin College
Grand Rapids, MI 49506

School Nickname: *Knights*

School Colors: *Maroon and Gold*

School Mascot: *The Calvin Knight*

School Newspaper: *The Chimes*

School Yearbook: *The Prism*

Alma Mater: *Calvin College Alma Mater*

Calvin, Calvin, sing we all to thee;
To Dear Alma Mater, We pledge fidelity.
Forever faithful to maroon and gold,
Thy name and honor we ever shall uphold!

Calvin, Calvin, God has been thy guide;
Dear Alma Mater, Thy strength he shall provide;
Be loyal ever to the faith of old,
God's name and honor we ever shall uphold!
Words by Celia Bruinooge, Class of '51
Music by Dale Grothenhuis, Class of '53

Central Michigan University
Mt. Pleasant, MI 48859

School Nickname: *Chippewas*

School Colors: *Maroon and Gold*

School Newspaper: *Central Michigan Life*

School Yearbook: *Chippewa*

Alma Mater: *Alma Mater, Hear Us Now*

>Alma Mater, hear us now;
>Ever more we praise thee.
>Hear us pledge our sacred vow,
>Ever to defend thee.
>
>Mighty Mother, Queen of Earth eternal,
>Precious emblem of our lives Supreme;
>Ever symbolizing truth and knowledge
>In glorified esteem.
>
>Alma Mater, hear us now;
>Ever more we praise thee.
>Hear us pledge our sacred vow,
>Ever to defend thee.
>   *By Ruth Mavis Williams, '29*

Fight Song: *CMU Fight Song*

>Come on and fight! Central, down the field.
>Fight for Victory -- Fight! Fellows never yield --
>We're with you, oh Varsity! Onward with banners bold,
>To our colors we'll be true! FIGHT for Maroon & Gold!
>Down the field for CMU!
>VARSITY! Rah, Rah. VICTORY! Rah, Rah.
>Chippewas we're proud of our nickname!
>Hear our song, loud and strong. CENTRAL is going to
>win this game!
>(repeat thru "Down the field for CMU!")
>   *Written by 'Howdy' Loomis, class of '35*

Eastern Michigan University
Ypsilanti, MI 48197

School Nickname: *The Hurons*

School Colors: *Green and White*

School Mascot: *The Huron Indian*

School Newspaper: *The Eastern Echo*

School Yearbook: *The Aurora*

Alma Mater: *Eastern, Sacred Alma Mater*

> Eastern sacred Alma Mater to your name we shall be true,
> Ever marching on to victory, we'll stand by to see you through,
> Softly floating on the breeze, verdant green with white of snow,
> This our banner we will carry in our hearts wher'er we go.

Fight Songs: *Go Green*

> Go Green, roll up the score
> Go Green, let's get some more.
> Raise a cheer for old Green and White
> Let's show them we came here to fight.
> Go Green, vic'try we'll claim
> Go Green, let's win this game.
> We'll always fight for old EMU
> Come on and let's Go Green!

Huron Fight Song

> Hurons, Hurons, Hats off to you!
> Fight, Fight, Fight for old EMU.
> Shout to the sky the Hurons' war cry
> The bravest we'll defy!
> Hold that line for old Green and White
> Loyal sons come show your might
> Fight! Fight! for old EMU and victory!

Ferris State College
Big Rapids, MI 49307

School Nickname: *Fighting Bulldogs*

School Colors: *Crimson and Gold*

School Mascot: *Bulldog*

School Newspaper: *Torch*

School Yearbook: *Ferriscope*

Grand Valley State College
College Landing
Allendale, MI 49401

School Nickname: *Lakers*

School Colors: *Blue, White and Black*

School Mascot: *The Laker*

School Newspaper: *Lanthorn*

Alma Mater: *Hail To Thee, Grand Valley*

> Hail to thee Grand Valley-
> We're loyal steadfast, true.
> Praise our Alma Mater-
> We pledge our faith to you.
> Keep your banners flying.
> Black & White & Blue.
> We sing to thee Grand Valley.
> United we're for you!
> *Arthur C. Hills*

Fight Song: *G.V.S.C. Victory*

> Grand Valley victory, as the Lakers we have pride.
> Our team will lead us on, Blue and White we're at your side.
> We want a Grand Valley victory, as our foes will quickly see.
> Raise! Your! Voices and cheer, for a VIC-TO-RY!
> *Lyrics, Kathy Ure-Maris Tracy*
> *Music, William Root*

Lawrence Institute of Technology
21000 West Ten Mile Rd.
Southfield, MI 48075-1058

School Nickname: *LIT or Lawrence Tech*

School Colors: *Blue and White*

School Mascot: *Blue Devils*

School Newspaper: *Tech News*

School Yearbook: *L Book*

Alma Mater: *The L. I. T. Hymn*

> Let them fly so very high our colors Blue and White
> Flowing free for all to see like a guiding light
> With our might for all that's right we march to victory
> We can't hide our lasting pride for good old L. I. T.
>
> We will sing and chimes will ring our praise of L. I. T.
> Rising loud with hearts so proud ringing true for thee
> Listen to her song it is calling you and me on
> To keep the banner flying for ol' L. I. T.
>
> May her fame and honored name be greater with each year
> May they last these mem'ries past that we hold so dear
> Fear not the rival lot who'd stop our cause so free
> Show our course with endless force and pray for L. I. T.

Fight Song: *Dear Old L. I. T.*

> Tho' time divides us all
> We shall never prove untrue,
> No matter what the call
> Our loyalty we pledge to you.
> Rah! Rah! Rah!
> Dear old L. I. T.
> We love the Blue and White you're flying,
> Thru the years to be
> 'Twill ever tell of love undying,
> And in the class or on the field
> We'll bring you honor, victory,
> All hail to thee
> Our alma mater L. I. T.
> Rah! Rah! Rah!
> > *Words and Music by*
> > *H. O'Reilly Clint*

Michigan State University
East Lansing, MI 48824

School Nickname: *Spartans*

School Colors: *Green and White*

School Mascot: *Sparty*

School Newspaper: *State News*

School Yearbook: *Red Cedar Log*

Michigan Technological University
Houghton, MI 49931

School Nickname: *Michigan Tech*

School Colors: *Silver and Gold*

School Mascot: *Huskies*

School Newspaper: *Lode*

School Yearbook: *Keweenawan*

Alma Mater: *Hail Alma Mater*

> Hail alma mater; hats off to you.
> Ever you'll find us loyal and true.
> Firm and undaunted always we'll be.
> Hail to our MTU,
> here's a toast to thee.

Fight Song: *Fight Tech Fight*

> We'll fight, Tech, fight Engineers,
> for banners bright Engineers.
> The northern hills will sound our cry.
> We'll ring your praises to the sky.
> Then fight, Tech, fight Engineers,
> for right with might Engineers.
> We'll win the game, the glorious name,
> of the Michigan, Michigan, Michigan Engineers.

Northern Michigan University
Presque Isle Ave.
Marquette, MI 49855

School Nickname: *Wildcats*

School Colors: *Old Gold and Olive Green*

School Mascot: *Wildcat*

School Newspaper: *The North Wind*

Alma Mater: *Hail Northern*

> Hail Northern, we thy sons and daughters
> Now bring thee tribute long deserved.
> Thou beacon light mid nature's grandeur
> Through passing decades well preserved.
> O may we labor with untiring zeal
> That when these golden days have flown
> We may with honor face the future
> And match thy courage with our own.
> > *Words and Music by*
> > *Luther S. West*

Fight Song: *Come Men of Northern*

> Come Men of Northern
> We're all behind you in this game
> Come Men of Northern
> Let's do our best to win acclaim
> You are the pride and joy
> Of every person young and old
> So do your best for Northern's glory
> Fight for the Olive and Gold.
> Fight On! Fight On!
> Rah, Rah, Rah, Rah
> Fight On! Fight On!
> Make this game another Northern victory.

Oakland University
Walton at Squirrel Rds.
Rochester, MI 48063

School Nickname: *The Pioneers*

School Colors: *White and Gold*

School Newspaper *Oakland Sail*

Saginaw Valley State College
2250 Pierce Rd.
University Center, MI 48710-0001

School Nickname: *SVSC or Saginaw Valley*

School Colors: *Cardinal Red, Blue and White*

School Mascot: *Cardinal*

School Newspaper: *Valley Vanguard*

Alma Mater: *Alma Mater*

> Alma Mater, hail to thee
> Hail to thee our college dear
> Thy light shall shine and guide the way
> Thy halls will e'er be near.
> Alma Mater, hail to thee
> Thy name will honored be
> We follow thee, we look to thee
> To thee our guiding flame.
> May we always sing thy praise,
> May we hail thy name.

Fight Song: *Cardinal Fight*

> Let's go Cardinals
> Let's win that game
> On to victory tonight
> Down the field let them know
> With the Cardinals we'll go
> To victory we'll fight!
> Let's go Cardinals
> Let's hear that sound
> Hit em hard, that 1-2-3
> Let's go! Win!
> Lead us on to victory!

University of Michigan
Ann Arbor, MI 48109

School Nickname: *Michigan*

School Colors: *Maize and Blue*

School Mascot: *Wolverine*

School Newspaper: *Michigan Daily*

School Yearbook: *Ensian*

Alma Mater: *The Yellow and Blue*

> Sing to the colors that float in the light;
> Hurrah for the Yellow and Blue!
> Yellow the stars as they ride thro' the night,
> And reel in a rollicking crew;
> Yellow the fields where ripens the grain,

And Yellow the moon on the harvest wain;
Hail! Hail to the colors that float in the light;
Hurrah for the Yellow and Blue!

Blue are the billows that bow to the sun
When yellow robed morning is due;
Blue are the curtains that ev'ning has spun,
The slumbers of Phoebus to woo;
Blue are the blossoms to memory dear,
And blue is the sapphire and gleams like a tear;
Hail! Hail to the ribbons that nature has spun;
Hurrah for the Yellow and Blue!

Here's to the college whose colors we wear,
Here's to the hearts that are true!
Here's to the maid of the golden hair,
And eyes that are brimming with blue!
Garlands of blue-bells and maize interwine;
And hearts that are true and voices combine;
Hail! Hail to the college whose colors we wear;
Hurrah for the Yellow and Blue.
>   *Charles M. Gayley, '78*
>   *Michael W. Balfe*

Fight Song: *The Victors*

Now for a cheer they are here, triumphant!
Here they come with banners flying,
In stalwart step they're nighing,
With shouts of vict'ry crying,
We hurrah, hurrah, we greet you now,
Hail!

Far we their praises sing,
For the glory and fame they've bro't us,
Loud let the bells them ring
For here they come with banners flying,
Far we their praises tell,
For the glory and fame they've bro't us,
Loud let the bells them ring,
For there they come with banners flying,
Here they come, Hurrah!
>   *Chorus*
Hail! to the victors valiant
Hail! to the conqu'ring heros,
Hail! Hail! to Michigan the leaders and best,
Hail! to the victors valiant,
Hail! to the conqu'ring heros,
Hail! Hail! to Michigan the champions of the West.
>   *Louis Elbel, '99*

The University of Michigan-Dearborn
4901 Evergreen Rd.
Dearborn, MI 48128-1491

School Colors: *Maize and Blue*

School Mascot: *Wolf*

School Yearbook: *Freshman Record*

Wayne State University
Detroit, MI 48202

School Nickname: *Tartars*

School Colors: *Forest Green and Old Gold*

School Mascot: *Tartar*

School Newspaper: *The South End*

Alma Mater: *Hymn To Wayne*

> To thee, our Alma Mater,
> Homage we bring.
> Brave hearts raise grateful voices
> Thy praise to sing.
> Young art thou, young and strong;
> Renowned shalt thou live, and long;
> Honors to thee will throng--
> And Fame to thee cling.
> We laud thee, Alma Mater,
> Guardian of Right.
> Thou art our guide, our mentor--
> Thy name shines bright.
> Keep Learning's light aflame,
> And hold Truth a sacred name,
> Honor, thy steadfast aim.
> All hail to thy might!
> *Nicholas Stanley Oates '29*

Fight Song: *War March Of The Tartars*

> On to vict'ry,
> Marching down the field,
> On the vict'ry,
> Our opponents yield.
> On to vict'ry,

Smash right through that line,
We are headed for that line,
Rah! Rah! Rah!
In the battle driving for a score.
Come the Tartars pushing to the fore.
They are fighting and we sing their praises
As they drive their way to victory.
                    Marvin Fricke and Paul Schuster
                    Karl L. King

Western Michigan University
Kalamazoo, MI 49008

School Nickname: *Broncos*

School Colors: *Brown and Gold*

School Mascot: *Bronco*

School Newspaper: *Western Herald*

School Yearbook: *Brown and Gold*

Alma Mater: *Western's Alma Mater*

> Western, we sing to you
> Brown and Gold.
> Western, we bring to you
> faith untold.
> You challenge and inspire;
> Your hope is our desire;
> We sing to you our Alma Mater,
> Brown and Gold.

Fight Song: *Fight Song*

> Fight on, Fight on for Western
> Take the ball, make a score,
> Win the game,
> Onward for the Brown and Gold,
> Push 'em back, push 'em back,
> Bring us fame!
> Fight on, Fight on for Western,
> Over one, over all
> We will reign.
> Fight Broncos Fight!
> Fight with all your might.
> Western win this game.

MINNESOTA

Bemidji State University
Bemidji, MN 56601

School Nickname: *BSU*

School Colors: *Kelly Green and White*

School Mascot: *Beavers*

School Newspaper: *Northern Student*

Fight Song: *Fight Song*

> Go Bemidji Beavers,
> Go you Green and White
> Go Bemidji Beavers,
> Fight with all your might.
>
> We are here to cheer you.
> We are out to bring you fame.
> So go Bemidji Beavers,
> Fight and win this game.

College of St. Thomas
2115 Summit Ave.
St. Paul, MN 55105

School Nickname: *The Tommies*

School Colors: *Purple and Grey*

School Mascot: *Tommy Tom Cat*

School Newspaper: *The Aquin*

School Yearbook: *The Aquinas*

Mankato State University
South Rd. and Ellis Ave.
Mankato, MN 56001

School Nickname: *MSU*

School Colors: *Purple and Gold*

School Mascot: *Maverick*

School Newspaper: *The Reporter*

Alma Mater: *Inaugural Hymn*

> Praise to the men who forged Mankato's key,
> Who set the living hinges of the door,
> Who have looked past us to our destiny,
> Who gave us what they had, and wished for more.
>
> As careful husbandmen they tended here,
> In the tree sheltered valley's modest shade,
> A school that gave the world, year after year,
> The men and women whom good labor made.
>
> Now past the honor of those years of birth,
> Our honor in the fertile present grows,
> And to the future of the changing earth,
> The minds of men, a larger hope bestows.
> > *Words by C. K. Waterman*
> > *Paul Karvonen*

Fight Song: *Mankato State College Fight Song*

> Hail to our colors the Purple and the Gold.

Fight on for victory we're back of you
so fight, fight, fight, and conquer our foes,
all you heroes brave and bold.
So fight on for M-A-N-K-A-T-O
Come on let's go. Let's go.

Moorhead State University
Moorehead, MN 56560

School Nickname: *Dragons*

School Colors: *Red and White*

School Mascot: *Dragon*

School Newspaper: *The Advocate*

Alma Mater: *MSU Alma Mater*

> Where flows the river through prairies to the frozen north,
> Seekers of truth built a place of light and liberty,
> That from its portals their sons and daughters might go forth,
> Throughout the nation till the truth be spread that sets us free.
> Hail, hail, Moorhead State to Thee with love and loyalty.
> We pass the torch from the past to the future bright.
> Hail, hail, Alma Mater, answ'ring ever to our country's call,
> Ever changing, ever constant, ever true, Our Alma Mater.

St. Cloud State University
St. Cloud, MN 56301

School Nickname: *St. Cloud State*

School Colors: *Red and Black*

School Mascot: *Husky*

School Newspaper: *Chronicle*

Alma Mater: *University Hymn*

> Sing to thee, our Alma Mater, high on oak-crowned banks,
> Emblem of our search for knowledge, symbol of our youthful ranks.
> Filled with fires of true ambition, let us ever be
> Loyal to thy fine tradition. Hail, St. Cloud, to thee!

By the river's flowing waters, by its islands fair,
May the loyal sons and daughters, they enduring friendship share.
May they with sincere ambition, through the years e'er be
Loyal to thy fine tradition. Hail, St. Cloud, to thee!

Fight Song: *Rouser*

Oh, here we are, the gang and all,
To cheer our team to victory.
St. Cloud State U. has heard the call,
We're here to show our loyalty, Rah! Rah!
Come on, let's fight, let's win this game,
And show our colors, black and red.
We'll sing our song, both loud and strong,
To victory, St. Cloud S. U.

University of Minnesota
6 Morrill Hall
100 Church St., S. E.
Minneapolis, MN 55455

School Colors: *Maroon and Gold*

School Mascot: *Golden Gopher*

School Newspaper: *Minnesota Daily*

Alma Mater: *Hail Minnesota*

Minnesota, Hail to thee!
Hail to thee, our college dear!
Thy light shall ever be
A beacon bright and clear.
Thy sons and daughters true
Will proclaim thee near and far.
They will guard thy fame and adore
thy name;
Thou shalt be their Northern Star.

Like the stream that bends to sea,
Like the pine that seeks the blue;
Minnesota, still for thee
Thy sons are strong and true.
From thy woods and waters fair;
From thy prairies waving far,
At thy call they throng with their shout
and song
Hailing Thee their Northern Star.
                    Truman E. Rickard, '04

Fight Song: *Minnesota Rouser*

> *Chorus*
> Minnesota, hats off to thee,
> To thy colors true we shall ever be,
> Firm and strong, united are we.
> Rah! Rah! Rah! for Ski-U-Mah,
> (shouted) Rah! Rah! Rah! Rah!
> Rah! for the U. of M.
> *Permission from Alumni Association*

University of Minnesota, Duluth
10 University Dr.
Duluth, MN 55812

School Nickname: *UMD*

School Colors: *Maroon and Gold*

School Mascot: *Bulldog*

School Newspaper: *Statesman*

Winona State University
8th and Johnson
Winona, MN 55987

School Nickname: *WSU*

School Colors: *Purple and White*

School Mascot: *Warriors*

School Newspaper: *Winonan*

Alma Mater: *Hail! Winona*

> Lo, in Mississippi's waters,
> Blue the eternal sky;
> In our hearts, O Alma Mater,
> Clear thy spirit high!
> *Chorus*
> Lift the chorus
> Send it ringing
> Far o'er hill and vale!
> Hail to thee, O Alma Mater!
> Hail, Winnona, hail!

Noble hills watch o'er the valley
Where thy dwelling lies;
Steadfast hearts, O Alma Mater,
Guard thy destinies.
 (Repeat Chorus)
Ever shall tomorrow better
What today hath won;
Lead thy children, Alma Mater,
On, forever on!
 (Repeat Chorus)
  By Charlotte Chorpenning

MISSISSIPPI

Jackson State University
1400 J. R. Lynch St.
Jackson, MS 39217

School Colors: *Blue and White*

School Mascot: *Tiger*

School Newspaper: *Blue and White Flash*

School Yearbook: *Jacksonian*

Alma Mater: *Jackson Fair*

> Jackson fair, Jackson dear
> Thee I love, my dear old College home
> Thee I love, wherever I may roam;
> Jackson fair, Jack dear.
>
> Jackson fair, Jackson dear
> Thee I love, thy colors rich and bright
> Thee I love, the blue and white;
> Jackson fair, Jackson dear.
> *Refrain*
> Hail, hail to thee, Yes hail to thee;

Hail to the College of my heart.
Hail, hail to thee, Yes hail to thee
Hail to the College of my heart.

Mississippi State University
Mississippi State, MS 39762

School Nickname: *Bulldogs*

School Colors: *Maroon and White*

School Mascot: *English Bulldog*

School Newspaper: *The Reflector*

School Yearbook: *Reveille*

Alma Mater: *Maroon and White*

> In the heart of Mississippi,
> Made by none but God's own hand
> Stately in her natural splendor
> Our Alma Mater proudly stands:
> State University of Mississippi,
> Fondest memories cling to thee
> Life shall hoard thy spirit ever,
> Loyal friends we'll always be.
>
> Thru our life some power may vanquish
> Loyalty can't be o'er run;
> Honors true on thee we lavish
> Until the setting sun;
> Live Maroon and White forever,
> Ne'er can evil mar thy fame,
> Nothing us from thee can sever,
> Alma Mater we acclaim.
> > *Chorus*
> Maroon and White, Maroon and White!
> Of thee with joy we sing;
> Thy colors bright, our souls delight,
> With praise our voices ring.

Fight Song: *Hail State*

> Hail, dear old State!
> Fight for that victory today,
> Hit that line and tote that ball,
> Cross that goal before you fall,

And then we'll yell, yell, yell, yell,
For dear old State we'll yell like HELL.
Fight for Mississippi State,
Win that game today.

The University of Mississippi
University, MS 38677

School Nickname: *Ole Miss*

School Colors: *Red and Blue*

School Mascot: *Colonel Rebel*

School Newspaper: *The Daily Mississippian*

School Yearbook: *The Ole Miss*

Alma Mater: *Alma Mater*

> Way down South in Mississippi there's a spot that ever calls
> Where among the hills enfolded stand old Alma Mater's Halls.
> Where the trees lift high their branches to the whisp'ring Southern breeze
> There Ole Miss is calling, calling to our hearts fond memories.
>
> With united heart we praise thee, all our loyalty is thine.
> And we hail thee, Alma Mater, may thy light forever shine;
> May it brighter grow and brighter, and with deep affection true,
> Our thoughts shall ever cluster 'round thee, dear old Red and Blue.
>
> May thy fame throughout the nation, through thy sons and daughters grow,
> May thy name forever waken, in our hearts a tender glow,
> May thy counsel and thy spirit ever keep us one in this,
> That our own shall be thine honor, now and ever, dear Ole Miss.
> *Words by Mrs. A. W. Kahle*
> *Music by W. F. Kahle '25*
> *Revised by Ruth McNeil '37*
> *Copyright 1987 University of Mississippi*

University of Southern Mississippi
Hardy St.
Hattiesburg, MS 39406

School Nickname: *USM (athletes - Golden Eagles)*

School Colors: *Black and Gold*

School Mascot: *Golden Eagles* Name: *Nugget*

School Newspaper: *Student PRINTZ*

School Yearbook: *The Southerner*

Alma Mater: *Alma Mater*

> We sing to thee, our Alma Mater, U. S. M. thy praises be.
> Southern mem'ries we shall cherish Loyalty we pledge to thee.
>
> Oh, give us courage to go forward to our tasks, and let us be.
> Men of trust for thy name's keeping U. S. M. we hallow thee.
>
> And now we pledge thee by our honor, Steadfast love and loyalty;
> Working ever for thy glory U. S. M. thy glory be.
>
> Spacious skies and land of sunshine, Verdant trees and shelt'ring walls
> Now our hearts lift ever to thee as we praise thy hallowed halls.

Fight Song: *Southern To The Top*

> Southern Mississippi to the top! to the top,
> So lift your voices high show them the reason why
> that Southern spirit never will stop.
> FIGHT! FIGHT! FIGHT!
> Southern Mississippi all the way
> Banners high and we will Fight!
> Fight! Fight! to victory, hear our battle cry!
> *Words and Music by Robert D. Hays*

MISSOURI

Central Missouri State University
Warrensburg, MO 64093

School Colors: *Crimson Red and Black*

School Mascot: *Mule*

School Newspaper: *The Muleskinner*

School Yearbook: *Rhetor*

Alma Mater: *Hail to Central State*

> Central State stands proud and noble,
> Serving all who ask,
> In the center of the nation,
> Joyful in her task;
> Red and black her colors fly;
> Faith and vision, dreams unite,
> Leading all who look for truth
> To hold her honor bright,
> Our beloved Alma Mater,
> Hail to Central State.

Central State the chimes are calling,
Hear their joyful sound,
In our hearts their echoes falling,
While we gather round;
Striving on with purpose clear,
Loyal to the school we love,
Let us never falter
While your banner flies above,
Our beloved Alma Mater,
Hail to Central State.

Lyrics by Carole G. Austin
Music by William Stoney

Fight Song: *"Go Mules"*

Go Mules! Fight to win for the team we love the best.
Go Mules! Don't give in, put our name above the rest.
Fight! Fight! Fight!
Go Mules! We're for you and we let the whole world know,
That at C-M-S-U, it's go, Mules go!

Written by Clifton A. Burmeister

Missouri Southern State College
Newman & Duquesne
Joplin, MO 64801

School Nickname: *Southern*

School Colors: *Green and Gold*

School Mascot: *Lion*

School Newspaper: *The Chart*

School Yearbook: *Crossroads*

Alma Mater: *Alma Mater*

Our Alma Mater, we honor thee,
shaping and guiding our destiny.
After we have parted as the years roll by;
we'll keep each memory hail, hail to thee.

Words by Mary Laird, Class of '39
Music by Emerson Jackson,

Missouri Western State College
4525 Downs Dr.
St. Joseph, MO 64507

School Nickname: *Griffons*

School Colors: *Black and Gold*

School Newspaper: *Griffon News*

School Yearbook: *Griffon*

Alma Mater: *MWSC Alma Mater*

> Gently flows the wide Missouri,
> Searching for the sea.
> Take me to my alma mater,
> Where it waits for me
> Though I leave and ever wander,
> This I know is true,
> When I dream of old Missouri,
> I'll remember you.
> Loyal hearts to her returning,
> Faithful, proud, and true,
> Missouri Western live forever.
> We sing in praise of you.
> > *Words by Daryl McDermott*
> > *Music by Michael Mathews*

Northeast Missouri State University
Kirksville, MO 63501

School Colors: *Purple and White*

School Mascot: *Bulldog*

School Newspaper: *The Index*

School Yearbook: *The Echo*

Alma Mater: *Old Missou*

> "Old Missou" and "Old Missouri"
> Our hearts the school has won,
> Fondly cling we to the mem'ry
> Of old "Missouri's Son."

Gladly thee our hearts we tender
By the dim and flick'ring light
Every lad a proud defender
Of the Purple and the White.
                Basil Brewer,'01

Northwest Missouri State University
Maryville, MO 64468

School Nickname: *Northwest*

School Colors: *Green and White*

School Mascot: *Bearcats*

School Newspaper: *Northwest Missourian*

School Yearbook: *The Tower*

Alma Mater: *Alma Mater*

Let your voices loudly ringing,
Echo far and near;
Songs of praise thy children singing
To thy mem'ry Dear.
            Chorus
Alma Mater! Alma Mater!
Tender, fair and true,
Grateful ones with love unfailing,
All their vows renew.

Years may dim our recollections,
Time its change may bring,
Still thy name in fond affection
Evermore we sing.

St. Louis University
St. Louis, MO 63103

School Nickname: *SLU*

School Colors: *Reflex Blue and White*

School Mascot: *Billiken*

School Newspaper: *University News*

School Yearbook: *Archives*

Southeast Missouri State University

900 Normal
Cape Girardeau, MO 63701

School Nickname: *SEMO*

School Colors: *Red*

School Mascot: *Indians - Otahkians*

School Newspaper: *Capaha Arrow*

School Yearbook: *Sagamore*

Alma Mater: *Alma Mater*

> High above the Mississippi,
> Ageless in majestic flow,
> Rise thy halls in native grandeur,
> Beacon light to all below,
>> *Chorus*
> Cape Girardeau, Alma Mater
> Forward press unceasingly,
> In the quest for truth untrammelled,
> Till humanity is free.
>
> 'Round thee Springtime flings her blossoms,
> June in verdure veils thy hill,
> Autumn paints in poignant beauty,
> Winter's snows fall soft and still.
>
> With the passing of the ages,
> Brighter still thy light shall glow;
> Sons and daughters more shall gather
> Here to laugh, and love, and grow.
>> *Bera Beauchamp Foard*
>> *Wilhelmina L. Vieh*

Southwest Missouri State University

901 S. National
Springfield, MO 65804

School Nickname: *Bears*

School Colors: *Maroon and White*

School Mascot: *"Boomer" the Bear*

School Newspaper: *The Standard*

School Yearbook: *Ozarko*

Alma Mater: *Alma Mater*

> Sing we praises
> Now to our Alma Mater!
> All hail, Maroon and White!
> SMS, we pledge devotion
> May you live
> Ever in truth and right.

University of Missouri-Columbia
Columbia, MO 65211

School Nickname: *Mizzou*

School Colors: *Black and Gold*

School Mascot: *Tiger* Name: *Mizzou*

School Newspaper: *Maneater*

School Yearbook: *Savitar*

Alma Mater: *Old Missouri*

> Old Missouri, fair Missouri
> Dear old Varsity,
> Ours are hearts that fondly love thee
> Here's a hail to thee.
>
> Proud art thou in classic beauty
> Of thy noble past
> With thy watchwords--honor, duty
> Thy high fame shall last.
>
> Every student, man and maiden,
> Swells the glad refrain,
> Till the breezes music laden
> Waft it back again.

Fight Song: *Fight Tigers*

> Fight, Tiger, fight for old Mizzou,
> Right behind you, everyone is with you.

Break the line and follow down the field,
And you'll be, on the top, upon the top;
Fight, Tiger, you will always win,
Proudly keep the colors flying skyward.

In the end we'll win the victory,
So Tigers, fight for Old Mizzou!

University of Missouri-Kansas City

5100 Rockhill
Kansas City, MO 64110

School Nickname: *UMKC*

School Colors: *Blue and Gold*

School Mascot: *Kangaroo*

School Newspaper: *University News*

School Newspaper: *The Kangaroo (sporadic publication)*

Alma Mater: *Alma Mater*

    Hail Alma Mater's UMKC
    Our University, Our destiny.
    Let Missouri's motto ring Salus Populi,
    Through our University UMKC

University of Missouri-Rolla

Rolla, MO 65401

School Nickname: *Miners (UMR)*

School Colors: *Silver and Gold*

School Mascot: *The Miner*

School Newspaper: *Missouri Miner*

School Yearbook: *The Rollamo*

Alma Mater: *Alma Mater Hymn*

    Through the years with honor glowing,
    Love for you is ever growing,
    From our hearts forever flowing,
    Alma Mater.

Wrought in Silver Forged in Gold.
Always in our hearts we'll hold
U - M Rolla, M. S. M. Alma Mater.
Words and Music by
Nancy Cook Mackman, 1984

Fight Song: *Fight Miners*

Go you Miners. hit 'em again;
Clap hands Miners, we're gonna win!
Roarin' scorin' as the season goes.
Ev'ry body knows there's nothing finer
Than a Miner!
Go Miners, we're on the ball;
Clap hands Miners,
we've got it all;
Clear the way, cause we're here to stay
Miner Gang from UMR!
Harold W. Cleveland

University of Missouri-St. Louis
St. Louis, MO 63121

School Nickname: *UMSL*

School Colors: *Red and Gold*

School Mascot: *Riverman/Riverwoman*

School Newspaper: *Current*

Washington University
St. Louis, MO 63130

School Nickname: *Washington*

School Colors: *Red and Green*

School Newspaper: *Student Life*

School Yearboook: *Hatchet*

Alma Mater: *Alma Mater*

Dear Alma Mater, Thy name is sweet to me.
Our hearts are all for thee Fair Washington.
Thy halls shall honored be Throughout this great country
For all eternity, Our Washington.

Those days of youth which All of us spent with thee
Form a dear history, Fair Washington.
Could they renewed be, We'd live our days with thee
For all eternity, Our Washington.

Webster University
St. Louis, MO 63119

School Nickname: *Gorloks*

School Colors: *Midnight Blue, Gold and White*

School Mascot: *Gorlok*

School Newspaper: *The Journal*

MONTANA

Montana State University
Bozman, MT 59717

School Nickname: *Bobcats*

School Colors: *Blue and Gold*

School Mascot: *Bobcat*

School Newspaper: *The Exponent*

School Yearbook: *Montanan*

Alma Mater: *Fair M.S.U.*

> Fling wide our colors bright and true,
> Sunlight gold and ether blue
> Fit emblem of our college days,
> Proudly we our banner raise.
> > *Chorus*
> Oh, M. S. U., right loyalty
> We offer songs of praise to thee;
> Long may thy pow'r enduring be,
> Alma Mater, hail to thee!

Montana's sons shall ever climb
Mountain heights in deeds sublime;
Her daughters' fame shall far out vie
Snowy peaks in purity.

Then rouse ye sons and daughters all,
Here our college honor call,
Be swift to dare and strong to do,
Ever zealous, ever true.

When years have borne us far away,
Memory shall keep today
We'll gladly owe to M. S. U.
What we are and hope to be.
            Words by Mabel Kinney Hall

Fight Song: *Stand Up and Cheer*

Stand up and cheer,
Cheer long and loud for dear Montana,
For today we raise
The blue and gold to wave victorious!
Our sturdy band now is fighting
And we are sure to win the fray
We've got the vim, we're here to win,
For this is dear Montana's day
Rah! Rah! Rah!
            Words by Edward A. Duddy
            Music by Paul P. McNeely

University of Montana
Missoula, MT 59812

School Nickname: *U of M   UM*

School Colors: *Copper, Silver and Gold*

School Mascot: *Grizzly Bear -- the Grizzlies*

School Newspaper: *Montana Kaimin*

School Yearbook: *Sentinel*

NEBRASKA

Creighton University
California at 24th St.
Omaha, NE 68178

School Colors: *Blue and White*

School Mascot: *Billy Bluejay*

School Newspaper: *Creightonian*

School Yearbook: *The Bluejay*

Fight Song: *The White and The Blue*

> The White and the Blue!
> Colors true, it is you we defend.
> Fearless for you,
> Our might to the fight we will lend.
> So wave, colors, wave,
> We will fight on for your glory.
> White and Blue!
> We will fight till the fight is won.
>
> The White and the Blue!
> The fame of your name we will sing.

Honor to you;
Praises fair on the air ever ring.
So hail, Creighton, hail!
Here's to you, our inspiration.
White and Blue;
All hail! All hail! To you!
Words and Music by Gordon Richmond

Kearney State College
Kearney, NE 68849

School Nickname: *Antelopes or Lopers*

School Colors: *Blue and Gold*

School Mascot: *B A Loper*

School Newspaper: *Antelope*

School Yearbook: *Blue and Gold*

Alma Mater: *Kearney State Alma Mater*

> Afar in the west where the green valleys run
> And the sweeping hills dip to the plain;
> Rise the gray, storied walls of the home that we love--
> Alma Mater! We hail thee again!
>
> 'Neath thy shade we have gazed over valley and plain
> On the scenes that enrapture the eye;
> And our hearts thrill with pride as the Blue and the Gold
> Proudly floats 'gainst the evening sky.

Fight Song: *K. S. C. Fight Song*

> Come on and fight K.S.C.
> come on and fight for victory
> Keep up your fighting spirit.
> We'll always cheer it
> That's what we're here for.
> Fight for the blue and gold.
> Rah! Rah! Rah!
> Cheer for the blue and the gold and
> as together we stand, proud
> of the best in the land.
> Fight for the blue and gold.

University of Nebraska-Lincoln
Lincoln, NE 68588

School Nickname: *Cornhuskers*

School Colors: *Scarlet and Cream*

School Mascot: *Herbie Husker*

School Newspaper: *Daily Nebraskan*

Alma Mater: *There Is No Place Like Nebraska*

There is no place like Nebraska,
Dear old Nebraska U.
Where the girls are the fairest,
The boys are the squarest
Of any old school that I knew.
There is no place like Nebraska,
Where they're all true blue.
We'll all stick together,
In all kinds of weather,
For dear old Nebraska U.
        Harry L. Pecha

Fight Song: *Hail Varsity*

Hail to the team
The stadium rings as everyone sings the scarlet and cream.
Cheers for a victory.
Echo our loyalty.
Son on mighty men.
The eyes of the land upon every hand are looking at you.
Fight on to victory.
Hail to the team of Nebraska U.
        Lyrics by W. Joyce Ayers
        Music by Wilbur Chenowet

NEVADA

University of Nevada, Las Vegas
4505 Maryland Pkwy.
Las Vegas, NV 89154

School Nickname: *Rebels*

School Colors: *Scarlet and Silver*

School Mascot: *Hey Reb*

School Newspaper: *Rebel Yell*

School Yearbook: *Epilogue*

Fight Song: *Win With The Rebels*

> Win with the Rebels a victory today!
> Win with the Rebels the crimson and gray
> From mountains that surround you to far across the sea
> We'll win with the Rebels of UNLV!

University of Nevada-Reno
Reno, NV 89557

School Nickname: *UNR*

School Colors: *Blue and Silver*

School Mascot: *Wolf Pack*

School Newspaper: *Sagebrush*

School Yearbook: *Artemisia*

Alma Mater: *The Mackay Song*

Where the Truckee's snow fed waters,
drop from mountains crest,
And the meadows meet the sagebrush,
by the sun caressed.
Cradled be the silver mountains 'neath
the western blue,
Stands our noble Alma Mater, our
Nevada U.
As the miner, on the desert, prospects
ev'ry place,
So Nevada seeks the future with an
upturned face.
Ev'ry where she gathers knowledge, all
that's good and true.
Gives she to her sons and daughters,
of Nevada U.
We will ever live to serve her, live
to give our best,
Live to make our Alma Mater pride of
all the West.
Let her praises wake the echoes, while
we pledge anew,
Hearts and minds and hands and voices
to Nevada U.

Fight Song: *Hail, Sturdy Men!*

Hail to our sturdy men, loyal and true,
March, march on down that field, O' Silver and Blue.
We'll give a long cheer for Nevada's men,
See them break through again.
Fighting for our own U of N--to victory!
Hurrah, hurray, hurrah, hurray--NEVAAAA-DA!
We'll give a long cheer for Nevada's men,
See them break through again,
Fighting for our own U of N--to victory!

NEW HAMPSHIRE

Dartmouth College
Hanover, NH 03755

School Nickname: *Big Green*

School Colors: *Dartmouth Green and White*

School Newspaper: *The Dartmouth*

School Yearbook: *The Aegis*

Alma Mater: *Men of Dartmouth*

> Men (we) of Dartmouth, give a rouse
> For the college on the hill!
> For the Lone Pine above her,
> And the loyal sons (ones) who love her,
> Give a rouse, give a rouse, with a will!
> For the sons (friends) of old Dartmouth,
> The sturdy sons (ones) of Dartmouth,
> Though 'round the girdled earth they roam,
> Her spell on them remains;
> They have the still North in their hearts,
> The hill-winds in their veins,
> And the granite of New Hampshire
> In their muscles and their brains.

They were mighty men of old
That she nurtured side by side;
Till like Vikings they went forth
From the lone and silent North,
And they strove, and they wrought, and they died;
But the sons of old Dartmouth,
The laurelled sons of Dartmouth,
The Mother keeps them in her heart
And guards their altar flame;
The still North remembers them,
The hillwinds know their name,
And the granite of New Hampshire
Keeps the record of their fame.

Men (we) of Dartmouth, set a watch
Lest the old traditions fail!
Stand as brother (sister) stands by brother!
Dare a deed for the old Mother!
Greet the world, from the hills, with a hail!
For the sons (friends) of old Dartmouth,
The loyal sons (ones) of Dartmouth,
Around the world they keep for her
Their old chivalric (romantic) faith;
They have the still North in their soul,
The hillwinds in their breath;
And the granite of New Hampshire
Is made part of them till death.

Traditional and contemporary versions
Richard Hovey '85
Harry Wellman '07

Fight Song: *Glory to Dartmouth*

Glory to Dartmouth,
Loyally sing,
Now all together,
Make the echoes ring for Dartmouth.
Our team's a winner,
We've got the stuff,
We wear the Dartmouth green and that's enough.

Keene State College
Keene, NH 03431

School Nickname: *Owls*

School Colors: *Red and White*

School Mascot: *The Horned Owl*

School Newspaper: *The Equinox*

School Yearbook: *The Kronicle*

Alma Mater: *Lift Voices High*

> On lilac paths we've strolled,
> Past halls in ivy twined,
> Neath Mount Monadnock rising bold,
> Our college stands enshrined,
> A toast to Keene to days gone by,
> For days to come,
> Lift voices high and sing.
>
> For Keene State College stands,
> Throughout the mist of time,
> Yet strong she spreads her knowledge
> grand eternally benign,
> A toast to Keene to days gone by,
> For days to come,
> Lift voices high and sing.
> > *Music by Ann Weeks, '59*
> > *Words by Katherine Day Bourne, '60*
> > *and Patricia Piper Bushey, '59*

New Hampshire College
Manchester, NH 03104

School Nickname: *NHC*

School Colors: *Blue and Gold*

School Mascot: *Penman*

School Newspaper: *The Observer*

School Yearbook: *Enterprise*

Plymouth State College
Plymouth, NH 03264

School Nickname: *PSC*

School Colors: *Green and White*

School Newspaper: *The Clock*

School Yearbook: *The Conning Tower*

Alma Mater: *Plymouth State College Alma Mater*

> Where the Pemi shines so fair,
> 'Neath Prospect calm to view
> Thru deep woods and gentle meadows,
> Flow its waters blue.
> Sound their message in our chorus
> Lift our voices free,
> Honor to our mem'ry glorious
> Plymouth, hail to thee!
>
> Clear, the vision of thy mountains
> Strong, thy rock-ribbed vales;
> Gentle are thy bending birches,
> Staunch against the gales.
>
> Sound their message in our chorus
> Lift our voices free;
> Honor to thy memory glorious,
> Plymouth, hail to thee.
>   *Anderson*

University of New Hampshire
Durham, NH 03824

School Nickname: *UNH*

School Colors: *Blue and White*

School Mascot: *Wildcat*

School Newspaper: *The New Hampshire*

School Yearbook: *The Granite*

Alma Mater: *Alma Mater*

> New Hampshire, alma mater,
> All hail, all hail to thee!
> Behind thee tow'r the mountains,
> Before thee roars the sea.
> Thy sons and daughters ever
> Thy praises loud will sing;
> New Hampshire, alma mater,
> Accept our offering.
>
> We love thee, old New Hampshire,
> And to the White and Blue,

Where'er our work shall call us,
We always will be true.
We'll ever guard thy honor,
Bright shall thy mem'ry be;
New Hampshire, alma mater,
All hail, all hail to thee!
H. F. Moore, '98
To the Hymn-tune, "Lancashire",
by Henry Smart

Fight Song: *New Hampshire Hymn*

Fair stands she, all glorious,
New Hampshire, strong and free.
Hail to thee victorious!
New Hampshire, dear to me;
When years bring shadows,
Dark'ning life's sea,
Then, radiant, all glorious,
New Hampshire, thou shalt be.
Words and Music by
A. E. Richard

NEW JERSEY

Camden College of Arts and Sciences - Rutgers
Camden, NJ 08102

School Nickname: *Ruccas*

School Colors: *Scarlet and Black*

School Newspaper: *The Gleaner*

School Yearbook: *Mneme*

Fairleigh Dickinson University
Florham-Madison, Rutherford and Teaneck-Hackensack, NJ

School Nickname: *Florham-Madison - Jersey Devils, Rutherford, Teaneck-Hackensack - Knights*

School Colors: *Columbia Blue, Maroon and White*

School Mascot: *Knights and Blue Devils*

School Newspaper: *Rutherford-Spectator, Teaneck-Hackensack - Gaunlet, Florham-Madison - Metro*

School Yearbook: *Rutherford-Castlelight, Teaneck-Hackensack - Cygnus, Madison-Columns*

Alma Mater: *Alma Mater*

> Praise to thee, O Alma Mater, loyally we sing,
> Thru the years your name resounding Fairleigh Dickinson
> Campus friends will e'er be with us, to them we will cling,
> Campus lights will ever cheer us till the fight be won.
> > *Chorus*
> Alma Mater, we will cherish each day of the years,
> We were privileged to spend here, tho' our parting nears.
>
> Praise to thee, O Alma Mater, faithfully we sing,
> Hear our joyful voices ringing, Fairleigh Dickinson.
> Campus halls, that oft recall us, memories will bring,
> Campus lights will ever guide us, when the day is done.
> > *Goodhart-Davis*

Glassboro State College
Rt. 322
Glassboro, NJ 08028

School Nickname: *Profs*

School Colors: *Brown and Gold*

School Mascot: *Dr. Who*

School Newspaper: *The Whit*

School Yearbook: *The Oak*

Alma Mater: *Alma Mater*

> Alma Mater, we greet thee. All praise to thy name;
> Thy banner unfurl to the breeze.
> Thy children salute thee and pledge to thy fame
> As soldiers who drink to the lees.
> All about thee arise the first temples of god,
> Lifting high, leafy arms to the sky
> And the flowers that bloom in the green of the sod
> Seem to love thee too fondly to die.
> > *Ada PSchiable '24*

Jersey City State College
2039 Kennedy Blvd.
Jersey City, NJ 07305

School Nickname: *Gothic Knights*

School Colors: *Green and Gold*

School Mascot: *The Gothic Knight*

School Newspaper: *Gothic Times*

School Yearbook: *Tower Yearbook*

Alma Mater: *Alma Mater*

> Green and gold, we honor thee,
> Symbol of our aim.
> Lead us onward to thy goal
> Ever for thy fame.
> All our hearts will ever hold
> Memories that are dear;
> And you always will remain
> Our Alma Mater dear.
> > *Will Hayes, '36*
> > *Aubrey M. Kemper, '36*

Kean College
Morris Ave.
Union, NJ 07083

School Nickname: *Cougars*

School Colors: *Columbia Blue and Silver*

School Mascot: *Cougar*

School Newspaper: *Independent*

School Yearbook: *Memorabilia*

Alma Mater: *Alma Mater*

> Kean College, Alma Mater
> This our song....,
> Kean College, Alma Mater,
> hear our joyous throng!
> Forever, in our hearts--,
> We shall remember you---
> Kean College, Alma Mater,
> we shall be true!
> > *Lowell Zimmer*
> > *Michael Montgomery*

Monmouth College
West Long Branch, NJ 07764

School Nickname: *Hawks*

School Colors: *Royal Blue and White*

School Mascot: *Hawk*

School Newspaper: *The Outlook*

School Yearbook: *The Shadows*

Alma Mater: *Alma Mater*

> Monmouth College Alma Mater,
> Glorious praise of thee we sing,
> Proudly bear thy mighty banner.
> Monmouth, let our voices ring.
> Light tomorrow thy blazing emblem,
> Brighter than the shining sea,
> Hail to Monmouth, Alma Mater,
> Honor and glory to thee we bring.
> > *Musical setting by Henry Smart*
> > *Lyrics and Arr. by William A. Wollman*

New Jersey Institute of Technology
323 Rev. Martin Luther King, Jr. Blvd.
Newark, NJ 07102

School Nickname: *NiJIT*

School Colors: *Red and White*

School Mascot: *Highlander*

School Newspaper: *Vector*

School Yearbook: *Nucleus*

Alma Mater: *Alma Mater*

> To Alma Mater fair and great
> Our voices now we raise;
> Our gratitude we demonstrate,
> Her steady torch we praise.
> Her challenge on us ever falls;
> A world of knowledge calls.

In heart and mind
Our trust we'll bind
To our NJIT.
We'll hold her memory ever dear
Her spirit we'll revere.
To her we promise loyalty Our own NJIT.
Music by James N. Wise
Lyrics by Fredereick Fernsler

Princeton University
Princeton, NJ 08544

School Nickname: *Old Nassau*

School Colors: *Orange and Black*

School Mascot: *Tiger*

School Newspaper: *The Daily Princetonian*

School Yearbook: *The Nassau Herald*

Alma Mater: *Old Nassau*

Tune every heart and every voice,
Bid every care withdraw;
Let all with one accord rejoice,
In praise of Old Nassau.
Chorus
In praise of Old Nassau we sing,
Hurrah! Hurrah! Hurrah!
Our hearts will give, while we shall live,
Three cheers for Old Nassau.

Let music rule the fleeting hour,
her mantle round us draw;
And thrill each heart with all her pow'r,
In praise of old Nassau.

And when these walls in dust are laid,
With reverence and awe
Another throng shall breath our song,
In praise of Old Nassau.

Till then with joy our songs we'll bring,
and while a breath we draw,
We'll all unite to shout and sing:
Long life to Old Nassau
H.P. Peck, '62

Fight Song: *The Princeton Cannon Song*

In Princeton town we got a team that knows the way to play.
With Princeton spirit back of them, They're sure to win the day.
With cheers and song we'll rally 'round The Cannon as of Yore,
And Nassau's walls echo with The Princeton Tiger's roar:

Crash through the line of blue
And send the backs on 'round to the end!
Fight! fight! for ev'ry yard,
Princeton's honor to defend Rah! Rah! Rah!
Tiger, sis boom ah!
And locomotives by the score!
For we'll fight with a vim
That is dead sure to win for Old Nassau.

J.F. Hewitt, '07 & A.H. Osborn, '07

Ramapo College of New Jersey

505 Rampo Valley Rd.
Mahwah, NJ 07430

School Nickname: *Roadrunners*

School Colors: *Red and Gold*

School Mascot: *Roadrunner*

School Newspaper: *Ramapo News*

School Yearbook: *The Arch*

Alma Mater: *Alma Mater*

Ramapo, we sing to you
Ramapo, with pride.
Prais'd-filled voices
Raised on High,
Fill your Mountainside.
In the time we've spent together
We have come to learn--
To have dignity,
A mind that's free
And celebrate Humanity.
Ramapo, As years go by
Rampo, with love.
Even when you're far away,
Forever we'll be one.

Lyrics by Michael Alasa
Music by David Welch

Rutgers, The State University of New Jersey
New Brunswick, NJ 08903

School Nickname: *Scarlet Knights*

School Colors: *Scarlet*

School Mascot: *The Scarlet Knight*

School Newspaper: *Targum*

School Yearbook: *Scarlet Letter*

Alma Mater: *On the Banks of the Old Raritan*

My father sent me to old Rutgers,
And resolv'd that I should be a man;
And so I settled down, in that noisy college town,
On the banks of the old Raritan.

Her ardent spirit stirred and cheered me
From the day my college years began;
Gracious Alma Mater mine;
Learning's fair and honored shrine;
On the banks of the old Raritan.

I love her flaming, far flung banner,
I love her triumphs proud to scan,
And I glory in the fame,
That's immortalized her name
On the banks of the old Raritan.

My heart clings closer than the ivy,
As life runs out its fleeting span,
To the stately, ancient walls
Of her hallowed, classic halls
On the banks of the old Raritan.

Then sing aloud to Alma Mater,
And keep the Scarlet in the van;
For with her motto high,
Rutgers' name shall never die,
On the banks of the old Raritan.
Chorus
On the banks of the old Raritan, my boys,
Where old Rutgers ever more shall stand,
For she has not stood
Since the time of the flood,
On the banks of the old Raritan.
Howard N. Fuller, '74

Fight Song: *Vive Les Rutgers' Sons*

Oh here's to the college that stands on the hill,
She's stood there for ages she's standing there still.

Oh here's to the Ivy on old Rutgers walls
Our heart strings like Ivy shall cling 'round her halls.

A friend on the left and a friend on the right
In jolly good fellowship let us unite.
Chorus
Vive les Rutgers sons
Vive les Rutgers sons.
Vive la, vive la, Vive l'amour,
Vive la, vive la, Vive l'amour,
Vive l'amore, Vive l'amore,
Vive les Rutgers sons.

Saint Peters College
2641 Kennedy Blvd.
Jersey City, NJ 07306

School Nickname: *Peacocks and Peahens*

School Colors: *Blue and White*

School Mascot: *Peacocks and Peahens*

School Newspaper: *Pauw Wow*

School Yearbook: *Peacock Pie*

Alma Mater: *Alma Mater*

Hail, Alma Mater,
Deathless Saint Peter's
Our loving hearts acclaim
Thy resurrected name.

Nor war nor time has power
to bind thee,
Thine is the spirit proud and free.
And as year on year comes winging,
We will still be singing praises to thy fame.

Hail, Alma Mater,
Hallowed Saint Peter's
With each new day we see
How much we owe to thee.

Truth is our guide, we shall not fail,
And our love will ever bind us
So that death will find us thine eternally.

Seton Hall University
South Orange Ave.
South Orange, NJ 07079

School Nickname: *The Pirates*

School Colors: *Blue and White*

School Newspaper: *The Setonian*

School Yearbook: *The Galleon (originally called The Blue and White)*

Stockton State College
Jimmie Leeds Rd.
Pomona, NJ 08240

School Colors: *Black and White*

School Mascot: *Osprey*

School Newspaper: *ARGO*

Trenton State College
Hillwood Lakes, CN 4700
Trenton, NJ 08650-4700

School Nickname: *Lions*

School Colors: *Blue and Gold*

School Mascot: *Lion* Name: *Linus*

School Newspaper: *The Signal*

School Yearbook: *The Seal*

Alma Mater: *Alma Mater*

Alma Mater, Blue and Gold!
Name still blazing as of old!
Hearts we pledge that thou shalt be.
Shining through eternity.

Brighter as the years unfold.
Alma Mater, Blue and Gold.
Trenton College, Blue and Gold.
Thy brave spirit ne'er grows old.
And though far our steps may lead.
Thou wilt guide our thought and deed
On to heights as yet untold,
Alma Mater, Blue and Gold.
                    Franklin Grapel, '33

Fight Song: *TSC Victory March*

Current fight song is music only.

William Paterson College
300 Pompton Rd.
Wayne, NJ 97470

School Nickname: *Pioneers*

School Colors: *Orange and Black*

School Mascot: *The Pioneer*

School Newspaper: *The Beacon*

School Yearbook: *The Pioneer*

Alma Mater: *Alma Mater*

To thee, our Alma Mater,
We raise our voices high.
In learning's path you'll lead us;
to follow you, we'll try.
We'll guard and share thy learnings,
Diffuse thy truth and light,
Enlighten eager children,
Add to our country's might.

The years may soon divide us.
Our hearts return to thee,
Thy lessons held and cherished,
Enshrined in memory.
We're Pioneers courageous;
We face a wider world,
Aiding the spread of knowledge,
Truth's banner bright unfurled.

NEW MEXICO

Eastern New Mexico University
Portales, NM 88130

School Colors: *Silver and Green*

School Mascot: *Greyhounds*

School Newspaper: *Eastern Sun Press*

School Yearbook: *Silver Pack*

Alma Mater: *Alma Mater*

> There's a spot in my heart
> and a feeling I would share
> for the school of the silver and green
> For the memories I cherish
> and the friends that I know there
> In those days of fellowship keen
> There are thoughts that can't be spoken
> In my memory of you
> So I'm singing the praises of Eastern University
> Alma Mater TRUE!

New Mexico State University
Las Cruces, NM 88003

School Nickname: *AGGIES*

School Colors: *Crimson and White*

School Mascot: *Pistol Pete*

School Newspaper: *Roundup*

School Yearbook: *The Phoenix*

Alma Mater: *Alma Mater*

> Hail to thee, New Mexico
> Mother of wise men and true;
> We, thy sons and daughters fair,
> Pledge our devotion to you;
> Bright as this enchanted land,
> Guardian of youth's fair prime,
> Long may you in honor stand
> Strong to the end of time.
>
> Still in age we'll sing thy fame
> Wearing the crimson and white,
> Through the years we'll shout thy name,
> Symbol of all that is right;
> Mem'ries, then, will never die
> And many dreams come true
> So to you a health we cry,
> To you, N.M.S.U.

Fight Song: *Aggie Fight Song*

> Aggies, oh Aggies,
> The hills send back the cry,
> We're here to do or die.
> Aggies, oh Aggies,
> We'll win this game or know the reason why.
>
> And when we win this game
> We'll buy a keg of booze,
> And we'll drink it to the Aggies
> 'Til we wobble in our shoes.
>
> Aggies, oh Aggies,
> The hills send back the cry,
> We're here to do or die.
> Aggies, oh Aggies,
> We'll win this game or know the reason why.

University of New Mexico
Albuquerque, NM 87131

School Colors: *Cherry Red and Silver*

School Mascot: *Wolf* Name: *Lobo*

School Newspaper: *Daily Lobo*

School Yearbook: *The Mirage (currently not in existence)*

Alma Mater: *Alma Mater*

New Mexico, New Mexico
We sing to honor thee,
This golden haze of college days
Will live in memory,
This praise we sing will ever ring
With truth and loyalty,
New Mexico, your fame we know
Will last eternally.

Fight Song: *Hail New Mexico*

Hail to thee, New Mexico
Thy loyal sons are we
Marching down the field we go
Fighting for thee
Rah! Rah! Rah!
Now we pledge our faith to thee
Never shall we fail
Fighting ever, yielding never
Hail! Hail! Hail!

NEW YORK

Adelphi University
South Ave.
Garden City, NY 11530

School Nickname: *Panthers*

School Colors: *Brown and Gold*

School Mascot: *Panther*

School Newspaper: *Delphian*

School Yearbook: *Oracle*

Alma Mater: *Alma Mater*

Our Alma Mater true
We sing in loyalty;
The glory of thy name shall e'er resound
With honor, love and hope that we have found.

"The truth shall make us free"
As we go our way.
Adelphi live forever!
The Brown and Gold for Aye!

Baruch College/The City University of New York

17 Lexington Ave.
New York, NY 10010

School Colors: *Blue and White*

School Newspaper: *The Ticker*

School Yearbook: *The Lexicon*

Alma Mater: *Baruch Alma Mater*

> Standing high above the city's mighty roar,
> Bernard Baruch, we sing to you now and evermore.
> Praising you for years, we will always be
> Proud to call you alma mater, jubilant and free.
> Knowledge of the world, the honor it will bring,
> Are what you have given us; that is why we sing.
> Your dignity and strength make our spirits soar;
> Bernard Baruch, we sing to thee forever more.
> > *By Miriam Blech*
> > *Rev. by Grace Schulman*

Brooklyn College/City University of New York

Avenue H and Bedford Ave.
Brooklyn, NY. 11210

School Colors: *Maroon and Gold*

School Newspaper: *Kingsman*

School Yearbook: *Broeklundian*

Alma Mater: *Brooklyn College Alma Mater*

> On campus green, with towers of marble
> Lifting white spires in air.
> Oh, Brooklyn is our Alma Mater,
> And she is wondrous fair.
> Within the gray halls ever lit,
> The Lamps of learning burn,
> And ever on to goals of glory
> Young eager spirits yearn.
>
> A loyal band of student comrades,
> Golden our laughter rings.
> To stars above we turn our faces,
> Soaring on sweeping wings.

Our friendship here is woven with learning.
Joy fills all our days,
So hail to thee, our Alma Mater:
Brooklyn, we sing thy praise.
Words, Robert Friend
Music, Sylvia Fine Kaye

Canisius College
2001 Main St.
Buffalo, NY 14208

School Colors: *Blue and Gold*

School Mascot: *Griffin*

School Newspaper: *The Griffin*

School Yearbook: *The Azuwur*

Alma Mater: *Canisius College Alma Mater*

With hearts and voices joined in chorus glad and strong
We sing our Alma Mater's praise,
And bid the echoes of our song
Awaken memories of our college days.

Canisius men and women, Golden Griffins proud,
We boast our Alma Mater's name.
We sing her praises long and loud
And dedicate ourselves to spread her fame.
Chorus
Then rally round, and swell the sound,
The stirring tune of old!
Our banner fair unfold
The royal Blue and Gold'.

With ringing cheer, from far and near,
Our loyalty renew!
Our hearts will be true
Canisius, to you!
Words, Rev. J.G. Hacker, S.J. '11
Music, Carl Mischka, '11
Rev. 1985 Rev. James M. Demske, S.J., '47
and Dr. David J. Greenman, '62

Fight Song: *Fight Song*

On with a march, march, march to victory.
Our hearts are gay today, we're in the fray today.

On with a step, step, step triumphantly
We'll raise a chorus strong
To sing this battle song;
Go up, go up, go up, never say done to Canisius men
Fight on, fight on, fight on tho you have won and won again
Cheer with a shout, shout, shout exultantly
Lift up your eyes to see
our Griffin victory
Hail to you blue and gold, the victory is ours today;
with loyal sons of old our youthful hearts and bold
will rush your banners onward thru the fray
And fight, fight, fight on you Griffin men
Till ev'ry foe is put to flight;
and onward thru the fray triumphantly
You march in your victorius might--!
Rev. Timothy J. Coughlin

City College/City University of New York
Covent Ave. and 137th St.
New York, NY 10031

School Nickname: *City*

School Colors: *Black and Lavender*

School Mascot: *Beaver*

School Newspaper: *The Campus*

School Yearbook: *The Microcosm*

Alma Mater: *Lavender, My Lavender*

Sturdy sons of City College,
Trusty hearts and mighty hands,
Rally where our streaming banner
With its dauntless emblem stands;
Send a cheer to heaven Ringing,
Voicing in a fond acclaim
Faith and pride in Alma Mater
And her never dying fame.

Daughters, wise, of City College,
Join your voices in the song.
To the lusty cheers of brothers,
Add your effort clear and strong.
Send a hymn to heaven Singing,
Filled with love and fond acclaim,

Faith and pride in Alma Mater
And her never dying fame.
> *Chorus*

Lavender, my Lavender! Lavender, my Lavender!
On the field of life's endeavor
Bound by ties that naught can sever,
Hail we Alma Mater ever, Lavender, my Lavender!
> *Words, Elias Lieberman, '03*
> *and Daniel T. O'Connell, '24*
> *Music, Walter R. Johnson, '03*

Fight Song: *CCNY Fight Song*

C.C.N.Y See the battle through! Oh can't you see,
C.C.N.Y. We're always all for you.
Valiant men of Lavender and Black,
We'll send you forth to battle,
And we'll always bring you back.
Keep courage, men, The battle's just begun,
So fight! Fight! Fight! until we've won!
C.C.N.Y Skies are turning blue,
Get in and fight for we're all for you.
Some day they're gonna get it from C.C.N.Y. 'n why not, Right now.
Some day they've gotta take it from C.C.N.Y. 'n why not, Right now.
The Beavers are busy, But the foe will be busier.
We'll toss'em around and around and around till they can't be any dizzier.
They're gonna get it, They've gotta take it,
'Cause We're gonna give it right now.
> *Fred Waring, Tom Waring, Pat Ballards*
> *Frank Hower*

Clarkson University
Potsdam, NY 13676

School Colors: *Green and Gold*

School Mascot: *The Golden Knight*

School Newspaper: *Intregator*

School Yearbook: *Clarksonian*

Alma Mater: *Alma Mater*

Hear us, Clarkson, hail to thee.
Hear us sing thy praise.
We cherish dear the memory
of golden College days.
Thy banner, green and gold,

shall stand until eternity.
Alma Mater, strong and grand,
Clarkson, hail to thee.

College of Staten Island/City University of New York
130 Stuyvesant Pl.
Staten Island, NY 10301

School Nickname: *CSI*

School Colors: *Maroon and Blue*

School Mascot: *Dolphin*

School Newspaper: *College Voice*

School Yearbook: *CSI Dolphin*

Columbia University
New York, NY 10027

School Nickname: *Colossus on the Hudson*

School Colors: *Pale Blue and White*

School Mascot: *Columbia Lion*

School Newspaper: *Columbia Daily Spectator, Acta Columbiana*

School Yearbook: *The Columbian*

Cornell University
Ithaca, NY 14853

School Nickname: *Big Red*

School Colors: *Red and White*

School Mascot: *Cornell Bear*

School Newspaper: *Cornell Daily Sun*

School Yearbook: *Cornellian*

Alma Mater: *Alma Mater*

> Far above Cayuga's waters,
> With its waves of blue,
> Stands our noble Alma Mater,
> Glorious to view.
> *Refrain*
> Lift the chorus, speed it onward,
> Loud her praises tell;
> Hail to thee, our Alma Mater,
> Hail, all hail, Cornell!
>
> Far above the busy humming
> Of the bustling town,
> Reared against the arch of heaven,
> Looks she proudly down.

Fight Song: *Give My Regards to Davy*

> Give my regards to Davy;
> Remember me to Teefy Crane;
> Tell all the pikers on the Hill
> That I'll be back again.
> Tell them of how I busted,
> Lapping up the high high ball;
> We'll all have drinks at Theodore Zinck's,
> When I get back next fall.

Empire State College
2 Union Ave.
Saratoga Springs, NY 12866

School Colors: *Blue and White*

School Newspaper: *ESC News*

Fordham University
Bronx, NY 10458

School Nickname: *Rams*

School Colors: *Maroon*

School Mascot: *Ram*

School Newspaper: *The Ram*

School Yearbook: *The Maroon*

Alma Mater: *Alma Mater Fordham*

O Alma Mater, Fordham,
How mighty is thy power
To link our hearts to thee in love
That grows with every hour.
Thy winding elms, thy hallowed halls,
Thy lawns, thy ivy mantled walls,
O Fordham, Alma Mater,
What memories each recalls.

Alma Mater, Fordham,
While yet the life-blood starts,
Shrined by thy sacred image
Within our heart of hearts.
And in the years that are to be,
May life and love be true to me,
O Fordham, Alma Mater,
As I am true to thee.

Words by Rev. H. A. Gaynor, S.J.
Music by Frederic Joslyn

Fight Song: *Fordham Ram*

Hail! men of Fordham, hail! on
to the fray!
Once more our foes assail in
strong array.
Once more the old Maroon,
waves on high
We'll sing our battle song.
We do or die.

With a Ram, a Ram, a Ram for victory
With a Ram, a Ram, a Ram for loyalty.
To the fight, to fight,
To win our laurels bright!

Hail! men of Fordham, hail! on
to the fray!
Once more our foes assail in
strong array.
Once more the old Maroon,
waves on high
We'll sing our battle song.
We do or die.

Hofstra University
1000 Fulton Ave.
Hempstead, NY 11550

School Nickname: *Flying Dutchman (women)*

School Colors: *Gold, White and Blue*

School Newspaper: *Hofstra Chronicle*

School Yearbook: *Nexus*

Alma Mater: *The Netherlands*

O Hofstra, to honor thy name we forgather,
Rejoicing in voicing thy praises anew;
By thee we are guided, with counsel provided;
Sustain us with thy strength in the paths we pursue.

You settlers of Nassau who cleared its broad acres,
You sailors and whalers, adventurers bold,
Your precepts uphold us, your visions enfold us,
Your spirit be emblazoned in blue and in gold!

As sons and as daughters to Hofstra united,
We never will sever the ties that us bind;
The years that pass by us shall never deny us
The memories we cherish in heart and in mind.

Hunter College/City University of New York
695 Park Ave.
New York, NY 10021

School Colors: *Purple and White*

School Newspaper: *Hunter Envoy*

School Yearbook: *Wistarion*

Alma Mater: *The Good Ship Alma Mater (no longer used)*

The good ship Alma Mater rides at anchor in the bay,
With all her colors flying in the summer wind today;
For years she stoutly bore us, but now the ocean's past,
And in the hoped-for haven she has landed us at last.

Oh good ship Alma Mater, we bid farewell to thee,
Stand stately in the harbors, ride queen like on the sea,

May never storm come nigh thee, may never tempest make
Thy mighty masts to quiver, thine oaken sides to shake.
Thy mighty masts to quiver, thine oaken sides to shake.

O you who sailed before us, in the good ship long ago,
We followed where you lead us, stars above and sea below;
You led us like a beacon, that lit the seething foam,
You led us like the glitter of a star that pointed home.
You led us like the glitter of a star that pointed home.

O you who shall come after, we give you all God-speed,
Stand by the Alma Mater and serve her at her need,
Till you, too, pass the billows that hold you from the shore,
Till you, too, ride at anchor, and plow the waves no more.
Till you, too, ride at anchor, and plow the waves no more.

O good ship Alma Mater, a long farewell at last,
We're hopeful for the future, we're grateful for the past,
Sail on through sunny water; with more than tongue can tell
Of sorrow at our parting, we speak the last farewell.
Of sorrow at our parting, we speak the last farewell.
Words, Helen Gray Cone '76
Music, Prof. Mangold

Iona College
715 North Ave.
New Rochelle, NY 10801

School Nickname: *Gaels*

School Colors: *Maroon and Gold*

School Mascot: *Frank Smith-a gael*

School Newspaper: *The Ionian*

School Yearbook: *Icann*

Alma Mater: *Iona Alma Mater*

Iona, Alma Mater,
Hail, all hail, to thee!
We raise a cry to glorify
Thy name where'er we be.
To thee we owe allegiance;
Abroad we spread thy fame;
Throughout the world we praise thee,
Proud to bear thy name.

Great Columba, trusted patron
Guide our College year by year.
Founder of the first Iona,
Sing we now in accents clear:
Iona, Alma Mater,
On high thy glories soar;
Ionians go forth again
To praise thee evermore.
G.P Lyons

Ithaca College
Ithaca, NY 14850

School Nickname: *Bombers*

School Colors: *Blue and Gold*

School Newspaper: *The Ithacan*

School Yearbook: *The Cayugan*

Alma Mater: *Ithaca Forever*

Ithaca Forever shine your light on me,
In my heart together we shall always be,
And here's to Ithaca, my Ithaca, how beautiful you are:
Your towers high upon South Hill reach from stone to star.

Ithaca forever I'll recall a smile,
Clasp a hand in friendship, walk a snowy mile.
And here's to Ithaca, my Ithaca-- Alma Mater true,
Although I leave Cayuga's shore, I'll remember you.

Ithaca, forever guide us on our way,
Like shining beacon light our night and day,
And here's to Ithaca, my Ithaca, how bright your vision seems;
May all your sons and daughters dare to live their dreams.
Music, Philip J. Lang, '33
Lyrics, Alicia Carpenter

Lehman College
Bedford Park Blvd. West
Bronx, NY 10468

School Colors: *Blue and Green*

School Mascot: *A Lancer*

School Yearbook: *Abstracts*

Alma Mater: *Alma Mater*

> The challenge of the coming years
> Is seen on ev'ry hand;
> Oh, help us, Lehman, quell the fears
> That rise within our land.
>
> Lehman, Lehman, hear this earnest cry,
> In your hands our futures lie;
> Guide our minds to waiting truth,
> Open up the eyes of youth.
>
> Oh Alma Mater, shape our lives
> Lift high our faith, our sight;
> Refine our hopes, our cares, our drives
> To strive for truth and light.
>
> Lehman, Lehman, hear this earnest cry,
> In your hands our futures lie;
> Guide our minds to waiting truth,
> Open up the eyes of youth.

Long Island University/Brooklyn Campus
Brooklyn, NY 11201

School Nickname: *LIU*

School Colors: *Blue and White*

School Newspaper: *Seawanhaka*

School Yearbook: *Sound*

Alma Mater: *Alma Mater*

> By the towers of the city,
> Crossroads of the trades and arts,
> In the melting pot of nations
> Stands the college of our hearts
> Welcome to our common yearning
> All the faces of mankind,
> To search the crucible of learning
> For the treasures of the mind.
> So onward Long Island U!
> Sing out our colors strong and true!
> The past and future join in you..
> Alma Mater L-I-U!

Manhattan College
Riverdale, NY 10471

School Nickname: *Jaspers*

School Colors: *Green and White*

School Newspaper: *Quadrangle*

School Yearbook: *Manhattanite*

Alma Mater: *Alma Mater*

> Hail to thee, our Alma Mater!
> Of thy fame we sing today;
> And our hearts exult within us,
> as this tribute we thee pay.
> For we love thy sacred precincts,
> thy fair banners bright and gay;
> And thy name shall live in honor,
> Old Manhattan ever more.
> And thy name shall live in honor,
> Old Manhattan ever more.

Mercy College
555 Broadway
Dobbs Ferry, NY 10522

School Nickname: *The Flyers*

School Colors: *Royal Blue and White*

School Newspaper: *Reporter's Impact*

Alma Mater: *Alma Mater*

> When first we saw the sunlight glimmer
> On thy fields and Hudson waters,
> We then were kindled by that spirit,
> Hearts inflamed as sons and daughters.
> Now our voices loud we're raising,
> Singing out for thee who taught us.
> Hail to Mercy-on-the-Hudson,
> Now we pledge our voices true,
> To thyself and to each other,
> Loyal to our white and blue.
> Ever onward, ever upward,
> Alma Mater in thy name,
> From Mercy College we go forward,

Hearts inspired by thy flame.
Hail to Mercy-on-the-Hudson,
Now we pledge our voices true,
To thyself and to each other,
Loyal to our white and blue.
Hail to Mercy-on-the-Hudson,
Standing high o'er land and sea,
May thy wisdom's light be carried
By our hands through our country.
Always serving, never yielding,
Here we stand for thine and thee.
Words by D. Sivack
Music adapted from Handel
by Dr. John Rayburn

New York Institute of Technology
Old Westbury, NY 11568

School Nickname: *New York Tech (athletes-Bears)*

School Colors: *Blue and Gold*

School Mascot: *Bear*

School Newspaper: *Campus Slate in Old Westbury; Scope in Manhattan*

School Yearbook: *Estate in Old Westbury; Edumator in Manhattan*

New York University
New York, NY 10012

School Nickname: *The Violets*

School Colors: *Violet*

School Mascot: *Bobcat*

School Newspaper: *Washington Square News*

School Yearbook: *The Torch*

Alma Mater: *The Palisades*

O grim, grey Palisades, thy shadow.
Upon the rippling Hudson falls,
And mellow mingled tints of sunset
Illumine now our classic halls;

While students gather 'round thy altars
With tributes of devotion true,
And mingle merry hearts and voices
In praise of N Y U.

Oh stately Square that lies before us,
These stony portals straight and strong,
The birthplace of our Alma Mater,
We'll ever praise in splendid song.
The archway ever stands triumphant,
Protecting all we seek to do,
With thee for e'er our inspiration,
O honored N Y U.

But college friendships all must sever,
And fade as does the dying day,
And closest kinships all be broken,
As out in life we wend our way:
And yet, whatever be life's fortune,
'Tho mem'ry fails and friends be few,
We'll love thee still, our Alma Mater,
Our dear old N Y U.
> *Duncan M Genns, '00*
> *Dorthy I Pearce, '48*
> *Arr. by Deems Taylor, '06*

Niagara University
Niagara University, NY 14109

School Nickname: *Purple Eagles*

School Colors: *Purple and White*

School Mascot: *Purple Eagle*

School Newspaper: *The Index*

School Yearbook: *Niagaran*

Alma Mater: *Alma Mater*

This is our home, our college home,
Though hard and strict she be;
The home of many a noble soul,
The shrine of purity.

We love her rocks and river,
Wher'er we chance to be,
Shout "Rah!" for Old Niagara,

And her lovely scenery,
Shout "Rah!" for Old Niagara,
And her lovely scenery.

Fight Song: *Fight Song*

Here's to Old Niagara,
Onward to Victory
We're out to win, boys,
Ever loyal, ever loyal we will be;
Get in the game and win, boys,
Though the odds be great or small;
For the glory of Niagara,
We'll give our all.

Pace University
New York, NY 10038
Pleasantville, NY 10570
White Plains, NY 10603

School Nickname: *Setters*

School Colors: *Blue and Gold*

School Mascot: *Irish Setter*

School Newspaper: *Pace Press, New York City; New Morning, Pleasantville; The Prestonian, White Plains*

School Yearbook: *The Legend, New York and Pleasantville; Vestigia, White Plains*

Alma Mater: *Pace Alma Mater*

Alma Mater hearts and voices sing to thee our everlasting praise;
Each and ev'ry heart rejoices at the thought of happy days.
Pace Oh Pace we'll ne'er forget you nor the friends we hold so dear;
Memories will linger ever and will brighten coming years.
Alma Mater, stand forever, love is strong as we go marching by;
So to thee we raise our voices with your standard held on high.
Pace Oh Pace we'll ever follow where thy beacons show the way;
True to thee we'll be forever as we labor day by day.
        Evan Fox, '54

Polytechnic University
Brooklyn, NY 11201

School Nickname: *Poly or Polytech*

School Colors: *Blue and Grey*

School Mascot: *Bluejay*

School Newspaper: *Bohican, Long Island Campus; Reporter, Brooklyn*

School Yearbook: *Polywog*

Alma Mater: *Alma Mater*

> Polytechnic, Alma Mater!
> Name that fills our hearts with pride
> We are toiling onward, upward,
> With you for our help and guide.
> You are Queen, and with your scepter,
> O'er each loyal heart hold sway,
> While we strive to win new honors
> For the Blue and Gray.
>
> Sons and daughters of Poly, raise
> Your voices in a joyous song.
> Boast her triumphs, sing her praises,
> Sing them loud and long.
>
> And when college days are over
> And we've said our last farewell,
> Then we try to probe the future,
> What it holds no one can tell.
> When into the world we wander,
> Each upon his chosen way,
> May we ever prove a credit
> To the Blue and Gray.
>
> Sons and daughters of Poly, raise
> Your voices in a joyous song.
> Boast her triumphs, sing her praises,
> Sing them loud and long.
>
> Freshman come and Seniors leave her
> Yet she ever firm will stay.
> Hail, all hail, O Polytechnic
> And the Blue and Gray.
>> *Lyrics, John R. Brierly, '10*
>> *Music, John La Barbara*

Rensselaer Polytechnic Institute
Troy, NY 12181

School Nickname: *Engineers*

School Colors: *Red and White*

School Mascot: *The Swarm*

School Newspaper: *Polytechnic*

School Yearbook: *Transit*

Alma Mater: *Here's to old RPI*

> Here's to old RPI
> her fame may never die.
>
> Here's to old Rensselaer,
> she stands today without a peer.
>
> Here's to those olden days,
> here's to those golden days,
> here's to the friends we've made,
> at dear old RPI.
> *Music by E. Fales*

Fight Song: *Hail, Dear Old Rensselaer*

> Hail dear old Rensselaer, The college of our heart.
> For dear old Rensselaer each man must do his part.
> True sons of Rensselaer we'll always strive to be.
> Now dear old Rensselaer, hail to thee!
> Hear the Tramp, Tramp, Tramp, of marching feet.
> Hear the rat-tat-tat-tat of drums that beat.
> Hear the voices ringing loud and sweet
> Hear that mighty shout of
> Hear that thund'ring cry of ...
> *Words and Music by Charles Root, '34*

Rochester Institute of Technology
Rochester, NY 14623

School Nickname: *RIT*

School Colors: *Burnt Umber, Orange and White*

School Mascot: *Tiger*

School Newspaper: *Reporter Magazine*

School Yearbook: *Techmila*

Alma Mater: *Alma Mater*

O Alma Mater, day by day
We strive to hold thine honor bright,
And pledge anew our loyalty,
Defend thy name with all our might.
We rise in gratitude to thee
For the message thou has taught
A message crowned with love and pow'r
Respledant through thy service wrought
Thy noble founders heard the cry
That surges o'er the world today
Their dauntless spirit sends us forth
That we their precepts may obey.

Fight Song: *Fight Song*

Our spirit shows
Everyone knows
We're from RIT
Endure we will
Reach higher still
On to victory.

Our goals will never fail
We'll prove we're best
And never rest
Triumphant over all.

Our spirit shows
For all to know
Our pride is RIT
Endure we will
Reach higher still
On to victory.

We'll show our might
And scale the heights
Tigers, Tigers, raise your
mighty roar
Stronger, faster, higher
watch us soar.

St. John's University
Jamaica, NY 11439

School Nickname: *Redmen*

School Colors: *Red and White*

School Mascot: *Indian Chief* Name: *Black Jack*

School Newspaper: *The Torch*

School Yearbook: *The Vincentian*

SUNY/at Albany
Albany, NY 12222

School Nickname: *Great Danes*

School Colors: *Purple and Gold*

School Mascot: *Great Dane*

School Newspaper: *ASP (Albany Student Press)*

School Yearbook: *Torch*

SUNY/at Binghamton
Binghamton, NY 13901

School Nickname: *SUNY-B*

School Colors: *Green and White*

School Mascot: *The Colonial (Sports), Pegasus (Academic)*

School Newspaper: *Pipe Dream*

School Yearbook: *Pegasus*

SUNY/ at Stony Brook
Stony Brook, NY 11794

School Nickname: *Patriots*

School Colors: *Red and Gray*

School Newspaper: *Statesman, The Stony Brook Press*

School Yearbook: *Specula*

Alma Mater: *Alma Mater*

> Sandy Shore
> Meeting the Northern Sea
> Ancient ground where Patriots yet arise
> Scarlet, gray
> Under azure skies
> The morning of a lifetime lies in Stony Brook
> Raise a grateful cheer for Stony Brook!
>
> Youthful joys
> Youthful folly, too
> Ancient wisdom seen through youthful eyes
> Lifelong friends
> Bound by youthful ties
> The morning of a lifetime lies in Stony Brook
> Raise a grateful cheer for Stony Brook!
> *Words by Winston Clark*
> *Music by Peter Winklen*

SUNY/College at Brockport
Brockport, NY 14420

School Colors: *Green and Gold*

School Mascot: *Eagle*

School Newspaper: *Stylus*

School Yearbook: *Saga*

Alma Mater: *Alma Mater*

> Alma Mater, thy children raise
> To thy shrine deserved praise.
> Hope and courage thou dost impart
> To each loyal student heart.
>
> Friendly flowers and stately trees
> Lend new perfume to the breeze.
> Dear old Campus, lofty halls,
> Alma Mater, we love thy walls.
>
> When the fleeting years divide
> Us from thee, our gentle guide;
> Still our thoughts with thee shall rest,
> Alma Mater, Dearest, Best.

SUNY/College at Buffalo
1300 Elmwood Ave.
Buffalo, NY 14222

School Nickname: *Buff State*

School Colors: *Orange and Black*

School Mascot: *Bengal Tiger*

School Newspaper: *The Record*

School Yearbook: *The Elms*

Alma Mater: *Our Finest Hour*

> A toast to State, to all the days,
> All the laughter, all the tears.
> You have made our friendships great,
>
> We'll triumph through the years.
> With hope anew we'll face the storm
> Beyond which stands our lofty tower.
> This will be our finest hour.
>
> In years to come we'll look to thee,
> Yearning for your guiding light,
> You'll not fail us, Alma Mater,
> Keep us through the night.
> When darkness comes and all hope dies
> You will give us strength and power.
> That will be our finest hour.
> *L. Harry Ray, '51*

SUNY/College at Cortland
Cortland, NY 13045

School Nickname: *Red Dragons*

School Colors *Red and White*

School Newspaper: *The Press*

School Yearbook: *Didascaleion*

Alma Mater: *Alma Mater*

By lofty elm trees shaded round,
Tioughnioga near,
Our grand old Cortland College stands,
To all of us now dear!

We'll sing to thee, dear Alma Mater,
Of love that shall never die,
We'll strive for thy glory eternal,
Keep thy stainless honor high.

Inspiring each son and each daughter
The noblest aims to try,
All thy fame and thy spirit, Thy might are ours
As the swift years hurry by.

SUNY/College at Fredonia
Fredonia, NY 14063

School Nickname: *Blue Devils*

School Colors: *Blue and White*

School Mascot: *Blue Devil*

School Newspaper: *The Leader*

School Yearbook: *Fredonian*

Alma Mater: *Alma Mater*

Near the shore of old Lake Erie
Stands our Alma Mater True.
Fredonia State we proudly honor,
With her colors white and blue.

Sing her glory and her praises,
Let them ring forever true--
Beloved is our Alma Mater,
Fredonia State, all hail to you.

SUNY/College at Geneseo
Geneseo, NY 14454

School Nickname: *Knights*

School Colors: *Blue and White*

School Newspaper: *Lamron*

School Yearbook: *Oh-Ha-Daih*

Alma Mater: *Alma Mater*

> Shine the sun down on her
> halls of wisdom
>
> Where mem'ries linger and our
> thoughts remain
>
> Sing her praises out across
> the valley that echoes our
> refrain
> Geneseo, Geneseo, send us on
> our way
>
> Geneseo, Geneseo, with life's
> work we'll repay
> *Ray Agnew '81*

SUNY/College at New Paltz
New Paltz, NY 12561

School Nickname: *SUNY/New Paltz*

School Colors: *Orange and Blue*

School Mascot: *Hawk*

School Newspaper: *The Oracle; Fahari; and Hermanos Latinos*

School Yearbook: *Paltzonian*

Alma Mater: *Alma Mater*

> In a valley fair and beautiful
> Guarded well by mount and hill
> Beats a heart whose pulse is rich and full
> Of life, and pow'r, and thrill.
> We love thee, Alma Mater dear,
> To thee our hearts are true.
> And we'll sing with voices strong and clear
> To the Orange and the Blue.
> New Paltz, forever our Alma Mater,
> We raise our songs to thee,
> The hills re-echo with glad crescendo
> Our praises full and free.

SUNY/College at Old Westbury
Old Westbury, NY 11568

School Colors: *Dark Green and Ivory*

School Mascot: *Panther*

School Newspaper: *Catalyst*

School Yearbook: *Our Special Place*

SUNY/College at Oneonta
Oneonta, NY 13820

School Nickname: *SUCO*

School Colors: *Red and White*

School Mascot: *Red Dragon*

School Newspaper: *State Times*

School Yearbook: *The Oneontan*

Alma Mater: *Alma Mater*

> Oneonta, Alma Mater,
> Glorious is thy view;
> We, thy children,
> Love thy honor,
> Love thy purpose true.
>
> On the distant strengthening hilltops,
> On the busy town,
> On the pines and shifting shadows,
> Look we fondly down.
>
> When the coming years shall part us
> From thy fostering care,
> We shall turn with fondest yearning
> To thy halls so fair.
> *Chorus*
> Shout the name...'tis Oneonta!
> Loud her glories sing!
> With her praises all, unnumbered,
> Let the dear hills ring!

SUNY/College at Oswego
Oswego, NY 13126

School Nickname: *SUNYCO, The Lakers, Oswego State*

School Colors: *Green and Gold*

School Mascot: *Seagull* Name: *Oswegull*

School Newspaper: *Oswegonian*

School Yearbook: *The Ontarian*

Alma Mater: *Hail Oswego*

Voices fill the air
Singing reverently
Pledging our school fair
Truth and loyalty
This our song we raise
In her name and praise
Oswego, Alma Mater
Hail to thee!

SUNY/College at Plattsburgh
Plattsburgh, NY 12901

School Nickname: *Cardinals*

School Colors: *Cardinal Red and White*

School Mascot: *Cardinal* Name: *Burghy*

School Newspaper: *Cardinal Points*

School Yearbook: *The Cardinal*

Alma Mater: *Alma Mater*

As the evening shades are falling,
And the day fades into night;
Pause a moment in the gloaming
To salute the Red and White.
Chorus
Flag of red, our badge of courage,
With your gleaming letters white;
Emblem of our Alma Mater
Guide us onward toward the right.

Though our ways may part forever,
In our hearts there shall be bright;
All the golden memories gathered
'Neath the banner Red and White.

Syracuse University
Syracuse, NY 13244

School Nickname: *SU*

School Colors: *Orange*

School Mascot: *Sports teams called Orangemen*

School Newspaper: *The Daily Orange*

School Yearbook: *The Onondagan*

Alma Mater: *Alma Mater*

Where the vale of Onondaga
Meets the western sky,
Loyal be thy sons and daughters
To thy memory.

When the evening twilight deepens
And the shadows fall,
Lingers long the golden sunbeam
On thy western wall.

When the shades of life shall gather,
Dark the heart may be,
Still the ray of youth and love shall
Linger long o'er thee.
        Refrain
Flag we love, Orange, float for aye,
Old Syracuse, o'er thee!
Loyal be thy sons and daughters to thy memory.
        Junius W. Stevens, '95

Fight Song: *Down the field*

Out up on the gridiron stands old Syracuse,
Warriors clad in Orange and in Blue,
Fighting for fame of Alma Mater.
Soon those Crouse chimes will be ringing,
Soon you'll hear those fellows singing.
On on daga's braves are out to win today,
The sons of Syracuse are ready for the fray,

The line holds like a wall and now the Orange has the ball;
So ready for that old long yell. Rah! Rah! Rah!
Down, down the field goes old Syracuse,
Just see those backs hit the line and go thro';
Down, down the field they go marching,
Fighting for the Orange staunch and true.
Rah! Rah! Rah! Vict'ry's in sight for old Syracuse,
Each loyal son knows she ne'er more will lose,
For we'll fight, yes we'll fight, and with all our might,
For the glory of old Syracuse,
Rah! Rah! Rah! cuse.

> *Ralph Murphy, '15*
> *C. Harold Lewis, '15*

United States Military Academy
West Point, NY 10996

School Nickname: *Black Knights (of the Hudson)*

School Colors: *Black, Gray and Gold*

School Mascot: *Mule*

School Newspaper: *Pointer View*

School Yearbook: *Howitzer*

Alma Mater: *The Alma Mater*

Hail Alma Mater dear,
To us be ever near,
Help us thy motto bear
Through all the years.
Let duty be well performed.
Honor be e'er untarned,
Country be ever armed,
West Point, by thee.

Guide us, thy sons, aright
Teach us by day, by night,
To keep thine honor bright,
For thee to fight.
When we depart from thee,
Serving on land or sea,
May we still loyal be,
West Point, to thee.

And when our work is done,
Our course on earth is run,
May it be said, "Well Done;
Be thou at peace."
E'er may that line of gray,
Increase from day to day.
Live, serve, and die, we pray,
West Point, for thee.
P.S. Reinecke, '11

Fight Song: *On Brave Old Army Team*

The Army team's the pride and dream
Of every heart in gray,

The Army line you'll ever find
A terror in the fray;

And when the team is fighting
For the Black and Gray and Gold,

We're always near with song and cheer
And this is the tale we're told:

The Army Team
Rah! Rah! Rah! BOOM!

On Brave old Army team,
On to the Fray;
Fight on to victory,
For that's the fearless Army way. (whistle chorus)

University of Rochester
Rochester, NY 14627

School Nickname: *UR*

School Colors: *Blue and Yellow*

School Mascot: *Yellowjackets*

School Newspaper: *Campus Times*

School Yearbook: *Interpres*

Alma Mater: *The Genesee*

Full many fair and famous streams beneath the sun there be,
But more to us than any seems our own dear Genesee.

We love thy banks and stately falls,
for to our minds they bring Our dear old Alma Mater's halls,
where sweetest memories cling.

No castled crags along her way romantic splendors cast,
No fabled or historic lay recalls the golden past,
But more than battlemented walls or legend they may hear,
Our Alma Mater's vine-clad halls and memories ling'ing there.

As flows the river, gathering force, along her steadfast way,
May we along life's devious course grow stronger day by day.
And may our hearts where'er we roam forever loyal be
To our beloved college home beside the Genesee!
Words, T. T. Swinburne, Class of '98
Music, Herve D. Wilkins, Class of 1866

Yeshiva University
New York, NY 10033

School Nickname: *Maccabees*

School Colors: *Blue and White*

School Newspaper: *Main, The Commentator; Midtown, The Observer*

School Yearbook: *Main, Masmid; Midtown, Kochaviah*

York College/City University of New York
Jamaica, NY 11451

School Nickname: *The Cardinals*

School Colors: *Crimson*

School Newspaper: *Pandora's Box*

School Yearbook: *Changes each year*

NORTH CAROLINA

Appalachian State University
Boone, NC 28608

School Nickname: *ASU*

School Colors: *Black and Gold*

School Mascot: *Yosef*

School Newspaper: *The Appalachian*

School Yearbook: *Rhododendron*

Alma Mater: *Alma Mater*

> Cherished vision of the Southland,
> Alma Mater in the hills;
> Thou dost point our minds to wisdom,
> Till the truth our spirit thrills.
> Appalachian, Alma Mater,
> Of our hearts the joy and pride;
> Lead us ever, lead us onward,
> Vanguard of the Hero's side.

Fight Songs: *Hail To The Brave Hearts*

> Hail to the brave hearts that love to fight for thee;
> Alma Mater, Hail! All Hail for Victory, Rah! Rah! Rah!
> Strong arms defend thee whatever be the game;
> Appalachian Hail! All Hail! for thy never ending fame.

Fight Song

> Hi-Hi-y-ike-us
> Nobody like us,
> We are the mountaineers, mountaineers, mountaineers,
> Always a-winning
> Always a-grinning
> Always a feeling fine
> You bet, hey.

Duke University
Durham, NC 27706

School Colors: *Navy Blue and White*

School Mascot: *Blue Devil*

School Newspaper: *Chronicle*

School Yearbook: *Chanticleer*

Alma Mater: *Dear Ole Duke*

> Dear ole Duke, Thy name we'll sing,
> To thee our voices raise, we'll raise
> To thee our anthems ring
> in ever lasting praise.
> And tho' on life's broad sea,
> Our fates may far us bear;
> We'll ever turn to thee,
> Our Alma Mater dear.
> > R.H. James, '24

Fight Song: *Blue and White Fighting Song*

> Duke we thy anthems raise,
> For thy praises untold
> We'll sing for the Blue and White
> Whose colors we unfold
> Firm stands her line of blue
> For they are loyal through and through

Fighting with the spirit true
All for the love of old D. U.
Fight we'll fight
With all our strength and might
Win we can! So here we give a hand:
Hey Rah Rah Rah Rah Rah D - U - K - E Rah.
G.E. Leftwich, Jr.

East Carolina University
East Fifth St.
Greenville, NC 27834

School Nickname: *ECU Pirates*

School Colors: *Purple and Gold*

School Mascot: *Pirate*

School Newspaper: *East Carolinian*

School Yearbook: *Buccaneer*

Alma Mater: *Alma Mater*

Praise to you name so fair,
Dear old East Carolina.
Your joys we'll all share
And your friends we'll ever be.
We pledge our loyalty
And our hearts' devotion
To thee, our Alma Mater,
Love and praise.

Fight Song: *Fight Song*

We're from East Carolina
the Purple and the Gold;
The Pirates of the country
No others quite as bold.
   -GO PIRATES-
Stand up for our Pirates
As we go to Victory
So let's give'em a hand
Come on folks, let's stand!
and show'em, we're from EC!

North Carolina Agricultural and Technical State University

1601 East Market St.
Greensboro, NC 27411

School Nickname: *Aggies*

School Colors: *Blue and Gold*

School Mascot: *Bulldog*

School Newspaper: *A & T Register*

School Yearbook: *Ayantee*

Alma Mater: *Alma Mater*

Dear A. and T., Dear A. and T.
A monument indeed!
Around thy base with grateful hearts
Behold thy students kneel.
We bless the power that gave thee birth
To help us in our need.
We'll ever strive while here on earth
All loyalty to yield.
    Chorus
With joy, with joy, dear A. and T.
Thy students turn from thee,
To spread thy trophies year by year
From Dare to Cherokee.

Dear A. and T., Dear A. and T.
The signet thou shalt be,
Set by our great commonwealth
Proud boaster of the free.
She'd have the record of her worth
On granite not inscribed,
Nay, let the children of her birth
Proclaim it by their lives.

Dear A. and T., Dear A. and T.
Henceforth our aim shall be,
By precepts wise and deeds more sure
To bless the State through thee.
The Arts of industry to wield
Against an idle foe,
A harvest rich from ripened fields
Of what thy students sow.

North Carolina Central University
1801 Fayetteville St.
Durham, NC 27707

School Nickname: *NCCU*

School Colors: *Burgundy and Gray*

School Mascot: *Eagles*

School Newspaper: *Campus Echo*

School Yearbook: *NCCU Yearbook*

North Carolina State University
Raleigh, NC 27695-7504

School Nickname: *The Wolfpack*

School Colors: *Red and White*

School Mascot: *Wolf*

School Newspaper: *Technician*

School Yearbook: *Agromeck*

University of North Carolina at Chapel Hill
Chapel Hill, NC 27514

School Nickname: *Tar Heels*

School Colors: *Carolina Blue and White*

School Mascot: *Ram*

School Newspaper: *The Daily Tar Heel*

School Yearbook: *Yackety Yack*

Alma Mater: *Alma Mater Song*

> Hark the sound of Tar Heel voices
> Ringing clear and true
> Singing Carolina's praises,
> Shouting N.C.U.!

Hail to the brightest star of all
Clear its radiance shine!
Carolina, priceless gem,
Receive all praises thine.

Fight Song: *Fight Song*

I'm a Tar Heel born, I'm a Tar Heel bred;
And when I die, I'm a Tar Heel dead.
So it's Ra Ra Carolina lina
    Ra Ra Carolina lina
    Ra Ra Carolina lina
Ra! Ra! Ra!

University of North Carolina at Charlotte
Charlotte, NC 28223

School Nickname: *The Forty Niners*

School Colors: *Green and White*

School Mascot: *The Forty Niner*

School Newspaper: *The Forty Niner Times*

University of North Carolina at Greensboro
1000 Spring Garden St.
Greensboro, NC 27412-5001

School Nickname: *UNCG*

School Colors: *Gold, White and Navy*

School Newspaper: *Carolinian*

School Yearbook: *Pine Needles*

Alma Mater: *The University Song*

We raise our voices; let them swell
In a chorus loud and strong;
The rolling hills send back the sound
Of our triumphant song.
For in one great unbroken band
With loyal hearts and true,
Your sons and daughters stand and sing,
University, to you.

Our college days run swiftly by
And all too soon we part;
But in the years that are to come
Deep-graven on each heart
Our motto, "Service," will remain,
And service we will do,
And as we serve, our hearts will turn
University to you.

Dear Alma Mater, strong and great,
We never shall forget
The gratitude we owe to you-
A never-ending debt;
All honor to your name we give,
And love we pledge anew,
Unfailing loyalty we bring,
University to you.
                    Laura Weill, '10

University of North Carolina at Wilmington
601 South College Rd.
Wilmington, NC 28403

School Nickname: *UNCW*

School Colors: *Green and Gold*

School Mascot: *Seahawk*

School Newspaper: *The Seahawk*

School Yearbook: *Fledgling*

Wake Forest University
Winston-Salem, NC

School Nickname: *Wake Forest*

School Colors: *Old Gold and Black*

School Mascot: *Demon Deacon*

School Newspaper: *The Old Gold and Black*

School Yearbook: *The Howler*

Alma Mater: *Dear Old Wake Forest*

Dear Old Wake Forest
Thine is a noble name
Thine is a glorious fame
Constant and true.
We give thee of our praise
Adore thine ancient days
Sing thee our humble lays
Mother, so dear.

Dear Old Wake Forest
Mystic thy name to cheer
Be thou our guardian near
Fore'er and aye.
We bow before thy shrine
Thy brows with boys entwine
All honor now be thine
Mother, today.

Fight Song: *O Here's to Wake Forest*

O Here's to Wake Forest
A glass of the finest
Red ruddy, Rhenish filled up
to the brim.
Her sons they are many
Unrivaled by any
With hearts o'erflowing, we
will sing a hymn.
  Chorus
Rah! Rah! Wake Forest Rah!
Old Alma Mater's sons are we
We'll herald the story
And die for her glory
Old Gold and Black is ever
waving high.

As frosh we adore her
As sophs we explore her
And carve our names upon her
ancient walls.
As juniors patrol her
As seniors extol her
And weep to leave for'er her
sacred halls.

Western Carolina University
Cullowhee, NC 28723

School Nickname: *WCU or Western*

School Colors: *Purple and Gold*

School Mascot: *Catamount*

School Newspaper: *The Western Carolinian*

School Yearbook: *The Catamount*

Alma Mater: *University Hymn*

> Hail to thee, our Alma Mater
> Faithful kind, and true;
> Every son and every daughter
> Offers praise to thee.
> *Chorus*
> Hail to the dearest spot of all;
> Hail to W.C.U.!
> Light and life and fond devotion
> All to thee are due.
>
> Purple robes and colors golden,
> Streaming everywhere,
> Swell our hearts with pride for olden
> Days and friendship dear.
>
> Under shade trees' friendly bowers,
> Voices, ever gay,
> Mingle with the breath of flowers
> And the song bird's lay
>
> Shout aloud with one long chorus,
> Voices clear and true,
> Lifted high in praise and honor,
> All for W.C.U.!
> *Copyright 1969, Western Carolina University*

Fight Song: *Fight on, You Catamounts*

> Fight on! you Catamount
> Fight for purple and gold
> Fight on to victory,
> True warriors bold.

Wave the royal banner high,
And let it fill the western sky.
So fight on! you Catamounts,
Fight to victory.
Western! Western! Go--Western! Go--Cats!

Words by Richard Craddock and Thomas Tyra
Music by Richard Trevarthen
Copyright 1980, Western Carolina University

NORTH DAKOTA

The University of North Dakota
Grand Forks, ND 58202

School Nickname: *Fighting Sioux*

School Colors: *Green and White*

School Newspaper: *Dakota Student*

Alma Mater: *Alma Mater*

> Hail to thee, O Alma Mater!
> Hail to thee with heart and tongue!
> Pride we feel and love yet greater,
> While we raise our grateful song.
>
> Home of lofty thought and learning,
> Beacon o'er our western land,
> Shrine whence still the every burning
> Torch is passed from hand to hand.
>
> Free as roam our winds the prairie
> Thought and speech here unconfined;
> Free as eaglets round their eyrie,
> Soar, proud offspring of the mind.

Love of freedom, love of duty,
Love of truth without a bound,
Valor in thy sons, and beauty
In thy daughters all, be found.

Alma Mater, thine the glory,
If a thought of ours or deed
Find a place in song or story,
Win endeavor's glorious meed.

Prosper even, fost'ring mother;
Down the ages long resound,
Loud thy fame, while many another
Finds in thee what we have found.
By Joseph Haydn and John Macnie

Fight Songs: *Stand Up And Cheer*

Stand up and cheer,
Stand up and cheer for North Dakota!
Pledge your loyalty,
For she's your Alma Mater true.

Our boys are fighting,
And we will help them see it thru.
We've got the team, we've got the team,
So North Dakota, here's to you!
Adapted by Roy LaMeter
and Norman Nelson

Fight On, Sioux!

Fight on Sioux, we're all for you,
We're thousands of strong and loyal souls.
We know you'll win every game you're in,
No matter how distant the goals.

And as we go, we'll show each foe
That we're the toughest tribe between the poles.
We're rough and tough it's true but we're sportsmen thru and thru,
We're the fighting Sioux from North Dakota U. Hi! (shout)
By Raymond "Aimee" Johnson

OHIO

Baldwin-Wallace College
Berea, OH 44017

School Nickname: *B-W*

School Colors: *Brown and Gold*

School Mascot: *Yellow Jacket*

School Newspaper: *Exponent*

School Yearbook: *Grindstone*

Alma Mater: *Alma Mater*

> Baldwin-Wallace hail thy name
> Praise to thee we bring
> Where'er we go throughout the land
> Our loyalty we'll sing
> Thy wisdom and thy friendship true
> Shall inspiration be
> O, Baldwin-Wallace College
> We pledge our hearts to thee.

Fight Song: *Fight Song*

Fight Baldwin-Wallace, fight Baldwin-Wallace
Fight and win this game
We're cheering for you, There's glory for you
We're on the road to fame
And in the battle, we'll prove our mettle,
We're loyal, square and brave
Victory will crown our might and in the breeze tonight
Our Brown and Gold shall wave.

Bowling Green State University
Bowling Green, OH 43403

School Nickname: *Falcons*

School Colors: *Brown and Orange*

School Mascot: *Freddie and Freida Falcon*

School Newspaper: *BG News*

School Yearbook: *The Key*

Alma Mater: *Alma Mater*

Alma Mater hear us,
As we praise thy name
Make us worthy sons and daughters
Adding to thy fame.

Time will treat you kindly
Years from now you'll be
Ever dearer in our hearts,
Our University.

From your halls of ivy
To the campus scene,
Chimes ring out with gladness
From our dear Bowling Green.

When all is just a mem'ry
Of the by-gone days,
Hear our hymn dear Alma Mater
As thy name we praise.

Fight Song: *Forward Falcons*

> Forward Falcons!
> Forward Falcons!
> Fight for victory,
> Show our spirit,
> Make them fear it,
> Fight for dear Bee Gee.
> Forward Falcons!
> Forward Falcons!
> Make the contest keen,
> Hold up the fame
> Of our mighty name
> And win for Bowling Green!

Case Western Reserve University
Cleveland, OH 44106

School Colors: *Royal Blue and Light Gray*

School Mascot: *Spartans*

School Newspaper: *The Observer*

School Yearbook: *The Annum*

Alma Mater: *University Hymn*

> Though the years may roll unending,
> and another cause we serve,
> still her loyal sons and daughters will remember Case Reserve.
> All the knowledge man is heir to,
> all the talents he can share,
> all the joys of new discovery can be found abundant there.
> though the years may roll unending,
> and other causes we serve,
> still her loyal sons and daughters
> will remember Case Reserve.
> *Written by Barbara Denison, '67*

Cleveland State University
Cleveland, OH 44115

School Nickname: *CSU*

School Colors: *Green and White*

School Mascot: *Hagar the Horrible and Viktorious Viking*

School Newspaper: *Cauldron*

School Yearbook: *Fanfare*

John Carroll University
University Heights, OH 44118

School Nickname: *Blue Streaks*

School Colors: *Blue and Gold*

School Newspaper: *Carroll News*

School Yearbook: *Carillon*

Alma Mater: *Alma Mater*

> Hail to Carroll, gather near her,
> Let your joyful anthem ring;
> Sound your mother's praise, revere her,
> Her fair name full proudly sing.
> Loyal ever brave and true, Daughters, Sons of Carroll U,
> Pledge our love to Alma Mater, to the Gold and Blue,
> Pledge our love to Alma Mater, to the Gold and Blue.
> *Words and Music by J. A. Kiefer, SJ*

Fight Song: *Fight Song*

> Onward, on John Carroll,
> For we're here to see you win, Gold and Blue,
> Onward, on John Carroll,
> Onto greater goals and vict'ries new,
> Onward, on John Carroll,
> For our faith in you is boundless and true,
> Dear Alma Mater, we're all for you,
> And for the Gold and Blue.

Kent State University
Kent, OH 44242

School Nickname: *Golden Flashes*

School Colors: *Blue and Gold*

School Mascot: *Golden Eagle* Name: *Flash*

School Newspaper: *Daily Kent Stater*

School Yearbook: *Chestnut Burr*

Alma Mater: *Hail to Thee, Our Alma Mater*

From the beauty land Ohio comes a universal praise,
'Tis the song of Alma Mater that her sons and daughters raise,
'Tis a Hail to Kent forever, on the Cuyahoga shore,
Now we join the loving thousands as they sing it o'er and o'er.
Hail to thee, our Alma Mater O, how beautiful thou art
High enthroned up on a hilltop, Reigning over every heart.

From the hilltop Alma Mater gazing on her portals wide,
Sees the coming generations as they throng to seek her side,
Seek her side to win her blessing, throng her gates to bear her name,
Leave her gates to sing her praises, go afar to spread her fame.
Hail to thee, our Alma Mater O, how young and strong thou art,
Planning for the glorious future, Firm enthroned in every heart.
Words by E. Turner Stump
Music by Dwight Steere

Fight Song: *Fight On For K.S.U.*

Fight on for K.S,U.
Fight! for the blue and gold.
We're out to beat the foe;
Fight on brave and gold.

Fight on to victory;
Don't stop until we're through.
We're all together; Let's go forward
K.S.U.
Words and Music by
Ed Silnnicki

Miami University
Oxford, OH 45056

School Nickname: *Miami Redskins*

School Colors: *Red and White*

School Mascot: *Chief Miami and Tom-O-Hawk*

School Newspaper: *The Miami Student (est. 1826)*

School Yearbook: *Recensio*

Alma Mater: *Old Miami*

Old Miami from thy hill crest,
Thou hast watched the decades roll,
While thy sons have quested from thee,
Sturdy hearted, pure of soul.

Aging in thy simple splendor,
Thou the calm and they the storm;
Thou didst give them joy in conquest,
Strength from thee sustained their arm.

Now of late thyself envigored,
Larger usefulness awaits;
Host's assemble for thy blessing,
Youth and maiden throng thy gate.

Thou shalt stand a constant beacon,
Crimson tow'rs against the sky;
Men shall ever seek thy guiding,
Pow'r like thine shall never die.
Refrain
Old Miami! New Miami!
Days of old and days to be;
Weave the story of thy glory,
Our Miami, here's to thee!
Music by R.H. Burke, '21; Words by A. H. Upham, '97

Fight Song: *Miami March Song*

Miami old, to thee our love we bring,
To thee our hearts and minds will ever cling,
Thy fame of other days thy gifts so free,
Call us today to sing our praise to thee.

Thy elms, thy hills, thy skies of azure hue,
To them is deepest inspiration due,
Thy stately tow'rs up on the hill top fair,
To them do we our grateful homage bear.

On land and sea, our hearts will ever be,
The truest bravest man can show to thee,
Our duty ever in our loyalty,
To guard thy name through all eternity.
Chorus
Love and honor to Miami, Our College old and grand,
Proudly we shall ever hail thee, Over all the land
Alma Mater now we praise thee, Sing joyfully this lay
O sing our love and honor to Miami, Forever and a day.
R.H. Burke

The Ohio State University
Columbus, OH 43210

School Nickname: *Ohio State*

School Colors: *Scarlet and Gray*

School Mascot: *Buckeye* Name: *Brutus*

School Newspaper: *The Lantern*

School Yearbook: *Makio*

Ohio University
Athens, OH 45701-2979

School Colors: *Kelly Green and White*

School Mascot: *Bobcat*

School Newspaper: *The Post*

School Yearbook: *The Athena*

Alma Mater: *Alma Mater*

> Whene're we take our book of mem'ries
> And scan its pages through and through
> We'll find no days that glow so brightly
> As those we spent at old O.U.
> Within our Alma Mater's portals
> We meet her children hand to hand,
> And when there comes the day of parting,
> Still firm and loyal we will stand.
>
> Alma Mater, Ohio, Alma Mater, brave and fair!
> Alma Mater, we hail thee, For we own thy kindly care.
> Alma Mater, Ohio, When we read thy story o'er,
> We revere thee and cheer thee
> As we sing they praise once more.

Fight Song: *Fight Song*

> Stand up and cheer!
> Cheer loud and long for old Ohio,
> For today we raise the green and white above the rest.
> Our boys are fighting

And they are bound to win the fray
We've got the team!
We've got the steam!
And this is Ohio's day.

University of Cincinnati
Cincinnati, OH 45221

School Nickname: *U.C.*

School Colors: *Red and Black*

School Mascot: *Bearcat (athletic) Mich and Mack (school)*

School Newspaper: *The News Record*

School Yearbook: *Cincinnatian*

University of Dayton
Dayton, OH 45469-0001

School Nickname: *U.D.*

School Colors: *Red and Blue*

School Mascot: *Rudy the UD Flyer*

School Newspaper: *Flyer News*

School Yearbook: *Daytonian*

The University of Toledo
Toledo, OH 43606

School Nickname: *UT Rockets*

School Colors: *Blue and Gold*

School Mascot: *Rocky the Rocket*

School Newspaper: *The Collegian*

School Yearbook: *Blockhouse*

Alma Mater: *Alma Mater*

> In tower shadows
> Voices now raising,
> To Alma Mater, Golden and Blue...
> Fair Toledo
> Praise to thee.
> Portal of learning ever be,
> Hallowed halls we shall revere,
> Vow to keep thy memory dear.

Fight Song: *Fight Song*

> U. of Toledo, we'll fight for you
> (Fight! Fight! Fight!)
> U. of Toledo, we love your gold and blue.
> (Fight! Fight! Fight!)
> Men of the Varsity, the enemy must yield
> We'll fight just like our ancestors
> And march on down the field.

Wright State University
Dayton, OH 45435

School Nickname: *Wright State*

School Colors: *Green and Gold*

School Mascot: *Raiders*

School Newspaper: *The Daily Guardian*

Alma Mater: *Wright State Alma Mater*

> Wright State stands above the valley,
> Glorious banner green and gold!
> Helping build Ohio's future
> With a vision grand and bold!
>
> First to fly were Dayton's brothers!
> Great deeds old inspire the new!
> Wright State is our Alma Mater!
> Hail Wright State! Hail Wright State U!
>
> School of promise, school of spirit!
> With great heritage endowed!
> We shall ever love and serve you!
> We shall strive to make you proud!

In the classroom, on the sportsfield,
We shall always honor you!
Wright State is our Alma Mater!
Hail Wright State! Hail Wright State U!

Faith and hope in our endeavors.
Ever onward day by day!
Bravely shaping new traditions,
Letting knowledge light the way!

Green and Gold, we'll not forget you!
Through the years we shall be true!
Wright State is our Alma Mater!
Hail Wright State! Hail Wright State U!

> *David Garrison, Thomas Whissen, William Steinohrt*
> *Copyright 1984 Wright State University*
> *all rights reserved*

Xavier University
3800 Victory Pkwy.
Cincinnati, OH 45207

School Nickname: *Musketeers*

School Colors: *Blue and White*

School Mascot: *D'Artagnan*

School Newspaper: *Xavier Newswire*

School Yearbook: *The Musketeer*

Alma Mater: *Alma Mater*

Dear Alma Mater Xavier!
Undying troth we pledge to you
That we the living shall hold true
The Faith that those of years now gone
Inviolate kept and thus passed on.
So may the trust within us dwell
And may this song our voices swell
Until resounds o'er hill and dell
Dear Alma Mater Xavier.

Fight Song: *Fight Song*

> Sing the song and sing it loud and long,
> Let it be our pledge today,
> Our Alma Mater proud and strong,
> Old Xavier for aye!
> Sing the song and sing it loud and long,
> Let it be our pledge today
> Our Alma Mater proud and strong
> Old Xavier for aye!

Youngstown State University
Youngstown, OH 44555

School Nickname: *Penguins*

School Colors: *Scarlet and White*

School Mascot: *Penguin*

School Newspaper: *Jambar*

School Yearbook: *Neon*

Alma Mater: *Alma Mater*

> All hail to thee, O Youngstown,
> Our Alma Mater fair;
> In sunlight and starshine
> We see thee in all thy glory.
> The Red and the White, thy glorious colors,
> Ever we praise and hold them
> High to the breeze as the symbol of our
> Most loyal allegiance.
> This anthem, O Youngstown,
> Our pledge of trust shall be
> That thy sons and daughters
> Shall keep faith with thee forever.

Fight Song: *Fight Song*

> The red and white are waving over the field
> Our boys are fighting, with a spirit that will not yield.
>
> Rah! Rah! Rah!
>
> Hail to thee, O Youngstown; we'll fight for you.
> Once again the Penguins will win for YSU.

OKLAHOMA

Cameron University
2800 W. Gore Blvd.
Lawton, OK 73505

School Nickname: *Aggies*

School Colors: *Black and Gold*

School Mascot: *Cowboy* Name: *Ole Kim*

School Newspaper: *Collegian*

School Yearbook: *The Wichita*

Alma Mater: *Cameron Pride*

> Give us truth to light the darkness,
> and visions to pursue,
> and faith to meet the challenge
> of a world we must renew.
> Cameron Pride, Cameron Pride,
> broader than the plains,
> for your guidance and your promise.
> Our praise and thanks to you.
> > *Text by Sherrey Cardwell*
> > *Music by Gene Smith*

Fight Song: *Aggies Fight*

>We'll fight to the end Cameron Aggies
>Fight for our honored name
>We'll back you all the way you know
>For spirit is in our fame
>So here's to the Cameron Aggies
>Here's to the Black and Gold
>Yes FIGHT, FIGHT, Cameron Aggies
>All the way!

Central State University

100 N. University
Edmond, OK 73060

School Nickname: *Bronchos*

School Colors: *Bronze and Blue*

School Mascot: *Broncho*

School Newspaper: *Vista*

School Yearbook: *Bronze Book*

Alma Mater: *Alma Mater*

>Morning Sun greets many banners,
>with its crimson hue
>Fair to us above all others,
>waves the bronze and blue.
>Bronze and blue, flag we love,
>floats for aye,
>Central State to thee,
>May thy sons be ever loyal, to thy memory.

Fight Song: *Fight Song*

>Fight, boys, fight for C. S. U.
>Fight, boys, fight today;
>Fight for the team, boys,
>All full of steam, boys,
>Hear our cheers for you:
>Rah! Rah! Rah! Fight Boys,
>Fight for bronze and blue;
>Fight, boys, fight today;
>Add one more victory
>To our team's history,

Rah! Rah! Rah! Rah!
Words and Music by J. J. "Pops" Gecks

East Central University
Ada, OK 74820

School Nickname: *Tigers*

School Colors: *Black, Orange and White*

School Mascot: *ECU Tiger*

School Newspaper: *The Journal*

School Yearbook: *Pesagi*

Fight Song: *ECU Fight Song*

> Fight on East Central,
> Fight on for your fame.
> Fight on East Central Tigers,
> Win this game.
>
> We're cheering for you,
> Cheering to the end.
> Fight on East Central Tigers,
> Win! Win! Win!

Northeastern State University
Tahlequah, OK 74464

School Nickname: *The Redmen*

School Colors: *Green and White*

School Newspaper: *The Northeastern*

School Yearbook: *Tsa La Gi (a Cherokee Indian word)*

Alma Mater: *The Northeastern State University Alma Mater*

> Our Alma Mater forever may you live.
> Knowledge and freedom with truth you gladly give.
> Roots from the Cherokees, and promises for our future,
> Oh! Northeastern State, we shall honor you!
> *Steve Wiles*

Fight Song: *Northeastern, Northeastern*

Northeastern, Northeastern,
Your sons are staunch and true.
Northeastern, Northeastern,
We'll always stand by you.
We'll fight boys, we'll win boys,
For the green and white we'll stand.
Northeastern, we love you,
The best in all the land.
Henri Mensky

Oklahoma State University
Stillwater, OK 74078

School Nickname: *OSU Cowboys*

School Colors: *Orange and Black*

School Mascot: *Pistol Pete*

School Newspaper: *The Daily O'Collegian*

School Yearbook: *The Redskin*

Alma Mater: *Alma Mater*

Proud and immortal
Bright shines your name
Oklahoma State, we herald your fame
Ever you'll find us
Loyal and true
To our Alma Mater, O..S..U..!
Robert L. McCulloh

Fight Song: *Ride 'Em*

Ride, Ride, Ride, Ride,
Ride 'Em Cowboys
Right down the field
Fight, Fight, Fight, Fight,
Fight 'Em Cowboys
And never yield
Ride, Ride, Ride, Ride,
Ride on Cowboys to victory
Cross (opponent's) Goal - And we'll sing Oklahoma State!
J. K. Long

Oral Roberts University

7777 S. Lewis Ave.
Tulsa, OK 74171

School Nickname: *Titans*

School Colors: *Royal Blue and White*

School Newspaper: *The Oracle*

School Yearbook: *The Perihelion*

Fight Song: *Spirit Song*

> Oh, O-R-U,
> Oh, O-R-U,
> Oh, O-R-University!
> Holy Spirit blessed,
> Seeking out the best,
> Of the human trinity.
>
> Oh, O-R-U,
> Oh, O-R-U,
> Ordained by holy destiny!
> May your torch still burn,
> At the Lord's return,
> And count for eternity!

Southeastern Oklahoma State University

Durant, OK 74701

School Colors: *Blue and Gold*

School Newspaper: *The Southeastern*

School Yearbook: *Savage*

Alma Mater: *Hymn to the Gold and Blue*

> Here's a hymn to the Gold and Blue,
> Hear our joyful cry,
> Sons and Daughters, Brave and True,
> Sing with heads held high.
> Striving here, we seek, we grow,
> Wise and strong and free.
> Alma Mater hail to you,
> hail to S.S.U.
> *By Walter C. Britt, '79*

Fight Song: *Fight Song*

> There's a school that we call Southeastern,
> Down south in the Red-chief's land.
> There floats the gold and blue
> Over hearts so true
> In that loyal Savage band
> For where'er we go,
> or what'er we do
> It is S. T. C.;
> It's the gold and blue;
> It is glory be
> to S. T. C.,
> The School of the Rising Sun.
>> *Lyrics by Julia Munson*
>> *Music by Julia E. Stout and Pearl Shull*

University of Oklahoma
Norman, OK 73071

School Nickname: *Big Red*

School Colors: *Crimson and Cream*

School Newspaper: *The Oklahoma Daily*

School Yearbook: *Sooner Yearbook*

Alma Mater: *Alma Mater*

> O-K-L-A-H-O-M-A
> Our chant rolls on and on
> Thousands strong join heart and song
> In Alma Mater's praise
> Of campus beautiful by day and night
> Of colors proudly gleaming red and white
> 'Neath a western sky
> OU's chant will never die.
> Live on University.

Fight Song: *Fight Song*

> Boomer Sooner. Boomer Sooner.
> Boomer Sooner. Boomer Sooner.
> Boomer Sooner. Boomer Sooner.
> Boomer Sooner. O-K-U.
> I'm a sooner born and a sooner bred
> and when I die I'll be sooner dead.
> Rah Oklahoma. Rah Oklahoma.

Rah Oklahoma. O-K-U
Oklahoma. Oklahoma. Oklahoma. Oklahoma.
Oklahoma. Oklahoma. Oklahoma. O-K-U.
I'm a sooner born and a sooner bred
and when I die I'll be a sooner dead.
Rah Oklahoma. Rah Oklahoma. Rah Oklahoma. O-K-U.

University of Tulsa
Tulsa, OK 74104

School Nickname: *Golden Hurricane*

School Colors: *Blue, Gold and Red*

School Newspaper: *The Collegian*

School Yearbook: *Kendallabrum*

Alma Mater: *Hail to Tulsa U.*

Hail to thee Alma Mater, gold and blue.
Praise from thy sons and daughters, old and true
Pride in our hearts, our voices let us raise.
Filled with devotion we will sing thy praise.
Alma Mater, now we honor, loyal, always true.
We will sound a toast in chorus, Hail to Tulsa U.

Alma Mater Tulsa U., we are of thee
To thy mem'ry we'll be true, to eternity
Long may thy halls be with honor
May we not bring thee dishonor
Always happiness Alma Mater Tulsa U.
To thee homage due
May thy reward be our reward we pledge thee Tulsa U.

Fight Song: *Hurricane Fight Song*

Down the field to victory
On Tulsa on.
Fight on University,
Battle on and on.
March to the goal line, oh Tulsa,
Score on mounting score.
March to the goal line, oh Tulsa,
Let that Hurricane roar.
Drive those (name opponent) back and back,
Fight 'em Tulsa, Fight!
Gold, Blue and Red, go right ahead,
Down the field to victory.

OREGON

Oregon State University
15th and Jefferson
Corvallis, OR 97331

School Nickname: *Beavers*

School Colors: *Orange and Black*

School Mascot: *Benny Beaver*

School Newspaper: *Barometer*

School Yearbook: *The Beaver*

Alma Mater: *OSU Alma Mater*

> Within a vale of western mountains,
> There's a college we hold dear.
> Her shady slopes and fountains
> Oft to me appear.
> I love to wander on the pathway
> Down to the Trysting Tree,
> For there again I see in fancy,
> Old friends dear to me.

Chorus
Carry me back to OSU
Back to her vine-clad halls;
Thus fondly ever in my mem'ry
Alma Mater calls.
       Words and Music by Homer Maris, '18

Fight Song: *OSU Fight Song*

OSU our hats are off to you
Beavers, Beavers, fighters thru and thru
We'll cheer for every man
We'll root for every stand
That's made for old OSU.

Watch our team go tearing down the field;
Men of iron, their strength will never yield.

Hail to old OSU.
       Words and Music by Harold A. Wilkins, '07

Portland State University
Portland, OR 97207

School Nickname: *Vikings*

School Colors: *Green and White*

School Mascot: *Viking*

School Newspaper: *The Vanguard*

School Yearbook: *The Viking (ceased publication in late 1970's)*

Fight Song: *Men of Ohio (music only)*

Southern Oregon State College
1250 Siskiyou Blvd.
Ashland, OR 97520

School Nickname: *SOSC or Southern*

School Colors: *Red and Black*

School Newspaper: *The Siskiyou*

School Yearbook: *The Raider*

Alma Mater: *Alma Mater*

> Where the hills in kingly splendor
> Tower to the skies
> There's a college we remember
> Her fame never dies.
> Southern Oregon! Alma Mater!
> Highest praise to thee
> May thy sons fore'er be loyal
> To thy memory.

University of Oregon
Eugene, OR 97403-1299

School Colors: *Green and Yellow*

School Mascot: *Ducks*

School Newspaper: *Oregon Daily Emerald*

School Yearbook: *Oregana (ceased publication in 1980)*

Alma Mater: *Oregon Pledge Song*

> Fair Oregon we pledge to Thee,
> Our honor and fidelity
> Both now and in the years to be.
> A never failing loyalty
> Fair Oregon Thy name shall be written high in liberty.
> Now, uncovered, Swear us everyone.
> Our pledge to Oregon.
> > *By John Stark Evans*

Fight Song: *Mighty Oregon*

> She is small our Alma Mater
> But she rules with strength and right,
> What she lacks in mass and numbers
> She makes up for in her fight
> Oregon is never beaten
> 'Till the final whistles call.
> Who can tell her tale of triumph?
> Scores can never show it all.
>
> Rally fellows, stand behind them,
> They are doing all they can.
> Back the team in sun and shadow,
> Back the captain, back each man.

They will carry home the vict'ry
To old Deady's hallowed hall.
Give the team the best that's in you.
Give your Alma Mater all.
> *Chorus*
Oregon, our Alma Mater.....
We will guard thee on and on....
Fellows gather round and cheer her....
Chant her glory Oregon....
Roar the praises of her warriors....
Sing the story Oregon....
On to Victory urge the heroes....
Of our mighty Oregon....
Oregon....

> *Words by De Witt Gilbert*
> *Music by Albert Perfect*

PENNSYLVANIA

Bloomsburg University of Pennsylvania
Bloomsburg, PA 17815

School Nickname: *Huskies*

School Colors: *Maroon and Gold*

School Mascot: *Husky*

School Newspaper: *Voice*

School Yearbook: *Obiter*

Alma Mater: *Alma Mater*

> Far above the river winding,
> Midst the mountains grand
> Stands our school so dear to students
> far throughout the land.
> *Chorus*
> Bloomsburg, Bloomsburg, Alma Mater
> up on College Hill
> Years to come shall find us ever
> True to Bloomsburg still.

California University of Pennsylvania
California, PA 15419

School Colors: *Red and Black*

School Mascot: *Vulcan*

School Newspaper: *California Times*

School Yearbook: *Monocal*

Alma Mater: *Alma Mater*

> California, alma mater
> Now we sing to thee
> California, dear forever
> In our memory.
> With our voices loudly ringing,
> Of thy fame we're ever singing.
> California, alma mater;
> Hail! All hail to thee.
>
> For the friends and joys you gave us,
> We give thanks to thee
> All thy knowledge we'll make worthy
> For Posterity.
> May thy reign be ever prosperous
> And thy name forever glorious.
> California, alma mater;
> Hail! All hail to thee.
> > *Phillip Rossi, '37*

Carnegie Mellon University
5000 Forbes Ave.
Pittsburgh, PA 15213

School Colors: *Tartan Plaid (gray and burgundy for sports uniforms)*

School Mascot: *Scottie*

School Newspaper: *The Tartan*

School Yearbook: *The Thistle*

Alma Mater: *Alma Mater*

> Here, where spangled wilderness
> Robed the mountains of the West,

Where the savage strife and stresses
Brought the settlers' crimson quest:
Land of legend, glory, graces,
Gypsy tide and toiling shore,
'Mid thy hilltops, Alma Mater
Stands enthroned forevermore.
Hail Carnegie! Alma Mater-
Stand enthroned forevermore!

Here was heard the musket's rattle,
' Round us rolled the thralling drum-
All is hushed, no more they startle,
Low we hear sweet labor's hum,
Art and science rule our battle,
In their pathway honor lies,
Hail Carnegie! Alma Mater-
Show the way that truth may rise!
Hail Carnegie! Alma Mater-
Show the way that truth may rise!

Show the way, arouse, awaken!
Bear aloft thy beacon bright,
That our minds be ever taken
Unto learning, into light.
Stand in daytimes storm unshaken,
Guide through gloom of deepest night!
Hail Carnegie! Alma Mater
Stand for progress, peace and right!
Hail Carnegie! Alma Mater
Stand for progress, peace and right!
Professor Charles Jay Taylor,'13

Fight Song: *Fight For The Glory of Carnegie*

Andy was the grand old man we loved so well,
Carnegie;
In the land where thistles grow he used to dwell,
O'er the sea;
Members of the clan that bears his name
Struggle for its glory and its fame.
Fight! for the glory of Carnegie.
Fight! for the glory of the clan.
Let your eyes be ever on the Tartan bright,
As we stand united ev'ry man fight, fight, fight,
Fight ev'ry loyal son of Skibo.
Fight till we win the victory.
The Kilties are coming, hurray, hurray,
The Kilties are coming, they'll win today,
For they're fighting for the glory of Carnegie!
Words and Music by Robert Schmertz, '21

Clarion University of Pennsylvania
Clarion, PA 16214

School Nickname: *Golden Eagles*

School Colors: *Blue and Gold*

School Mascot: *Golden Eagle*

School Newspaper: *The Call*

School Yearbook: *Sequelle*

Alma Mater: *Alma Mater*

> Oh, Clarion, dear Clarion
> Oh college on the hill
> To all the joys of student life
> Our hearts will ever thrill
> Your silent winding river
> It haunts me still.
> Oh, Clarion, dear Clarion
> We pledge our faith to you
> With lasting love and loyalty
> In everything we do
> To you dear Alma Mater
> We'll ever be true.

Fight Song: *Fight Song*

> Carry on for Clarion,
> We're gonna shout it one and all,
> Rah! Rah! Rah!
> It's so grand to be in the Eagle band
> Sounding Clarion's call.
> Watch the Eagles, Golden Eagles,
> Soaring on and on.
> So there will be another victory
> For mighty Clarion.

Duquesne University
Pittsburgh, PA 15282

School Nickname: *Dukes*

School Colors: *Red and Blue*

School Mascot: *Duke*

School Newspaper: *The Duquesne Duke*

School Yearbook: *L 'Esprit Du Duc*

Alma Mater: *Alma Mater*

> Alma Mater, old Duquesne guide and
> friend of our youthful days,
> we, thy sons and daughters all,
> our loyal voices raise.
> The hours we spent at thy mothers knee,
> and drank of wisdom's store,
> shall e'er in mem'ry treasured be,
> tho' we roam the whole world o'er.
> Then forward ever, dear Alma Mater, o'er our
> hearts unrivaled reign,
> Onward ever, old Alma Mater!
> All hail to thee, Duquesne!
> > *Written by John Mallory, C.S.Sp.*

Fight Song: *Fight Song*

> We'll sing hurrah for the Red and Blue,-
> A big hurrah for the Red and Blue.....
> For the flag we love, on to victory,
> and when the foe is downed,
> we will raise a mighty shout
> and sing hurrah for the Red and Blue.-
> We're all your sons and we're all true-
> So with all your might,
> give them FIGHT, FIGHT, FIGHT, FIGHT,
> For the grand ole Red and Blue.-
> > *Written by Rev. Thomas J. Quigley, C.S.Sp.*

East Stroudsburg University
East Stroudsburg, PA 18301

School Colors: *Red and Black*

School Mascot: *Warrior*

School Newspaper: *The Stroud Courrier*

School Yearbook: *The Stroud*

Alma Mater: *Alma Mater*

> Alma Mater, thy halls so majestically stand

On the hill overlooking the town;
With the vine-covered walls and thy maple trees trim,
We treasure thy smile and thy frown.
A mystical charm binds thy children to thee,
Each incoming class feels its spell;
Those who leave thee regretful thy beauties recall,
Which deep in their memories dwell.
Dear College, thy honor is safe in their hands,
Their deeds by thy precepts are led;
Thy students and athletes fresh victories each year,
Shall win for the Black and the Red.
We'll strive with our might thy fond name to exalt,
We'll sacrifice self to thy aim.
And united in hand and in heart we'll achieve,
Only deed's that shall add to thy name.

Fight Song: *Fight Song*

Hail, dear old Stroudsburg, we're out to win.
Always victorious, never give in.
We're "champs" and then some, victors o'er all.
C'm, gang, lots of pep
Rah! Rah! Rah!

Edinboro University of Pennsylvania
Edinboro, PA 16444

School Nickname: *Fighting Scots*

School Colors: *Red and White*

School Mascot: *Fighting Scots and Lady Scots*

School Newspaper: *Spectator*

School Yearbook: *Tartan*

Alma Mater: *Alma Mater*

Hail to Thee, our Alma Mater Glorious,
Fresh Wreaths we bring to bind Thy brow
Trials have past and Thou hast stood victorious
Never fairer never statelier than now,
O Edinboro, Edinboro
Ever praising Thee in song
While class speeds class as swift years pass
To Thee our hearts belong.

Fight Song: *Scotland the Brave*

Gannon University
University Square
Erie, PA 16541

School Nickname: *The Gannon Knights*

School Colors: *Maroon and Gold*

School Mascot: *The Gannon Knight*

School Newspaper: *Gannon Knight*

School Yearbook: *The Lance*

Indiana University of Pennsylvania
Indiana, PA 15705

School Nickname: *IUP*

School Colors: *Crimson and Gray*

School Mascot: *Indians*

School Newspaper: *The Penn*

School Yearbook: *The Oak*

Alma Mater: *Alma Mater*

> To our noble Alma Mater's name
> We, her children, sing a joyful lay
> And to her a new allegiance pledge,
> That lives beyond a day.
>> *Refrain*
> Sing, O Sing, Our Alma Mater's praise,
> Hail, O Hail, her colors' gleaming hue!
> Give to her our homage and our love
> And to her name be true.

Fight Song: *Fight Song*

> Hail, IUP! Give a rousing cheer!
> Go, IUP, for victory is near!
> Drive, IUP! Push on toward the goal!
> Hail, IUP! So onward roll!

Kutztown University
Kutztown, PA 19530

School Colors: *Maroon and Gold*

School Mascot: *Golden Bear*

School Newspaper: *The Keystone*

School Yearbook: *The Keystonia*

Alma Mater: *Alma Mater*

>Where stately trees are bending,
>Where Nature's glories shine,
>And loveliness unending
>In beauty rare combine,
>There rise the Kutztown towers,
>And there the College stands,
>The wellspring of our powers,
>The shrine our love commands.
>
>And we will ever love her
>And live to serve her fame;
>Our lives shall add new lustre
>Unto her glorious name.
>As guardian of her new day
>Our work will ever be
>To labor so that she may
>Achieve her destiny.
>   *Clyde Francis Lytle*

Pennsylvania State University
University Park, PA 16802

School Nickname: *Penn State; Nittany Lions*

School Colors: *Blue and White*

School Mascot: *Nittany Lion*

School Newspaper: *The Daily Collegian*

School Yearbook: *La Vie*

Alma Mater: *Alma Mater*

>For the Glory of Old State
>For her founders strong and great,

For the future that we wait,
Raise the song, raise the song.

Sing our love and loyalty
Sing our hopes that bright and free
Rest, O Mother dear, with thee,
All with thee, all with thee.

When we stood at childhood's gate,
Shapeless in the hands of fate,
Thou didst mold us, dear old State,
Dear old State, dear old State.

May no act of ours bring shame
To one heart that loves thy name,
May our lives but swell thy fame,
Dear old State, dear old state.
By Fred Lewis Pattee

Fight Song: *Fight on State*

Fight on State, Fight on State,
Strike your gait and win,
Victory we predict for thee,
We're ever true to you, dear old White and Blue.
Onward State, Onward State
Roar Lions roar,
We'll hit that line, roll up the score,
Fight on to victory evermore,
Fight on, on
On, on, on
Fight! on, on
Penn State!
By F. E. Wilbur

Robert Morris College
Coraopolis, PA 15108

School Colors: *Blue and White*

School Newspaper: *Minuteman*

School Yearbook: *Patriot*

Alma Mater: *Alma Mater*

Hail to thee dear Robert Morris,
Let the anthem ring

Hand in hand and with one voice
Your praises we do sing,
And as the long years roll by,
With mem'ry fond and true,
We'll still salute your colors
Of shining white and blue.
With ideals high to guide us,
The path ahead is clear;
We'll be reminded of the bright days
Spent at our alma mater dear.

Saint Joseph's University
Philadelphia, PA 19131

School Colors: *Crimson and Gray*

School Mascot: *Hawk*

School Newspaper: *The Hawk*

School Yearbook: *The Greatonian*

Alma Mater: *Alma Mater*

Saint Joseph's hail! In song we praise
Our mother dear and fair.
In life's grim battle, we'll march on
With Faith and strength to dare.
For valiant deeds make stout our hearts
To prove your sons are true.
Let us rejoice and with one voice
Pledge loyal love to you.

Saint Joseph's hail! Our blood runs proud
To hold tradition's fame,
For words of gold on history's scroll
Shed glory on your name.
To honor God, to love all men,
Crusaders for each fray,
Against the sky our colors fly,
Deep crimson folds and gray.

Fight Song: *When the Hawks Go Marching In*
(same words and tune as "When the Saints Go Marching in")

Shippensburg University
Shippensburg, PA 17257

School Nickname: *Ship*

School Colors: *Red and Blue*

School Mascot: *Red Raider*

School Newspaper: *Slate*

School Yearbook: *Cumberland*

Alma Mater: *Alma Mater*

> In the dear old Cumberland valley
> 'Neath the glowing sky
> Proudly stands our Alma Mater
> On the hilltop high.
>
> Mid the waving golden cornfields
> Just beyond the town
> Stands the ivy-covered buildings
> As the sun goes down.
>
> When we leave our Alma Mater
> We will praise her name
> Ever live to raise the standards
> Of her glorious fame.
> *Chorus*
> Swell the chorus ever louder
> We'll be true to you
> Hail to thee our Alma Mater
> Dear old Red and Blue.

Slippery Rock University
Slippery Rock, PA 16057-1326

School Nickname: *The Rock/The Rockets*

School Colors: *Green and White*

School Mascot: *Rocky*

School Newspaper: *The Rocket*

School Yearbook: *Saxigena*

Alma Mater: *Alma Mater*

> Where the Slippery Rock creek wanders,
> With its sparkling falls.
> There in stately grace and beauty
> Stand old SR halls.
> *Chorus*
> Sing her praises loud resounding,
> Speed them on their way.
> We'll be true to thee, O, S.R.
> True for aye and aye.

> All the halls the day in dying
> Crowns with golden light,
> And the morn in waking splendor
> Greets thee in thy might.

> Long may you, our Alma Mater
> Shed your light abroad,
> As your loyal sons and daughters
> Live for you and God.

Temple University
Philadelphia, PA 19122

School Colors: *Cherry and White*

School Mascot: *Owl*

School Newspaper: *Temple News*

School Yearbook: *Templar*

University of Pennsylvania
Philadelphia, PA 19104-6380

School Nickname: *Penn*

School Colors: *Red and Blue*

School Newspaper: *Daily Pennsylvanian*

School Yearbook: *The Record*

Fight Song: *Fight Song*

(No official Fight song, 59 popular songs)

University of Pittsburgh
Pittsburgh, PA 15260

School Nickname: *PITT*

School Colors: *Navy and Gold*

School Mascot: *Panther*

School Newspaper: *The Pitt News*

School Yearbook: *Panther Prints*

Alma Mater: *Alma Mater*

> Alma Mater, wise and glorious
> Child of life and Bride of Truth
> Over Fate and Foe victorious,
> Dowered with eternal youth
> Crowned with love of son and daughter
> Thou shall conquer as of yore
> Dear old Pittsburgh, Alma Mater
> God preserve thee, evermore!

Fight Song: *Victory Song*

> Fight on for dear old Pittsburgh
> And for the glory of the game
> Show our worthy foe that the Panther's on the go
> Pitt must win today
> Cheer loyal sons of Pittsburgh
> Cheer on to victory and fame
> For the Blue and Gold will conquer as of old
> So Fight! Pitt! Fight!
> FIGHT PITT FIGHT, FIGHT PITT FIGHT!

University of Scranton
Scranton, PA 18510

School Colors: *Purple and White*

School Mascot: *Royals Rooster*

School Newspaper: *The Aquinas*

School Yearbook: *The Windhover*

Alma Mater: *University of Scranton Alma Mater*

The hours too quickly slip away.
And mingle into years.
But mem'ries of our Scranton days
Will last whatever next appears.
The legacy from those before is briefly ours to hold.
We leave the best behind for others.
As the coming years unfold.

With faith in lives that touch us here.
And paths that ours have crossed
We know that reaching for the rising sun
Is surely worth the cost.
May God be ever at our side,
May goodness fill our days.
We hail as loving sons and daughters
Alma mater ours always.
                    Words and Music By Kathleen M. Fisher, '80
                    and Edward Gannon

Villanova University
Villanova, PA 10985

School Nickname: *Wildcats*

School Colors: *Blue and White*

School Mascot: *Wildcat*

School Newspaper: *Villanovan*

School Yearbook: *Belle Aire*

Alma Mater: *Villanova University Anthem*

When the twilight shadows gather
Out upon the Campus green,
When the blue and purple night
Comes stealing on the scene
Loyal heirs of Villanova
Sing a hymn of praise
To our dear old ALMA MATER
And our College days.

Villanova, Villanova
When we leave your shelt'ring walls,
We shall leave an echo ringing

Through your treasured halls
We will leave an echo ringing
In the silent night
While our memories are singing
Of the Blue and White.

When the last big game is over
And the last roll call is heard
When the oldest pedagogue
Has had his final word
We shall come to ALMA MATER
In our dreams again
With a prayer for Villanova
And a sweet amen.
> *By Al Dubin and Joseph Burke*

Fight Songs: *"V" For Villanova ("V" For Victory)"*

"V" for Villanova "V" for Victory
"B" for Blue and "Double-U" for White
For the Blue and White, we will fight! fight!
fight! fight!
Fight! for VILLANOVA! Fight for Victory.
For we're out to win the fray,
VILLANOVA lead the way
With a capital "V" for Victory!

VILLANOVA! VILLANOVA
"V" for Victory! V-I-C-T-O-R-Y
It's a tooth for a tooth, and an eye for an eye
And a "V" for a V-I-C-T-O-R-Y!!!
"V" for Villanova "V" for Victory
"B" for Blue and "Double-U" for White
For the Blue and White, we will fight! fight!
fight! fight!
Fight! for VILLANOVA! Fight for Victory.
For we're out to beat the foe
Show the enemy we know
How to win with a "V" for Victory.
> *By Les Irving*

The March of the Wildcats

March, you Wildcats-march right on
We are out to win the day
We'll·march straight through to victory
So onward let us go-Rah! Rah!
Let us fight, fight, fight, fight!
Villanovans one and all

Join to sing a praise to Alma Mater
Hail, Blue and White.
By Carmen Giordano, '36

West Chester University
West Chester, PA 19383

School Colors: *Purple and Gold*

School Mascot: *Ram*

School Newspaper: *Quad*

School Yearbook: *Serpentine*

Alma Mater: *Alma Mater*

West Chester, hail, all hail, noble and strong.
To thee with loyal hearts we raise our song,
Swelling to heaven high, our praises ring,
West Chester, hail, all hail, of thee we sing.

Majesty as a crown rests on thy brow;
Pride, honor, glory, love before thee bow;
Ne'er can thy spirit die, thy walls decay,
West Chester, hail, all hail, for thee we pray.

West Chester, hail, all hail, guide of our youth,
Lead thou thy children on to light and truth,
Thee, when we hence depart, others shall praise,
West Chester, hail, all hail, through endless days.
West Chester, hail, all hail, through endless days.
Adapted-Charlotte N. Hardee

York College of Pennsylvania
York, PA 17403

School Nickname: *Spartans-YCP*

School Colors: *Kelly Green and White*

School Mascot: *Spartans*

School Newspaper: *Spartan*

School Yearbook: *Horizon*

Alma Mater: *Alma Mater*

The Years shall pass, but we will not forget
Our Alma Mater dear.
Resound the hallowed halls with homage yet;
Keeping faith without fear.
Consecrated to the Truth and Right;
Our pledge to thee, old Green and White.
Let the chorus fill the air;
Let the song go ev'rywhere;
Ev'ry heart sing bold and free;
Giving praise, Old York, to thee,
E'en to eternity.

RHODE ISLAND

Brown University
Providence, RI 02912

School Nickname: *Brunonia*

School Colors: *Brown and White*

School Mascot: *Bear*

School Newspaper: *Brown Daily Herald*

School Yearbook: *Liber Brunensis*

Alma Mater: *Alma Mater*

> Alma Mater we hail thee with loyal devotion,
> And bring to thine alter our off'ring of praise;
> Our hearts swell within us with joyful emotion
> As the name of Old Brown in loud chorus we raise.
> The happiest moments of youth's fleeting hours
> We've passed 'neath the shade of these time-honor'd walls;
> And sorrows as transient as April's brief showers
> Have clouded our life in Brunonia's halls.
> > *By James A. DeWilf 1861*

Fight Song: *Ever True to Brown*

> We are ever true to Brown
> For we love our college dear,
> And wherever we go,
> We are ready with a cheer.
> And the people always say,
> That you can't outshine Brown men and women,
> With a Rah! Rah! Rah! and Ki! Yi! Yi!
> And a B-R-O-W-N.
> > *Traditional version by Donald Jackson '09*

Bryant College
450 Douglas Pike
Smithfield, RI 02917-1284

School Nickname: *Indians*

School Colors: *Black and Gold*

School Mascot: *Indians*

School Newspaper: *The Archway*

School Yearbook: *The Ledger*

Alma Mater: *Alma Mater*

> Bryant College Alma Mater,
> let us sing our praise to you,
> grand traditions, ling-ring mem-ries,
> domes and archways, fountains, view.
> Black and gold we carry onward
> love and friends and knowledge gained
> Be forever in our vision,
> lovingly your name proclaim.
>
> Bryant College Alma Mater,
> source of knowledge sound and true,
> Ever growing, ever striving,
> bringing business strength anew,
> Caring, sharing hope and wisdom;
> Greatness strived for and obtained
> Bryant College, proudly do we hold your torch
> respect your name.

Johnson and Wales College
Providence, RI 02903

School Colors: *Blue and White*

School Newspaper: *Campus Herald*

School Yearbook: *Johnsonian*

Providence College
River Ave.
Providence, RI 02918

School Nickname: *PC*

School Colors: *Black and White*

School Newspaper: *The Cowl*

School Yearbook: *Veritas*

Alma Mater: *Alma Mater*

> Mother of Truth, we proudly pledge to thee
> Undying love and steadfast loyalty.
> From thee we learned the wonderous work of God,
> His goodness, grace, and holy power;
> Clear has thou shown what pathways must be trod;
> All fearless now we brave life's hour!
>
> Through failure frown, though kindly fortune smile,
> Firm our advance, naught can us e'er beguile.
> To honor bound, to love virtue sworn,
> Lift we our voice in full acclaim
> Our lives shall thee with noble deeds adorn;
> Hail Providence! we praise thy name!
> *From "Findandia" by Jan Sibelius*

Rhode Island College
Providence, RI 02908

School Colors: *Gold and White (Burgundy as an accent color)*

School Mascot: *Anchor*

School Newspaper: *The Anchor*

School Yearbook: *Denouemont*

Alma Mater: *Alma Mater*

> Dear Alma Mater wise and kind,
> To thy fair name shall e'er belong
> our grateful praises and our love,
> The tribute of our song.
> Thou guardian of the sacred shrine
> of truth that makes us free.
> We cherish thy beloved fame and pledge our loyalty.
> Rhode Island College hail to thee!
> All hail to Alma Mater!
> Enshrined thou art within the heart of ev'ry son and daughter.
>> *Grace E. Bird and Helen S. Leavitt*
>> *Copyright Rhode Island College.*
>> *Used by permission*

University of Rhode Island
Kingston, RI 02881-0807

School Nickname: *Rams - men; WRams - women*

School Colors: *Light Blue and White*

School Mascot: *Rams*

School Newspaper: *Good 5 Cent Cigar and The University Pacer*

School Yearbook: *Renaissance*

Alma Mater: *Alma Mater*

> All Hail to thee Rhode Island
> We pledge our faith anew
> While our heroes bring thee honor
> With our banner of white and blue.
> In truth we owe her much for she's shown us the way
> To achieve and be of service to the world.
> So hail our Alma Mater,
> Rhode Island, our guide what'er we do.

Fight Song: *Rhode Island Born*

> We're Rhode Island born
> We're Rhode Island bred
> And when we die
> We'll be Rhode Island dead.

We're here to play
And we're here to win,
And when we play
We play like sin.
    Chorus
For it's Rah! Rah! Rhode Island, Island,
Rah! Rah!, Rhode Island, Rah, Rah,
Rhode Island R.I. State.

SOUTH CAROLINA

Bob Jones University
Greenville, SC 29614

School Colors: *Blue and White*

School Yearbook: *Vintage*

Clemson University
Clemson, SC

School Nickname: *Tigers*

School Colors: *Burnt Orange and Northwestern Purple*

School Mascot: *Tiger*

School Newspaper: *The Tiger*

School Yearbook: *Taps*

Alma Mater: *Alma Mater*

> Where the Blue Ridge yawns its greatness;
> Where the Tigers play;
> Here the sons of dear Old Clemson,

Reign supreme alway.
We will dream of great conquests
For our past is grand,
And her sons have fought and conquered
Every foreign land.

Where the mountains smile in grandeur
O'er the hill and dale
Here the Tiger lair is nestling
Swept by storm and gale.

We are brothers strong in manhood
For we work and strive;
And our Alma Mater reigneth
Forever in our lives.
Chorus
Dear Old Clemson, we will triumph
And with all our might,
That the Tiger's roar may echo
O'er the mountains height.

Words by A.C.Corcoran,'19
Music by Dr. Hugh McGarity

Fight Song: *Tiger Rag (music only)*

College of Charleston
Charleston, SC 29424

School Nickname: *The College*

School Colors: *Maroon and White*

School Mascot: *The Cougar*

School Newspaper: *The Meteor*

School Yearbook: *The Comet*

Alma Mater: *Alma Mater*

Hail to thee, our Alma Mater.
Hail to thy time-honored name.
Proud traditions hover 'round thee;
May we never bring thee shame.
Loyal sons and daughters love thee,
Strive to conquer and prevail.
We will sing the praises ever--
College of Charleston, hail, all hail.

South Carolina State University
Orangeburg, SC 29117

School Nickname: *The Bulldogs*

School Colors: *Garnet and Blue*

School Mascot: *Bulldog*

School Newspaper: *Collegian*

School Yearbook: *The Bulldog*

Alma Mater: *Alma Mater*

> Sing the praise of Alma Mater
> Let us rally to her calls
> Lift our voices, send them ringing
> Thru the groves and classic halls.
> *Chorus*
> Hail! Hail! Dear Alma Mater
> Hail! Hail! Dear S.C.C.
> We'll defend and honor
> Love and cherish thee.
>
> We are loyal sons and daughters
> Proud to own the name we bear
> For the truths that thou has taught us
> Ready all to do and dare.

University of South Carolina
Columbia, SC 29208

School Nickname: *Fighting Gamecocks*

School Colors: *Garnet and Black*

School Mascot: *Gamecock* Name: *Cocky*

School Newspaper: *The Gamecock*

School Yearbook: *The Garnet and Black*

Alma Mater: *Here's A Health to Carolina*

> We hail thee, Carolina and sing thee high praise
> With loyal devotion, remembering the days
> When proudly we sought thee, thy children to be:
> Here's a health, Carolina, forever to thee!

Since pilgrims of learning, we entered thy walls
And found dearest comrades in thy classic halls,
We've honored and loved thee as sons faithfully;
Here's a health, Carolina, forever to thee!

Generations of sons have rejoiced to proclaim
Thy watchword of service, thy beauty and fame;
For ages to come shall their rallying cry be:
Here's a health, Carolina, forever to thee!

Fair shrine of high honor and truth, thou shalt still
Blaze forth as a beacon, thy mission fulfill,
And be crowned by all hearts in a new jubilee:
Here's a health, Carolina, forever to thee!

Fight Song: *Fight Song*

Hey! let's give a cheer, Carolina is here!
The fighting Gamecocks lead the way.
Who gives a care if the going gets rough?
'Cause when it gets tough, that's when the 'Cocks'
get going.
Hail to our colors of Garnet and Black!
In Carolina, pride have we.
So, go Gamecocks, go!
Drive for that goal!
USC will win tonight! "GO COCKS"
So, let's give a cheer, Carolina is here!
The fighting Gamecocks all the way!

Winthrop College
Rock Hill, SC 29733

School Colors: *Garnet and Gold*

School Mascot: *Eagles*

School Newspaper: *The Johnsonian*

Alma Mater: *Alma Mater*

The Chapel holds our history,
Each new day Tillman rings,
Your halls are rich with memories
to which we'll always cling.
A part of each one here remains
as a part of you we claim,
Alma Mater may your name be grand,
Winthrop College ever stand.

The friends we've made, the memories,
Will last a lifetime long.
We soar to reach the goals we've set
As Eagles bold and strong.
May others see our loyalty
Ever honored you will be,
Alma Mater may your name be grand,
Winthrop College ever stand.

Words, Donna Durst and Lisa Breland, '87
Music, Donna Durst, '83, copyright holder

SOUTH DAKOTA

South Dakota State University
Box 2201
Brookings, SD 57002

School Nickname: *SDSU Jackrabbits*

School Colors: *Yellow and Blue*

School Mascot: *Jackrabbit*

School Newspaper: *Collegian*

School Yearbook: *South Dakota State University Jackrabbit*

Alma Mater: *The Yellow and Blue*

"We come from the Sioux and Missouri,
The Cheyenne and the Jim,
From the pine-clad peaks of the Black Hills,
Brim-ful of vigor and vim;
We sing the song of the prairie,
The home of the Yellow and Blue.
The gleaming gold of the cornfield,
The flax of azure blue."

Refrain
Oh, S. D. S. C., Hurrah for the Yellow and Blue;
Old S. D. S. C., All honor and glory to you;
Forever raise the song in praise
Both loud and long with loyal hearts true.
Oh, loyal hearts and true.

The glorious haze of the harvest
Where sky and prairie meet
The golden gleam of the sunrise,
The blue of violets sweet;
The yellow and blue of the rainbow.
The azure of noon-day sky
The golden hair of the maiden,
The blue of her sparkling eye.

The yellow and blue of our banner,
The cups that are won on the field;
The golden words of orations
That honors unto us yield;
We sing the song of the prairie
Where many a mile we may scan,
And blizzard breath from the northland
Develops the fighting man.

The bronchos we break for the round-up
And ride the range all day.
We kill the coyote and gray wolf
As snarling they sneak away;
The peace pipe smoke with the red man
And listen to legends of gore,
The loud tum tum of the Sioux drum
The tomahawk dance of war.

Then forth to a bold life of action
Both stirring and grand for all,
As knights of old battled evil
So we are heeding the call;
We scorn the faint hearted coward,
A slave for the galley is he;
We cheer the knights of the present
And fight on to victory.
                Francis J. Haynes and N. E. Hansen

Fight Song: *Ring the Bells*

Ring the bells for South Dakota
The yellow and the blue;

Cheer the team from South Dakota
With loyal hearts so true;
Win the game for South Dakota
The school that serves us well;
We will fight for South Dakota
So lets ring, ring, ring those bells.
Words by Stan Schleuter

The University of South Dakota
414 East Clark
Vermillion, SD 57069

School Colors: *Red and White*

School Mascot: *Coyote*

School Newspaper: *Volante*

School Yearbook: *Coyote*

Alma Mater: *Alma Mater*

South Dakota, how dear to thy children thy name
How daring the tales oft retold
Of the builders who first to thy wilderness came;
Theirs a glory that never grows old.
O, the pine crested peaks of the storied Black Hills
The Missouri that ribbons thy plains;
Where the slant summer sunshine so lavishly spills
Over prairie and pasture and grain.

Fight Song: *Fight Song*

Hail, South Dakota
Pride of the West
Our Alma Mater
Noblest and best.
We rally 'round thee,
Marching abreast
Hail thee! Hail thee
Riding the crest
Our sons and daughters ever will be
Loyal and true to thee
Varsity, varsity, hail varsity, U.S.D.

TENNESSEE

Austin Peay State University
College St.
Clarksville, TN 37044

School Nickname: *APSU*

School Colors: *Red and White*

School Mascot: *The Governors* Name: *Gov. "P"*

School Newspaper: *The All State*

School Yearbook: *Governors' Pride*

East Tennessee State University
Johnson City, TN 37614

School Nickname: *The Buccaneers*

School Colors: *Blue and Gold*

School Mascot: *Parrot* Name: *"Pepper"*

School Newspaper: *East Tennessean*

School Yearbook: *Buccaneer*

Alma Mater: *Alma Mater*

> In the shadow of the mountains,
> Under skies of blue,
> Stands our dear old Alma Mater,
> Glorious to view,
> Sound the chorus, speed it onward;
> Thee we'll never fail!
> Hail to thee, our Alma Mater--
> Hail to thee, all Hail!
>
> In thy halls we formed our friendships,
> Dear old college home;
> And to thee we pledge our hearts,
> Wherever we may roam,
> Sound the chorus, speed it onward;
> Thee we'll never fail!
> Hail to thee, our Alma Mater--
> Hail to thee, all hail!

Fight Song: *Fight Song*

> Fight, fight, fight, with all your might,
> Vic-to-ry will our slogan be;
> Dear alma mater, fairest of all,
> Thy loyal sons will obey thy call,
> To fight, fight, fight, with all your might,
> Ever the goal to gain,
> Into the game for old "state's" fame,
> Fight on to vic-to-ry!

Memphis State University
Memphis, TN 38152

School Nickname: *Tigers*

School Colors: *Blue and Gray*

School Mascot: *Live Bengal Tiger* Name: *TOM (Tigers of Memphis)*

School Newspaper: *The Helmsman*

School Yearbook: *DeSoto*

Alma Mater: *Alma Mater*

> Stand firm, O Alma Mater,
> Through all the years to come;
> In days of youth and beauty
> Thy halls have been our home.
> In time of preparation
> Great lessons didst thou teach
> Til now, O Alma Mater,
> The stars we'll strive to reach.

Fight Song: *Go Tigers Go*

> Go Tigers Go, go on to victory,
> Be a winner thru and thru,
> Fight Tigers fight
> 'cause we're going all the way Fight Fight
> For the blue and grey, and say let's Go Tigers Go,
> Go on to victory see our colors brite and true
> It's Fight now with out a fear
> Fight now let's shout a cheer,
> Shout for dear old MSU
> Go Tigers Go
> Go Tigers Go
> Yea-----------Tigers!
> *Tom Ferguson*

Middle Tennessee State University
Murfreesboro, TN 37132

School Nickname: *MTSU*

School Colors: *Blue and White*

School Mascot: *Hound Dog*

School Newspaper: *Sidelines*

School Yearbook: *The Midlander*

Alma Mater: *Second Alma Mater*

> We sing thy praises faithful guide of youth;
> Through all the ages affirmed and strong in truth.
> Alma Mater Middle Tennessee
> We proudly offer our hearts in loyalty.
> *Douglas Williams, '53*

Fight Song: *MTSU Fight Song*

> Come see those Blue Raiders ride today
> Watch our mighty fighting men
> And while they're riding high
> We'll shout our battle cry
> And see them charge on down the line again
> MTSU Raiders never fail
> That's our motto and our pride
> All through the years of history
> Our mighty varsity
> Has brought us victory
> And so it's always bound to be
> Whenever big Blue Raiders ride.
> > *Arr. by Paul Yoder*

Tennessee State University
3500 John A Merritt Blvd.
Nashville, TN 37209

School Nickname: *TSU*

School Colors: *Blue and White*

School Mascot: *Tiger*

School Newspaper: *The Meter*

School Yearbook: *The Tennessean*

Alma Mater: *Alma Mater*

> In the land of golden sunshine,
> By the Cumb'rland's fertile shore.
> Stands a school for greatest service
> One that we adore.
> Alma Mater, how we love thee,
> Love thy white and blue
> May we strive to meet thy mandates
> With faith that's true.
>
> Many come to Thee for knowledge,
> Come from East, North, South and West.
> For they know that Thou dost offer
> Such a rich bequest.
> Alma Mater, all thy children
> Worship at Thy shrine;
> May the God of nations bless thee
> With gifts divine.

Send forth sons both strong and valiant,
Send forth daughters wise and true.
Filled with hope and dauntless courage
Motives sane and true.
Alma Mater, kindly mother
Smile on Tennessee
May she lift her head towards heaven
Honor Country, God and Thee.
                        L. M. Averitte
                        Clarence Hayden Wilson

Fight Song: *Fight Song*

I'm so glad I go to TSU!
I'm so glad I go to TSU!
I'm so glad I go to TSU!
Singing Glory Hallelujah, I'm so glad!

Tennessee Technological University
Cookeville, TN 38505

School Nickname: *Tech*

School Colors: *Purple and Gold*

School Mascot: *Golden Eagle* Name: *Awesome Eagle*

School Newspaper: *The Oracle*

School Yearbook: *The Eagle*

Alma Mater: *Tennessee Tech Hymn*

The quiet hills stand steadfast round walls of russet brown.
On halls serene and campus green the smoky hills look down;
And steadfast may I cherish what thou hast giv'n to me.
Oh Alma Mater Tennessee Tech, God prosper thee.

Deep purple stand the mountains and golden sets the sun.
We proudly wear these colors fair until our goal is won;
We pledge thee faithful service, our love and loyalty.
Oh Alma Mater Tennessee Tech God, prosper thee.
                        Mrs Everett Derryberry

Fight Song: *Tennessee Tech Fight Song*

There they go again today, what a team
Yea, the Eagles, you'll hear everybody say

Better get on the ball with the Eagles
Make that touchdown play again
see them running up the score, for
We'll be leading all the way
with our own Tech Golden Eagles.
     Paul Yoder

University of Tennessee
Knoxville, TN 37996

School Nickname: *Volunteers or Vols (registered trademarks)*

School Colors: *Orange and White*

School Mascot: *Blue-Tick Hound* Name: *Smokey*

School Newspaper: *The Daily Beacon*

School Yearbook: *The Volunteer*

Alma Mater: *Alma Mater*

On a hallowed hill in Tennessee,
Like beacon shining bright
The Stately walls of old U.T.,
Rise glorious to the sight.

What torches kindled at that flame
Have passed from hand to hand!
What hearts cemented in that name
Bind land to stranger land!

O, ever as we strive to rise
On Life's unresting stream
Dear Alma Mater, may our eyes
Be lifted to that gleam!
    Refrain
So here's to you old Tennessee,
Our Alma Mater true
We pledge in love and harmony
Our loyalty to you!
    Mrs. John Lamar Meek, '28

Fight Song: *Fight! Vols, Fight!*

Fight, Vols, fight with all your might
For the Orange and White
Never falter, never yield

As we march on down the field--
Keep Marching
Let the Spirit of the Hill
Every Vol with courage fill
Your loyalty means our victory
So fight, Vols, fight!
> *Words by Gwen Sweet*
> *Music by Thornton W. Allen and Milo Sweet*

University of Tennessee at Chattanooga
Chattanooga, TN 37403

School Nickname: *Moccasins, "Mocs"*

School Colors: *Blue and Gold*

School Mascot: *Indian Chief* Name: *Moc-A-Nooga*

School Newspaper: *Echo*

School Yearbook: *Moccasin*

Alma Mater: *UTC Alma Mater*

Lookout Mountain o'er us guarding
Ceaseless watch doth keep.
In the valley stands our college,
Where the shadows creep.
Chattanooga, Chattanooga
Loud the anthem swell;
Sing O sing of Alma Mater,
All her praises tell.

University of Tennessee at Martin
Martin, TN 38238

School Nickname: *Pacers*

School Colors: *Orange and Blue*

School Mascot: *Roadrunner* Name: *Pacer Pete*

School Newspaper: *The Pacer*

School Yearbook: *The Spirit*

Vanderbilt University
West End Ave.
Nashville, TN 37240

School Nickname: *Vandy*

School Colors: *Black and Gold*

School Mascot: *The Commodore*

School Newspaper: *The Hustler*

School Yearbook: *The Commodore*

TEXAS

Abilene Christian University
Abilene, TX 79699

School Nickname: *Wildcats*

School Colors: *Purple and White*

School Mascot: *Willie the Wildcat*

School Newspaper: *Optimist*

School Yearbook: *Prickly Pear*

Alma Mater: *Oh, Dear Christian College*

> Oh, Dear Christian College, we love you,
> Our dear Alma Mater, today;
> Like the stars shining brightly above you,
> Your fame shall shine brightly for aye.
> To you we'll prove faithful and loyal
> While ever up-holding the right,
> And gladly we'll give forth the royal
> Three cheers for the purple and white.

We gathered while safe in your keeping
Bright jewels of wisdom and truth,
Preparing life's field for the reaping,
Improving the days of our youth.
Whenever the call comes for service,
We'll answer with hearts true and right,
In home, field, shop, pulpit or office,
We'll honor the purple and white.

Still upward and onward we're pressing
To win the great battle of life,
True courage and brave hearts possessing,
We'll never grow faint in the strife.
And when our life's journey is ended,
And sunset is shrouded by night,
In the warm after glow we'll see blended
The beauteous purple and white.
Chorus
Then we'll pledge our love to Christian,
To her is honor due;
While we gaily sing let praises ring
For our Alma Mater true.
Adapted by Dr. G. C. Morlan
Arr. by Leonard Burford

Angelo State University
2601 W. Avenue N.
San Angelo, TX 76909

School Nickname: *ASU*

School Colors: *Blue and Gold*

School Mascot: *Rams*

School Newspaper: *RamPage*

School Yearbook: *Rambouillet*

Baylor University
Waco, TX 76798

School Nickname: *Bears*

School Colors: *Kelly Green and Gold*

School Mascot: *Bear*

School Newspaper: *The Lariat*

School Yearbook: *The Round-up*

Alma Mater: *That Good Old Baylor Line*

> That good old Baylor line,
> That good old Baylor line
> We'll march forever down the years,
> As long as stars shall shine.
> We'll fling our Green and Gold afar,
> To light the ways of time,
> And guide as we onward go,
> That good old Baylor line.
> > *Enid E. Markham*
> > *Copyright Baylor University, 1952*

East Texas State University
Commerce, TX 75428

School Nickname: *Lions*

School Colors: *Blue and Gold*

School Mascot: *Lion*

School Newspaper: *East Texan*

School Yearbook: *Locust*

Alma Mater: *Alma Mater*

> Let our voices loudly ringing,
> Echo far and near,
> Songs of praise thy children singing,
> To thy memory dear.
> > *Chorus*
> Alma Mater, Alma Mater,
> Loud her praises be,
> Hail to thee, our Alma Mater,
> Hail, all hail, E.T.
>
> All the days we've been together
> Foundly we recall,
> Days of fair or stormy weather,
> Thou hast gladdened all.

Years may dim our recollection,
Time its changes bring,
Still thy name in fond affection
Evermore we sing.

Fight Song: *E. T. Fight Song*

Fight! Fight! Fight! for Alma Mater dear;
We're gonna win that game today.
Let our voices ring loud and clear
In the old East Texas way.
Yell! Yell! Yell! East Texas you're all right;
You are the best of all.

We're gonna down those Bobcats
And then come home tonight,
With a Lion victory call.
Fight, Team! Fight! Fight! Fight!
East Texas Lions are marching on today,
Onward to victory.

Lamar University
Beaumont, TX 77710

School Nickname: *Cardinals*

School Colors: *Red and White*

School Mascot: *Big Red*

School Newspaper: *University Press*

Alma Mater: *Alma Mater*

Lamar to thee we're singing.
Voices raised on high.
We will forever love thee.
Laud thee to the sky
We will ever need thee
As our guiding star.
To us you'll always be
Our Glorious Lamar.
            G. Rhodes Smartt

Fight Song: *Fight Song*

Fight Lamar University Cardinals
For Alma Mater, Fight Glory

In the Triumph for the
Red and the White.
Faithful to your colors
We will ever be fighting
Ever fighting for Lamar
University victory.
Let's go B-I-G R-E-D
Big Red, Big Red

Midwestern State University
3400 Taft Blvd.
Wichita Falls, TX 76308

School Colors: *Maroon and Gold*

School Mascot: *Indians*

School Newspaper: *The Wichitan*

School Yearbook: *Wai-Kun*

Alma Mater: *Alma Mater*

Hail to Midwestern, hail maroon and gold.
We praise Alma Mater, as days of old.
Here's to the Indians, long may they stand.
Onward to victory, on hand in hand.

Pan American University
1201 W. University Dr.
Edinburg, TX 78539

School Nickname: *Pan Am*

School Colors: *Green and White*

School Mascot: *The Broncs*

School Newspaper: *The Pan American*

School Yearbook: *El Bronco*

Prairie View A&M University
Prairie View, TX 77446

School Nickname: *Panthers*

School Colors: *Purple and Gold*

School Mascot: *Panther*

School Newspaper: *Panther Newspaper*

School Yearbook: *Pantherland*

Alma Mater: *Dear Prairie View*

> Dear Prairie View, our song to thee we raise,
> In gratitude we sing our hymn of praise,
> For mem'ries dear, for friends and recollections,
> For lessons learned while here we've lived with thee
> For these we pledge our hearts full of devotion
> To serve thee now, and through eternity.
>
> As days go by, our hearts will not grow cold,
> We'll love thy purple royal and thy gold,
> We'll through our lives exemplify thy teachings,
> We'll always strive a blessing to be.
> Thy children we our love and pride confessing,
> We'll love thee now, and through eternity.
> *Words by O. Anderson Fuller*

Fight Song: *Mighty Panther*

> We're the Mighty Panthers
> We are Panthers until we die
> We're Mighty Mighty Panthers
> And I'll tell you that ain't no lie
>
> We're the Marching Panthers
> We are Panthers until we die
> We're Mighty Marching Panthers,
> And I'll tell you that ain't no lie
>
> .... Panthers!
> .... Panthers!
> .... Panthers!

Rice University
6100 South Main St.
Houston, TX 77005

School Colors: *Confederate Blue and Gray*

School Mascot: *Owl*

School Newspaper: *The Rice Thresher*

School Yearbook: *Campanile*

Alma Mater: *Rice's Honor*

>All for Rice's Honor, we will fight on.
>We will be fighting when this day is done;
>And when the dawn comes breaking.
>We'll be fighting on, Rice.
>For the Gray and Blue. We will be loyal
>To Rice be true.
>>*1922*

Fight Song: *Rice Fight Song*

>Fight for Rice,
>Rice fight on,
>Loyal sons arise,
>The Blue and Gray for Rice today,
>Comes breaking through the skies.
>Stand and cheer,
>Victory's near,
>Sammy leads the way,
>Onward go!
>To crush the foe,
>We'll fight for Blue and Gray
>>*Louis Girard '41*

Sam Houston State University
Huntsville, TX 77341

School Nickname: *Sam*

School Colors: *Orange and White*

School Mascot: *Bearkat*

School Newspaper: *The Houstonian*

School Yearbook: *The Alcalde*

Alma Mater: *Alma Mater*

>Hail, Alma Mater
>Hats off to you,
>Ever you'll find us
>Loyal and true;
>Firm and undaunted,

Ever we'll be,
Here's to the school we love
Here's a toast to thee.

Southern Methodist University
Dallas, TX 75275

School Nickname: *Mustangs*

School Colors: *Harvard Red and Yale Blue*

School Mascot: *Peruna*

School Newspaper: *Daily Campus*

School Yearbook: *The Rotunda*

Alma Mater: *Varsity*

> Oh, we see the Varsity, Varsity, Varsity
> As she towers o'er the hill over there
> and our hearts are filled with joy
> SMU - SMU
> Alma Mater, we'll be true forever.

Fight Song: *Fight Song*

> Here's to the Red and the Blue
> We're the Mustangs from SMU
> Give a cheer, give a fight
> There's a victory in sight
> And our battle cry will be
> Fight! Fight! Fight!
> Spirit's the best in the land
> And right to the end we'll stand
> for the M-U-S-T-A-N-G-S
> FIGHT! FIGHT! FIGHT!

Southwest Texas State University
San Marcos, TX 78666

School Nickname: *SWT*

School Colors: *Maroon and Gold*

School Mascot: *Bobcat*

School Newspaper: *The University Star*

School Yearbook: *The Pedagog*

Alma Mater: *Alma Mater*

O, Alma Mater, set up on the green hills,
With turrets pointing upward to the sky;
We yield to thee our love and our devotion,
Mother of hopes and aspirations high.

Thy feet are laved by pure and limpid waters,
Fair rivers flowing to the sea;
Thy hills are crowned with ancient oak and laurel,
Fit emblems they of strength and victory.

Thy spirit urges us to deeds of valor,
Raising the fallen, cheering the oppressed;
Thy call will echo clearly down the ages,
Dear Alma Mater, mother loved and blessed.

Stephen F. Austin State University
1936 North St.
Nacogdoches, TX 75962

School Nickname: *SFA*

School Colors: *Purple and White*

School Mascot: *Lumberjacks and Ladyjacks*

School Newspaper: *Pine Log*

School Yearbook: *Stone Fort*

Tarleton State University
Stephenville, TX 76402

School Nickname: *Tarleton Texans*

School Colors: *Purple and White*

School Mascot: *Texan Rider*

School Newspaper: *J-TAC (John Tarleton Agriculture College)*

School Yearbook: *Grassburr*

Alma Mater: *Tarleton Color Song*

> Oh, Our Hearts with joy are filling
> When the Tarleton Colors Wave.
> And our Spirits rise with rapture
> When Tarleton sons are brave.
> Fight for Victory, Fight for Honor,
> And success will crown the fight;
> ALL HAIL the proud defenders of the
> Purple and the White!

Fight Song: *On Ye Tarleton*

> On Ye Tarleton,
> On Ye Tarleton,
> Break right through that line
> Ever forward, ever onward
> We'll get there or die.
> On Ye Tarleton, On Ye Tarleton
> Fight for Victory;
> Fight, Texans, Fight, Fight, Fight!
> And win this game.

Texas A & I University
Kingsville, TX 78363

School Nickname: *Javelinas*

School Colors: *Gold and Blue*

School Mascot: *Porky*

School Newspaper: *South Texan*

Alma Mater: *Alma Mater*

> Hail A & I
> We pledge anew
> Aims that are high.
> Devotion deep and true
> And though we may part
> And though the years roll by,
> Still loyal each heart,
> To A & I!

Fight Songs: *Fight Song*

> Fight, Fight, for ole A & I!

Hail that grand old name.
Fight, fight, no one can deny
We're out to win this game.
So never stop
'Til the last gun is fired
And the score is told.
Sock their kabinas, you Javelinas
Blue and Gold.

Go you Javelinas
Fight for A & I!

Bust their old machines
Right between the eyes.

Hit 'em high, hit 'em low
Give 'em everything you've got.
Rah, rah, rah, rah, rah, rah, rah,
Yea team! Yea team!

Go, you Javelinas,
Fight for A & I!

Jalisco

Ay, Jalisco, Jalisco
Jalisco tu tienes
Tu novia
Que es Guadalajara.
Muchacha bonita
La perla mas rara
De todo Jalisco
Es mi Guadalajara.

Ay, Jalisco no te rajes
Me sale del alma
Gritar con calor.
Abrir echar este grito
Que lindo es Jalisco,
Palabra de honor.

Texas A & M University
College Station, TX 77843-5000

School Nickname: *Aggieland; Aggie*

School Colors: *Maroon and White*

School Mascot: *Registered Collie*   Name: *Reveille*

School Newspaper: *Battalion*

School Yearbook: *Aggieland*

Fight Songs: *The Aggie War Hymn*

> Hullaballo, Caneck! Caneck!
> Hullaballo, Caneck! Caneck!
> Good-bye to Texas University,
> So long to the Orange and White
> Good luck to dear old Texas Aggies,
> They are the boys that show the real old fight.
> "The eyes of Texas are upon you..."
> That is the song they sing so well,
> So good-bye to Texas University,
> We're going to beat you all to-
> Chig-ga-roo-gar-em!
> Chig-ga-roo-gar-em!
> Rough! Tough!
> Real Stuff! Texas A&M.
> > *Lyrics by James V. "Pinky" Wilson '21*
> > *Music by George Fairleigh*

Saw Varsity's Horns Off

> Saw Varsity's horns off!
> Saw Varsity's horns off!
> Saw Varsity's horns off!
> Short!
> Varsity's horns are sawed off!
> Varsity's horns are sawed off!
> Varsity's horns are sawed off!

Texas Christian University
Fort Worth, TX 76129

School Nickname: *TCU*

School Colors: *Purple and White*

School Mascot: *Horned Frog (phrynosoma cornutum)*

School Newspaper: *The Skiff*

School Yearbook: *Horned Frog (ceased publication in 73)*

Alma Mater: *Alma Mater Hymn*

> Hail-All Hail T. C. U.!
> Memr'ies sweet, Comrades true
> Light of faith, Follow through
> Praise to thee, T. C. U.
>
> Hail-All Hail Glory bright!
> Purple Frogs, Honor White;
> Victory! Spirits true
> Praise to thee, T. C. U.
> *Glenn Canfield '28*

Fight Songs: *Horned Frogs We Are All For You*

> We'll raise a song, both loud and strong,
> to cheer our team to victory;
> For T.C.U so tried and true
> we pledge eternal loyalty;
> Fight on boys fight,
> With all your might,
> Roll up the (touch-downs/scores for) T.C.U.
> Hail white and purple
> flag whose heroes never lag;
> Horned frogs we are for you.
> *Words by Mrs. Butler Smiser*
> *Music by Claude Sammis*

Frog March
> Come, join in a cheer or two,
> Like jolly good fellows and true,
> There's nothing so fine as the big Froggy line,
> And the backs of old T-C-U
> With rushes that gladden the soul,
> As over the gridiron we roll,
> A pass and a punt with an end running stunt,
> Will take us across the goal!
> Then it's fight! fight! fight! boys!
> Fight as we always do!
> With snap and dash we're off in a flash and
> there's nothing can stop us as onward we crash!
> And we'll win! win! win! boys!
> Win ere the fight is through:
> Come watch the way we carry the day for old T.C.U
> Then it's T.C.U. Hooray!
> *Fitz G. Lanham '31*

Texas Southern University
3100 Cleburne Ave.
Houston, TX 77004

School Nickname: *TSU*

School Colors: *Maroon and Gray*

School Mascot: *Tigers*

School Newspaper: *The Herald*

School Yearbook: *The Tiger*

Alma Mater: *Alma Mater*

The air is filled as our voices ring
From earth to the heav'ns above.
With voices raised; we're singing praise
To the school we dearly love.

Hail, Hail, Hail to Texas Southern
Hail to our dear Maroon and Gray
Undivided we will stand
By the greatest in the land,
T-S-U, T-S-U, we love you.

All roads lead to Texas Southern
Paved with light for one and all.
T.S.U.'re a shining star
And we're proud of what you are.
T-S-U, T-S-U, we love you.

Hail, Hail, Hail to Texas Southern
Hail to our Chiefs in reverence we sing
In our hearts you'll always stay
As you lead us on our way.
T-S-U, T-S-U, we love you.
Words and Music by C. A. Tolbert

Fight Song: *TSU Fight Song*

We are the Tigers of TSU,
And we love our school and colors too,
And we'll Fight! Fight! Fight!
Hooray for Maroon and Grayyyyyyy!

Texas Tech University
Lubbock, TX 79409

School Nickname: *Texas Tech*

School Colors: *Red and Black*

School Mascot: *Black Quarter Horse* Name: *Midnight Raider*

School Newspaper: *University Daily*

School Yearbook: *La Ventana*

Texas Woman's University
Denton, TX 76204

School Nickname: *Pioneers*

School Colors: *Red and White*

School Mascot: *Pioneer Woman*

School Newspaper: *Daily Lass-O*

School Yearbook: *Pioneer*

Alma Mater: *Alma Mater*

> Hail Alma Mater! Hail! Joyous we sing;
> Voices a-tune with love shall loudly ring.
> Thy daughters sing today praises to thee,
> Hail, Texas Woman's University!
>
> Strong ties of friendship true bind us to thee,
> Hours spent with thee are dear to memory
> With loyal love a-glow sing we our song,
> Hail! Let our voices glad the notes prolong!
>
> On broad and rolling plains, 'neath Texas skies,
> There, crowned with majesty, thy buildings rise.
> Thou hast with purpose new lighted our way.
> Hail! Alma Mater! Hear our songs today.

University of Houston-Clear Lake
2700 Bay Area Blvd.
Houston, TX 77058

School Colors: *Red and White*

School Newspaper: *Uhclidian*

University of Houston-Downtown
One Main St.
Houston, TX 77002

School Nickname: *UH-Downtown*

School Colors: *Red and White*

School Mascot: *Cougar*

School Newspaper: *Dateline*

Alma Mater: *Alma Mater*

All hail to thee
Our Houston University
Our hearts fill with gladness
When we think of thee.
We'll always adore thee
Dear old varsity,
And to thy memory cherished
True we'll ever be.
Words and Music by Harmony Class of '42

University of Houston-University Park
4800 Calhoun Rd.
Houston, TX 77004

School Colors: *Red and White*

School Mascot: *Shasta*

School Newspaper: *Daily Cougar*

School Yearbook: *Houstonian*

Alma Mater: *Alma Mater*

All hail to thee
Our Houston University
Our hearts fill with gladness
When we think of thee.

We'll always adore thee.
Dear old varsity,
And to thy memory cherished
True we'll ever be.
                    Words and Music by Harmony Class '42

Fight Song: *Fight Song*

Cougars fight for dear old U. of H.
For our Alma Mater cheer.
Fight for Houston University for victory is near.
When the going gets so rough and tough,
We never worry because were hot stuff
So fight fight fight for the red and white
And we will all go to victory.
                    Lyrics by Forest Fountain
                    Music by Marion Ford

University of North Texas
Denton, TX 76203

School Nickname: *Eagles*

School Colors: *Green and White*

School Mascot: *Eagles*

School Newspaper: *North Texas Daily*

School Yearbook: *Aerie*

Alma Mater: *Glory to the Green and White*

We're right behind North Texas,
She always leads the way;
Her fame has endured through ages long;
As the students come and go
Their fervent hopes will ever grow,
And their love for Alma Mater spurs them on:

We're with her on the platform,
We're with her on the field,
We cheer the Eagles on with all our might;
Alma Mater's stood the test,
Always planning for the best
As she proudly waves her colors green and white:

Chorus
Singing glory to the green,
Singing glory to the white,
For we know our Alma Mater's ever
Striving for the right;
Down the corridor of years,
We'll forget the joys and tears,
But North Texas, North Texas, we love!
Lyrics by Charles Langford
Music by Julia Smith

Fight Song: *Fight, North Texas*

Let's give a cheer for North Texas State;
Cheer for the Green and White.
Vict'ry's in store; but what e're the score,
Our men will ever fight, fight, fight, fight.
Shoulder to shoulder, they march along--
Men with a purpose true.
Playing the game for the honor and fame
of North Texas State and you.
Words and Music by Francis Stroup

University of Texas
Austin, TX 78712

School Nickname: *UT*

School Colors: *Burnt Orange and White*

School Mascot: *Texas Longhorn* Name: *Bevo*

School Newspaper: *Daily Texan*

School Yearbook: *Cactus*

University of Texas at Arlington
Arlington, TX 76019

School Nickname: *UTA*

School Colors: *Orange and White* (*Athletic Colors: Blue and White*)

School Mascot: *Maverick*

School Newspaper: *The Shorthorn*

School Yearbook: *The Reveille (last published in 1982)*

Alma Mater: *Alma Mater*

> Dear School we love,
> You are our Alma Mater,
> And Through the years
> Our Faith we shall proclaim.
>
> We are each one,
> A loyal son or daughter
> Our song of praise
> Shall glorify your name.
> Dear school we love,
> Forever, Arlington.

Fight Song: *Fight Song*

> M-A-V-E-R-I-C-K
> M-A-V-E-R-I-C-K
> M-A-V-E-R-I-C-K
> Mavericks, Mavericks
> Fight! Fight! Fight!

University of Texas at Dallas
Richardson, TX 75083-0688

School Colors: *Orange and Green*

School Newspaper: *UTD Mercury*

University of Texas at El Paso
El Paso, TX 79968

School Nickname: *UTEP*

School Colors: *Orange, White and Columbia Blue*

School Mascot: *Paydirt Pete*

School Newspaper: *The Prospector*

School Yearbook: *Dzong-La "The Fortress at the Pass"*

University of Texas at San Antonio
6900 Loop 1604 W.
San Antonio, TX 78285

School Nickname: *UTSA*

School Colors: *Orange, Navy Blue and White*

School Mascot: *Roadrunner*

School Newspaper: *The Roadrunner*

Alma Mater: *Hail UTSA*

> From our hills of oak and cedar
> To the Alamo,
> Voices raised will echo
> As, in song, our praises flow.
> Hail Alma Mater!
> Through the years our loyalty will grow.
> The University of Texas -- San Antonio.
> > *Words by Allen E. Craven*
> > *Music by Clarence J. Stuessy*

West Texas State University
Canyon, TX 79016

School Nickname: *Buffaloes; Buffs*

School Colors: *Maroon and White*

School Mascot: *Buffalo* Name: *Ladee*

School Newspaper: *The Prairie*

School Yearbook: *Le Mirage*

Alma Mater: *Alma Mater*

> Over boundless reach of prairie,
> Over rolling plain,
> Over cliff and crag and canyon,
> Alma Mater reigns.
> To maroon and white, our colors,
> We will faithful be;
> Hearts as bold as western breezes,
> Souls as pure and free.
>
> Round the image, Alma Mater,
> Hallowed memories twine;
> Bless the sacred ties of friendship,
> Pledged before thy shrine.

Alma Mater! Alma Mater!
We will faithful be,
Through the years that lie before us,
We'll remember thee!

Fight Song: *The Buffalo Fight Song*

On, On, Buffaloes,
We are right for the fight tonight.
Hold that ball and hit that line;
Every Buffalo will shine,
And then we'll Fight
For maroon and white,
And we'll roar for that old Varsity.
We will kick, pass and run
Til those (opponent's name) are done,
And we'll bring home the Victory!

UTAH

Brigham Young University
Provo, UT 84602

School Nickname: *BYU or "Y"*

School Colors: *Blue and White*

School Mascot: *Cosmo the Cougar*

School Newspaper: *The Daily Universe*

School Yearbook: *The Banyan*

Alma Mater: *College Song*

> All Hail the College that we love
> At the throne, the throne of wisdom's sway.
> O let us lift our songs above
> The thronging multitude today.
> No pride nor riches here may sue,
> The head, the heart, the hand, united must be true.
> Be true to thee our white and blue.
> When they join our happy band.

Chorus
Then cheer anew for BYU
We've come to work, to live to do.
We'll raise our standard, bear it through.
Our hearts are true, to the BYU

We are met this special morning
Greeting friends both old and new
And remembering happy times together
In the years we spent at BYU
College Hall-Room D-were meeting places,
Hearts beat faster-and-we studied too.
We are proud to grace these halls of learning
As alumni of BYU

Proms and hops and matinee dances
All were held at Ladies Gym
Social units vied for recognition
Destinies-Our guests would soon begin.
Football games were scored as moral victories,
We were loyal to dear old White and Blue.
Thuough the years we've cherished all these memories
As Alumni of BYU
                    Words by Merrill McDonald

Fight Song: *Alma Mater*

We praise our Alma Mater, our Alma Mammy, too.
We cheer for Yale and Harvard, with boola, boola, boo.
You've heard the "Sons of Utah" with A.C. anthems sung.
So here's a song we offer, at the shrine of Brigham Young.
                    Chorus
Our Alma Mater, for you we're fighting
To hear our Cougars scream victory.
His fangs are dripping with blood of battle,
Come on we'll FIGHT, FIGHT, FIGHT for thee.

It's in your honor we cheer our warriors,
Our songs are ringing, our banners flung.
We're sons of Brigham, united ever,
To fight for Brigham Young.
                    Words by Glenn S. Potter
                    Music by Walt Daniels

University of Utah
Salt Lake City, UT 84112

School Nickname: *The Utes*

School Colors: *Red and White*

School Mascot: *Ute Indian*

School Newspaper: *The Daily Utah Chronicle*

Fight Song: *Utah Man*

> I am a Utah man sir and I live across the green,
> Our gang it is the jolliest that you have ever seen.
> Our coeds are the fairest and each one's a shining star,
> Our yell you hear it ringing through the mountains near and far.
>
> Up to snuff, we never bluff, we're game for any fuss
> No other gang of college men dare meet us in the muss.
> So fill your lungs and sing it out and shout it to the sky,
> We'll fight for dear ol' crimson for a Utah man am I.
> *Chorus*
> Who am I sir? A Utah man am I,
> A UTAH man, and will be till I die, Ki Yi!

Utah State University
Logan, UT 84322

School Nickname: *USU*

School Colors: *Navy Blue and White*

School Mascot: *Aggies*

School Newspaper: *Statesman*

School Yearbook: *Buzzer (ceased publication)*

Alma Mater: *Alma Mater Hymn*

> Across the quad at eventide as shadows softly fall,
> The tower of Old Main appears and peace rests over all.
> The lighted "A" upon the hill stands out against the blue;
> Oh, Alma Mater, USU, my heart sings out to you.
>
> And through the years as time rolls on and student friendships grow,
> We'll ne'er forget the joys we had, those days we used to know,
> Thy mem'ries ever will be new, thy friends be ever true.
> Oh, Alma Mater, USU, my heart sings out to you.
> *Composed by Theodore M. Burton*

Fight Song: *Hail the Utah Aggies*

> Hail the Utah Aggies
> We'll play the game with all our might
> See the colors flying,
> The azure blue and tender white
> How they stir us onward
> We'll win the victory all right,
> Hail the Utah Aggies
> We're out to win so fight fight fight.

Weber State College
375 Harrison Blvd.
Ogden, UT 84408

School Nickname: *Wildcats*

School Colors: *Purple and White*

School Mascot: *Waldo Wildcat*

School Newspaper: *Signpost*

Alma Mater: *Purple and White*

> Proudly waving o'er ole Weber
> An Ensign of truth and right
> The flag I love, it waves above.
> I love it with all my might.
> Oh, royalty lies in its purple,
> And purity in its white.
> A king I'll be, if true to thee,
> And dare to do the right.
>
> I will e'er be true, O Weber
> To thy virtue high and rare,
> I will adore forever more..
> Thy name forever bear.
> So here's to thee, Alma Mater,
> For thy glory and thy might.
> Thy flag shall be the flag for me,
> Forever the purple and white!
> > *Chorus*
> Oh, I'll be true to thee, O purple and white!
> And I will stand by thee in any fight:
> For truth and right will always be
> Close by thee, O flag!
> All thy children honor thee,

Honor thine forever be.
Thou are mine forever,
Purple and white!

Fight Song: *We are the Wildcats*

We are the Wildcats...Scratching, Snarling
We're going to win this game.
Upward and onward fighting wildcats
With pride and honor on to fame.

We'll never quit 'til we have won
Our purple and white will reign.
We will scratch and snarl and show we rate
'Cause we are Weber State, Weber State..Great Great Great!!

VERMONT

University of Vermont
Burlington, VT 05405

School Nickname: *UVM*

School Colors: *Green and Gold*

School Mascot: *Catamount*

School Newspaper: *Cynic*

School Yearbook: *Ariel*

VIRGINIA

College of William and Mary
Williamsburg, VA 23185

School Nickname: *W&M*

School Colors: *Green, Gold and Silver*

School Mascot: *Indians, Tribe*

School Newspaper: *The Flat Hat*

School Yearbook: *The Colonial Echo*

Alma Mater: *Alma Mater*

>Hark the students' voices swelling,
>Strong and true and clear
>Alma Mater's love they're telling
>Ringing far and near.
>
>All thy sons are faithful to thee
>Through their college days;
>Singing loud from hearts that love thee
>Alma Mater's praise.

330 / GEORGE MASON UNIVERSITY

Iron shod or golden sandaled
Shall the years go by-
Still our hearts shall weave about thee
Love that cannot die.

God, our father, hear thy voices
Listen to thy cry
Bless the college of our fathers
Let her never die.
> *Chorus*
William and Mary loved of old
Hark, upon the gale,
Hear the thunder of our chorus
Alma Mater hail!
> *James Southall Wilson, '02*

Fight Song: *Tribe Fight Song*

Oh, we will fight fight fight for the Indians
When the Big Green team appears.
We will yell like hell for the Indians
And they will heed our mighty cheers.
We will lead our team on to victory
And give a shout for the Indians bold
We'll have a Touchdown, Touchdown, Indians!
And raise the Green and Gold!

George Mason University
Fairfax, VA 22030

School Nickname: *Patriots*

School Colors: *Green and Gold*

School Mascot: *Patriot*

School Newspaper: *Broadside*

School Yearbook: *By George!*

Hampton University
Hampton, VA 23668

School Nickname: *HU*

School Colors: *Blue and White*

School Mascot: *Pirate*

School Newspaper: *Script*

School Yearbook: *Hamptonian*

Alma Mater: *Alma Mater*

> O Hampton, a thought sent from heaven above,
> To be a great soul's inspiration;
> We sing thee the earnest of broad human love,
> The shrine of our heart's adoration.
> Thy foundation firm and thy roof tree outspread,
> And thy sacred alter fires burning;
> The sea circling 'round thee, soft skies overhead,
> Dear Hampton, the goal of our yearning!
> > *Refrain*
> O Hampton, we never can make thee a song,
> Except as our lives do the singing;
> In service that will thy great spirit prolong,
> And send it through centuries ringing!
>
> Kind mother, we'll treasure the dear happy days,
> We've spent here in life's preparation;
> Yet go with brave hearts upon our chosen ways,
> Of service to God and our nation;
> Still wearing our colors, the blue and the white,
> As pledge that our fond hearts will cherish;
> A love which for thee ever shines true and bright,
> A loyalty that ne'er can perish!
> > *Words by Sarah Collins Fernandis, 1882*
> > *Music by Chauncey Northern, '24*

James Madison University
Harrisonburg, VA 22807

School Nickname: *The Dukes*

School Colors: *Purple and Gold*

School Mascot: *Bulldog*   Name: *Duke Dog*

School Newspaper: *The Breeze*

School Yearbook: *The Bluestone*

Alma Mater: *Alma Mater*

Madison, James Madison, we'll stay forever true
Our loyalty will always be to JMU.
While friends remain within our hearts and knowledge guides
our way.
James Madison will lead us on to conquer each new day.
James R. Riley

Norfolk State University
Norfolk, VA 23504

School Nickname: *Spartans*

School Colors: *Green and Gold*

School Mascot: *Spartan Warrior*

School Newspaper: *The Spartan Echo*

School Yearbook: *Spartan Reflections*

Alma Mater: *Alma Mater*

By Virginia's golden shore,
There's a place that we adore
Where Norfolk's sun shines bright
Down on our campus site.
The walls of Brown Hall
Will always give a call
To all striving to succeed,
Forging onward, bound to lead.

Though the years we spend are few
You will teach us what to do.
In splendor we'll relive
The glorious time you give.
We'll wave the green and gold
To praise thee a thousand-fold.
A guiding light to us you've been
Unwav'ring to the end.
Chorus
Oh, Norfolk State we love you.
Oh, Norfolk State we'll always be true.
And when we leave we'll shed a tear,
For to us you've been so dear.
And leaving shed a joyful tear,
For our Alma Mater dear.
Words and Music by Carl W. Haywood

Fight Song: *Fight Song*

> Say Yeah!!! for the VIC-TO-RY
> That's sure to be
> For NSU we're here to fight
> And we will fight for!!!
> The GREEN and GOLD our Alma Mater
> We pledge our loyalty
> Say Yeah!!! (Yeah) for VIC-TO-RY
> Say Yeah!!! YEAH!!! YEAH!!!
> For NSU, we'll fight
> Fight team
> Fight on
> To VIC-TO-RY for N-S-U.
> > *Words and Music by Paul Adams*

Old Dominion University
Norfolk, VA 23529

School Nickname: *ODU*

School Colors: *Blue and Silver*

School Mascot: *Monarchs (symbolized as a lion)*

School Newspaper: *The Mace and Crown*

School Yearbook: *Troubadour*

Alma Mater: *Hail Alma Mater*

> Hail to thee our Alma Mater
> blue and silver, all hail!
> By the ocean's billows flying
> see them proudly sail.
> University, young and strong,
> we lift our voices in this song
> this our song of alma mater
> Old Dominion Hail!
> > *Robert Jager*

Radford University
Radford, VA 24142

School Nickname: *Highlanders*

School Colors: *Red, Blue, White and Green*

School Mascot: *Rowdy Red*

School Newspaper: *The Tartan*

School Yearbook: *The Beehive*

Alma Mater: *Alma Mater*

> Hail, all hail! to our Alma Mater,
> Bare our heads, make the welkin ring;
> Her's our hearts and our fond allegiance,
> Honors to her we bring.
> Praise her broad and her lofty aim,
> Her purpose ne'er will fail.
> Hail to thee, our Alma Mater, Hail, all Hail!
> Hail, all hail! to Radford University
> Give three cheers and then one cheer more;
> Let the praise of our Alma Mater Echo from shore to shore.
> She is ours, and our loyalty will never , never fail.
> Hail to thee, our Alma Mater, Hail, all Hail!

University of Richmond
Richmond, VA 23173

School Nickname: *Spiders*

School Colors: *Red and Blue*

School Mascot: *Spider*

School Newspaper: *The Collegian*

School Yearbook: *The Web*

Alma Mater: *Alma Mater*

> Mid the pines and rolling hills
> Stand the halls we cheer;
> Hallow'd place our mem'ry fills:
> Alma Mater dear.
> Hail to thee,
> Hail to thee,
> Hail to Red and Blue
> To thy hallow'd memory
> May we e'er be true.

Alma Mater, gracious name;
We thy children praise;
Home of honor, worth and fame
Love we all our days.
Hail to thee,
Hail to thee,
Hail to Red and Blue
To thy hallow'd memory
May we e'er be true.

Fight Song: *Spider Born*

I'm spider born and spider bred
And when I die I'll be spider dead,
So, 'Ray, 'ray for Richmond, Richmond,
'Ray, 'ray for Richmond, Richmond
'Ray, 'ray for Richmond,
'Ray, 'ray, 'ray!

The Spiders are all out today
And with this game they're gonna walk away,
So, 'Ray, 'ray for Richmond, Richmond,
'Ray, 'ray for Richmond, Richmond,
'Ray, 'ray for Richmond,
'Ray, 'ray, 'ray!

University of Virginia
Charlottesville, VA 22903

School Nickname: *U Va.*

School Colors: *Orange and Blue*

School Mascot: *Cavalier*

School Newspaper: *The Cavalier Daily and The University Journal*

School Yearbook: *Corks and Curls*

Virginia Commonwealth University
Richmond, VA 23284-0001

School Colors: *Black and Gold*

School Mascot: *Ram*

School Newspaper: *VCU Today and Commonwealth Times*

Virginia Polytechnic Institute & State University
Blacksburg, VA 24061

School Nickname: *Virginia Tech*

School Colors: *Chicago Maroon and Burnt Orange*

School Mascot: *Virginia Tech Hokie*

School Newspaper: *Collegiate Times*

School Yearbook: *Bugle*

Alma Mater: *Alma Mater*

> Sing praise to Alma Mater dear,
> For V.P.I. we'll ever cheer;
> Come lift your voices, swell the song
> Our loyalties to her belong.
> *Chorus*
> So stand and sing, all hail to thee.
> V.P., all hail to thee.
>
> The Orange and Maroon you see,
> That's fighting on to victory;
> Our strife will not be long this day,
> For glory lies within this fray.
>
> All Loyal sons of V.P.I.
> We raise our banner to the sky;
> Our motto brings a spirit true,
> That we may ever serve for you.

Fight Song: *Tech Triumph*

> Techmen, we're Techmen, with spirit true and faithful
> Backing up our teams with hopes undying;
> Techmen, O Techmen, we're out to win today.
> Showing pep and life with which we're trying.
> VP, old VP, you know our hearts are with you
> In our luck that never seems to die;
> Win or lose, we'll greet you with a glad returning--
> You're the pride to VPI.
> *Chorus*
> Just watch our men, so big and active,
> Support the Orange and Maroon. Let's go, Tech.

We know our ends and backs are stronger
With winning hopes we fear defeat no longer.
To see our team plow through the line, boys,
Determined now to win or die; so give a
Hokie, Hokie, Hokie, Hi--
Rae Ri, old VPI.

WASHINGTON

Central Washington University
Ellensburg, WA 98926

School Nickname: *Wildcats*

School Colors: *Crimson and Black*

School Mascot: *Wildcat*

School Newspaper: *Observer*

School Yearbook: *Hayakem (no longer published)*

Eastern Washington University
Cheney, WA 99004

School Colors: *Red and White*

School Mascot: *Eastern Eagle*

School Newspaper: *The Easterner*

School Yearbook: *Aquila*

Alma Mater: *Alma Mater*

All hail to Eastern Washington,
Thy colors red and white!
You stand as a symbol,
Of our strength and might!
All hail to Eastern Washington,
A leader brave and true!
We sing the praise of college days,
All hail to you!
                George W. Lotzenhiser

Pacific Lutheran University
Tacoma, WA 98447

School Colors: *Black and Gold*

School Newspaper: *The Mast*

School Yearbook: *SAGA*

Alma Mater: *Alma Mater*

> 'Neath lofty trees and mountain grand
> A blessed place she firmly stands.
> Alma Mater P.L.U.
> That she may grow in strength and name.
> Live and rule without disdain,
> Forever may our hearts be true
> To Alma Mater P.L.U.

Fight Song: *PLU Fight Song*

> PLC your students hail thee
> As queen of all the land
> Where students all are carefree
> And for thine honor stand
> May the light be ever glorious
> And always to the end
> Reign o'er all victorious
> Our alma mater friend.
>
> Come join our band
> We'll give a cheer for PLC
> Down through the years
> We'll sing our song of victory
> Pacific for you
> Each loyal comrade, brave and true
> With might and main
> Sing this refrain
> Forever and forever PLC.

Seattle University
Seattle, WA 98122

School Nickname: *Chieftans*

School Colors: *Scarlet and White*

School Newspaper: *Spectator*

School Yearbook: *Aegis (no longer published)*

University of Puget Sound
Tacoma, WA 98416

School Nickname: *Loggers*

School Colors: *Maroon and White (Academic) Green and Gold (Athletic)*

School Mascot: *Logger*

School Newspaper: *The Puget Sound Trail*

School Yearbook: *Tamanawas*

Alma Mater: *Alma Mater*

> All hail to Alma Mater,
> The best that can be found,
> The spirit of the westland,
> All hail to Puget Sound.
> Her guardian is the mountain
> Beside the silver sea;
> All hail to Alma Mater,
> All hail, all hail to thee.

Fight Song: *Fight Song*

> Fight, Fight, Fight for UPS, boys,
> Fight, fight, fight for Puget Sound
> Pull together,
> Courage ever,
> On to victory bound.
> Fight, fight, fight for UPS, boys,
> Let your colors fly.
> Rah, rah, we are the best.
> Triumphant to the test.
> UPS, let's do or die.

University of Washington
Seattle, WA 98195

School Nickname: *UW, "U-DUB"*

School Colors: *Purple and Gold*

School Mascot: *Husky*

School Newspaper: *The Daily*

School Yearbook: *Tyee*

Alma Mater: *Alma Mater*

> To her we sing who keeps the ward
> O'er all her sons from sea to sea,
> Our Alma Mater, Washington!
> A health! a health! we give to thee!
> Child of the mighty western land,
> You're the mother of a mighty race,
> Silent her gentle vigil holds in strength,
> purity and grace.
> > *Chorus*
> All hail! O Washington!
> Thy sons and daughters sing glad acclaim,
> Through years of youth and loyalty;
> And still in age we sing thy fame.
> In honor thy towers stand,
> Thy battlements shine in dawning light,
> And glow again in sunset rays
> All hail! O Washington!
> > *Words by Riley Allen, '03*
> > *Music by George Hager, '09*

Fight Songs: *Bow Down to Washington*

> Bow down to Washington, Bow down to Washington
> Mighty are the men who wear the Purple and the Gold,
> Joyfully we welcome them within the victor's fold.
> We will carve our name in the Hall of Fame
> To preserve the memory of our devotion.
> Heaven help the foes of Washington;
> They're trembling at the feet of mighty Washington.
> The boys are there with bells,
> Their fighting blood excels,
> It's harder to push them over the line
> Than pass the Dardanelles.
> Victory! The cry of Washington.

Leather lungs together with a Rah! Rah! Rah!
And o'er the land our joyous band
Will sing the glory of Washington for ever.
Words and Music by Lester J. Wilson, '13

Vict'ry For Washington

HAIL HUSKY, once again the band is playing, for husky conquest.
HAIL HUSKY, as the cheering crowd is swaying,
Chanting again the fighting refrain for vict'ry.
FIGHT! FIGHT! FIGHT! for WASHINGTON! RAH!
Vict'ry for Washington, for the purple and the gold.
Vict'ry for Washington hear the husky cry of old to win.
The husky pack is fighting on again, hear the loyal rooters sing
With vict'ry for Washington Alma Mater shall ring.
Words by Tom Herbert. '36
Music by George Larson, '37
Reprinted with permission of the Univ. of Wash.

Washington State University
Pullman, WA 99164

School Nickname: *Cougars*

School Colors: *Crimson and Gray*

School Mascot: *Butch*

School Newspaper: *Daily Evergreen*

School Yearbook: *Chinook*

Alma Mater: *Washington, My Washington*

Washington, my Washington,
The Crimson and the Gray!
'Tis the songs of memory
That we sing today.
When the sad hours come to you,
And sorrows 'round you play,
Just sing the songs of Washington,
The Crimson and the Gray,
Just sing the songs of Washington,
The Crimson and the Gray.
Words and Music by J.De Forest Cline

Fight Song: *The Fight Song*

Fight, fight, fight for Washington State!
Win the victory
Win the day for Crimson and Gray!
Best in the West, we know you'll all do your best,
So on, on, on, on! Fight to the end!
Honor and Glory you must win!
So fight, fight, fight for Washington State and Victory!
Words by Zella Melcher, '19
Music by Phyllis Sayles, '19

Western Washington University
Bellingham, WA 98225

School Nickname: *Vikings*

School Colors: *Blue and White*

School Newspaper: *Western Front*

Alma Mater: *Alma Mater*

Far above the bay's blue waters stands our own Sehome
Guarded all around by mountains, crowned by Baker's dome
Nestling there among the grandeur, reigns the White and Blue.
Colors of our Alma Mater, hail all hail to you.
Here the youth from farm and seashore gather for the year
Learning truths that shall be cherished, forming friendships dear.
Soon the ties must all be severed, but they leave with you,
Happy memories and best wishes for the White and Blue.
Ada Hogle Abbott
Not currently used

Fight Song: *Viking Victory March*

Come join the Vikings
Marching onward beneath the blue and white
With purpose steady
We will safely reach our goal,
And prove the Vikings' might.
Keep marching onward,
We stand united
With a courage undaunted, brave and true,
We'll cheer Western Washington
Until every victory's won,
So Vikings, we're all for you.
Don Walters
Not currently used

WEST VIRGINIA

Fairmont State College
Fairmont, WV 26554

School Nickname: *Fighting Falcons*

School Colors: *Maroon and White*

School Mascot: *Falcon*

School Newspaper: *The Columns*

School Yearbook: *The Mound*

Alma Mater: *Alma Mater*

> Among the hills of time,
> There stands a school so fair,
> As pure as the sky above,
> With all the stars up there,
> And when we bow to thee,
> Dear Fairmont State,
> Our hearts with rapture thrill,
> So here's to the school we love,
> The College 'on the Hill'.

Fight Song: *FSC Fight Song*

> Fairmont State College we love you,
> And to your colors, we'll e'er be true,
> Your colors stand for fighting spirit,
> And this is what they mean,
> Rah Rah for Fairmont College
> Maroon the color of fighters,
> White is for sports pure and clean,
> We fight to win and we love our fellows
> Fairmont State College team.

Marshall University
Huntington, WV 25701

School Nickname: *Thundering Herd*

School Colors: *Green and White*

School Mascot: *Buffalo* Name: *Marco*

School Newspaper: *The Parthenon*

School Yearbook: *The Chief Justice*

Alma Mater: *Marshall Alma Mater*

> Marshall, gracious Alma Mater
> We thy name revere;
> May each noble son and daughter
> Cherish thine honor dear.
> May thy lamp be ever bright
> Guiding us to truth and light;
> As a beacon o'er dark water
> This is for thee our prayer.
>
> May the years be kind to Marshall
> May she grow in fame;
> May her children fail her never,
> True to her beacon flame.
> May her spirit brave and strong,
> Honor right and conquer wrong,
> This is the burden of our song,
> Ever her truth proclaim.

Fight Songs: *Sons of Marshall*

> We are the sons of Marshall
> Sons of the great John Marshall
> Year after year we go to Marshall U.
> Cheering for our team and gaining knowledge, too
> Proudly we wear our colors
> Love and loyalty we share
> Sure from far and near
> You'll always hear
> The wearing of the green
> For it's the Green and White of Marshall U.

Fight On

> Show me a Scotchman
> Who doesn't love a thistle
> Show me an Englishman
> Who doesn't love a rose
> Show me a true-heart
> A son of dear old Marshall
> Who doesn't love to win. Hey!
> M-A-R-S-H-A-L-L
> Fight, Fight for dear old Marshall U.

West Virginia State College
Institute, WV 25112

School Nickname: *Yellow Jackets*

School Colors: *Old Gold and Black*

School Mascot: *Yellow Jacket*

School Newspaper: *The Yellow Jacket*

School Yearbook: *The Arch*

Alma Mater: *Alma Mater of West Virginia State College*

> There is a place we love so dear
> Its name we'll ever praise and revere
> 'Tis West Virginia State we love
> Just one more step from there is heaven above
> West Virginia's praise we'll sing
> Lift our voices 'til heavens ring
> As we gaily march along

We'll sing a song for Alma Mater how we love her
Pride of all our loyal hearts
From her we will never part
Thoughts of thee will ne'er be few
Alma Mater we love you.

We'll love her more as days go by,
And send her praise to the sky;
To place her over all the rest,
And keep her e'er the dearest and the best.

Shadowed 'neath a deep blue sky;
Is State for whom we'll live and we'll die-
Arise! O men of God and sing;
We're loyal. and to her we'll always cling.
                    Ernest Wade, '30
                    Martha Spencer, '31

Fight Song: *Hail To The Team*

Hail to the team boys,
Victory's the goal of our team today.
Hail to ole State girls,
West Virginia'll triumph all along the way.

Hail to the team whose conquering might
Brings fears to all foes they play,
Here's to the colors of Gold and Black
This is our vict'ry day.

Charge 'em, charge 'em, hit'em hard and low.
Onward, onward, goal to goal we go.
Sock'em! Rock'em! Knock'em! Sock'em
RAH! RAH! RAH! RAH!.

Hail to the team boys,
Victory's the goal of our team today.
Hail to ole State girls,
West Virginia'll triumph all along the way.

Hail to the team whose conquering might
Brings fears to all foes they play,
Here's to the colors of Gold and Black
THIS IS OUR VICT'RY DAY. HEY!
                    Words by Fannin S Belcher, '48
                    Music by Joseph W. Grider

West Virginia University
Morgantown, WV 26506

School Nickname: *The Mountaineers*

School Colors: *Old Gold and Blue*

School Mascot: *The Mountaineer*

School Newspaper: *The Daily Athenaeum*

School Yearbook: *Monticola*

Alma Mater: *Alma Mater*

> Alma, our Alma Mater,
> The home of Mountaineers.
> Sing we of thy honor,
> Everlasting through the years.
> Alma, our Alma Mater,
> We pledge in song to you.
> Hail, all hail, our Alma Mater,
> West Virginia "U."

Fight Song: *Fight Song*

> Lets give a rah for West Virginia,
> And let us pledge to her anew.
> Others may like black or crimson,
> But for us it's gold and blue.
> Let all our troubles be forgotten,
> Let college spirit rule,
> We'll join and give our loyal efforts
> For the good of our old school.
>
> It's West Virginia, it's West Virginia,
> The pride of every Mountaineer,
> Come on you old grads, join with us young lads,
> It's West Virginia now we cheer. (rah! rah!)
>
> Now is the time boys to make a big noise
> No matter what people say.
> For there is naught to fear, the gang's all here,
> So hail to West Virginia, Hail!!

WISCONSIN

Marquette University
Milwaukee, WI 53233

School Nickname: *Warriors*

School Colors: *Royal Blue and Gold*

School Mascot: *Bluteaux*

School Newspaper: *Marquette Tribune*

School Yearbook: *Marquette Hilltop*

Alma Mater: *Marquette University Anthem*

> Hail Alma Mater thee we do call.
> We're here to greet thee, Dearest friend to all.
> We're here to show thee our love is strong.
> Hail Alma Mater! Marquette! Hear our song.
> *Words and Music by Liborius Semmann*

Fight Song: *Ring Out Ahoya!*

> Ring out Ahoya with an M. U. Rah Rah,
> M.U. Rah Rah, M.U. Rah Rah Rah Rah Rah

Ring out A hoya with an M. U. Rah, Rah,
M.U. Rah Rah for Old Marquette. Rah! Rah! Rah!
Arr. by Olive Glueckstein, '29

University of Wisconsin-Eau Claire
Eau Claire, WI 54701

School Nickname: *Blugolds*

School Colors: *Blue and Gold*

School Newspaper: *The Spectator*

School Yearbook: *The Periscope*

Alma Mater: *University Hymn*

> Oh School of Eau Claire, our voices we raise;
> Accept thou this anthem of undying praise.
> We pledge to be faithful, stout hearted and strong.
> And cherish thy mem'ry as our lives are long.
>
> Give honor to thee, and sing out thy name.
> Oh college of ours, we dearly acclaim.
> Instill thou within us a feeling of pride.
> We pray Alma Mater forever abide.

University of Wisconsin-Green Bay
Green Bay, WI 54301-7001

School Nickname: *UWGB*

School Colors: *Red, White and Green*

School Mascot: *Phoenix*

School Newspaper: *The Fourth Estate*

Alma Mater: *Alma Mater*

> Let us rise above these waters,
> Men and women of Green Bay.
> Rise in knowledge,
> Rise in wisdom,
> Rise in friendship sealed today.

As the Phoenix rose from flame,
Let us rise and still proclaim,
That we pledge our Alma Mater,
And the memories of her name.

University of Wisconsin-La Crosse
La Crosse, WI 54601

School Nickname: *Indians (men) Roonies (women)*

School Colors: *Maroon and Gray*

School Newspaper: *Racquet*

School Yearbook: *La Crosse*

Alma Mater: *Alma Mater*

Morning sun greets many banners on its westward way,
Fair to us above all others waves maroon and gray.
Colors dear, flag we love, float for aye, Old La Crosse to thee.
May your sons for e'er be loyal, to thy memory.

Fight Song: *La Crosse*

We're going to cheer, La Crosse,
Because we're here, La Crosse,
Let us make it clear.
We're going to fight, La Crosse,
With all our might, La Crosse,
Victory is near.
So let's dig in, La Crosse,
We're going to win, La Crosse,
Go Maroon and Grey.
We're going to fight, win,
Show that we're the best
Because we are La Crosse, La Crosse.
Words and Music by Joyce Grill
Copyright Joyce Grill, 1987

University of Wisconsin-Madison
Madison, WI 53706

School Nickname: *Badgers*

School Colors: *Cardinal Red and White*

School Mascot: *Bucky Badger*

School Newspaper: *Daily Cardinal and Badger Herald*

School Yearbook: *Badger Yearbook*

Alma Mater: *Alma Mater*

> Varsity, varsity
> U-rah-rah Wisconsin
> Praise to thee, we sing
> Praise to thee, our alma mater
> U-rah-rah, Wisconsin.

Fight Song: *Fight Song*

> "On Wisconsin! On Wisconsin!
> Plunge right through that line!
> Run the ball clear down the field,
> A touchdown sure this time.
> On Wisconsin! On Wisconsin!
> Fight on for her face--
> Fight, fellows, fight, fight, fight,
> We'll win this game."

University of Wisconsin-Milwaukee
Box 413
Milwaukee, WI 53201

School Nickname: *UWM*

School Colors: *Black and Gold*

School Mascot: *Panther* Name: *Victor E. Panther*

School Newspaper: *The UWM Post*

Alma Mater: *UWM Alma Mater*

> To Thee we give allegiance,
> to you UWM
> To Thee we sing our praises
> as we gather here again-
>
> Alma Mater hail to thee
> our university
> Our loyalty to Black and Gold
> we remember from days of old.

To Thee we give allegiance
to UWM
To Thee we turn our hearts and voices
UWM
To Thee we turn our hearts and voices
UWM.

Copyright Ralph Hermann, '65

Fight Song: UWM Fight Song

Fight-Fight-Fight for UWM
Fight to the end,
Win it again
Fight-Fight-Fight for the Black and Gold
Our teams brave and bold
To victory we'll hold
Fight-Fight-Fight for UWM
Fight for her fame
We'll win this game
And when the panther on the prowl
gives a howl and a growl
We'll Fight-Fight-for UWM.

Copyright Ralph Hermann, '65

University of Wisconsin-Parkside
Kenosha, WI 53141

School Nickname: *Rangers*

School Colors: *Green, White and Black*

School Mascot: *Ranger Bear*

School Newspaper: *Parkside Ranger*

Fight Song: *Parkside Fight Song*

Parkside Rangers hats off to thee,
Brave and strong united are we,
Heads held high with spirit and pride,
Never daunted ever onward
Green and White will show us the way,
Banners flying triumph today,
So fight and fight to show your might
And lead us to victory,
Rah, Rah, Rah.

Wegner-Thomason

University of Wisconsin-Platteville
Platteville, WI 53818

School Nickname: *Pioneers*

School Colors: *Orange and Blue*

School Mascot: *Pioneer Pete*

School Newspaper: *The Exponent*

School Yearbook: *Pioneer*

Alma Mater: *Alma Mater*

> Alma Mater grand and glorious
> we shall ever be victorious.
> Loyal are we to dear Platteville
> Pioneers we'll be.
> We shall win her honor.
> Praise be ever on her.
> Onward, upward to the fore,
> none shall falter evermore.
> Alma Mater grand and glorious
> wrought by loyalty.

Fight Song: *Fight Song*

> Come on you Pioneers of Platteville.
> Come on you sons of orange and blue.
> We are with you one and all,
> Men of Platteville strong and tall.
> You're the best team, we're for you.
> Come on you Pioneers of Platteville.
> Come on our heroes all by name.
> We will Fight! Fight! Fight!
> With all our might
> And we'll win, win this game.

University of Wisconsin-River Falls
River Falls, WI 54022

School Colors: *Red and White*

School Mascot: *Falcon*

School Newspaper: *Student Voice*

School Yearbook: *Meletean (ceased publication)*

Alma Mater: *Alma Mater*

> To thee River Falls we pledge all our love
> And to thy banner floating above
> May we in passing, add just a gem
> To shine forever in thy diadem.

University of Wisconsin-Stevens Point
Stevens Point, WI 54481

School Colors: *Purple and Gold*

School Mascot: *Pointer Dogs* Names: *Stevie and Stephanie*

School Newspaper: *The Pointer*

School Yearbook: *Horizon*

Alma Mater: *The Purple and The Gold*

> Other schools of valor boast,
> Of victories galore,
> Of laurels never lost,
> Of triumphs by the score;
>
> Let them tell you of their prowess,
> Of warriors strong and bold,
> But their colors ever lower
> To the Purple and the Gold.

Fight Song: *On, On Stevens Point*

> On, On Stevens Point!
> We are ripe for the fight tonight,
> Get that ball and toe that line,
> Every Pointer star will shine,
> So fight, fight, fight!
>
> For the team that's right,
> As we cheer on our ole' Varsity,
> We will kick, pass and run
> 'till the battle is won,
> And we'll bring home a victory!
> GO POINT!

University of Wisconsin-Stout
Minomonie, WI 54751

School Nickname: *Blue Devils*

School Colors: *Blue and White*

School Mascot: *The Blue Devil*

School Newspaper: *Stoutonia*

School Yearbook: *The Tower*

Alma Mater: *Alma Mater to the Stout Institute*

> On the Banks of Lake Menomin,
> Stands Alma Mater true, with Tower
> high and brilliant "S" for her we'll
> dare and do. We'll sing her praises
> many, We'll glorify her name, and
> on thro'out the years of time, our
> love for Stout proclaim.

Fight Song: School Fight Song

> Stand for our team.
> For Stout we'll fight evermore.
> And while we're fighting, we're cheering,
> We're piling up a mighty score.
> U! Rah! Rah!
> Raise high our flag,
> The ever valiant blue and white
> For Alma Mater true,
> For Stout we'll fight! Fight! Fight!

University of Wisconsin-Whitewater
Whitewater, WI 53190

School Nickname: *Warhawks*

School Colors: *Purple and White*

School Mascot: *Willie Warhawk*

School Newspaper: *Royal Purple*

School Yearbook: *Minneiska*

Alma Mater: *Whitewater Alma Mater*

Hark the strains of our Alma Mater,
Fill our hearts with loyal thoughts and true;
The purple and the white stand firmly for the right,
Hail the scenes of our college campus
Hail our gone mem'ries thrilling us
Alma Mater! Alma Mater! Alma Mater! Whitewater!

WYOMING

University of Wyoming
Laramie, WY 82071

School Nickname: *Cowboys*

School Colors: *Brown and Gold*

School Mascot: *Cowboy Joe*

School Newspaper: *Branding Iron*

School Yearbook: *WYO*

Alma Mater: *Alma Mater*

> Where the western lights' long shadows
> Over boundless prairies fling
> And the mountain winds are vocal
> With thy dear name, Wyoming.
> There it is the Brown and Yellow
> Floats in loving loyalty,
> And the College throws its portals
> Open wide to all men free.

Refrain
And so our songs we bring.
Our Alma Mater sing,
To her our hearts shall cling,
Shall cling forever more.

Yonder we can see it standing,
Circled by purple hills,
While the flaming fire of sunset
Every western window fills;
'Tis the College! Ah, we know it!
Shrine of many joys and tears,
And the rays that light upon it
Are prophetic of its years.

Fight Song: *Cowboy Joe*

SCHOOL NAME INDEX

SCHOOL COLOR INDEX

SCHOOL MASCOT INDEX

About the Compilers

LINDA SPARKS is Associate Librarian at the University of Florida, Gainesville.

BRUCE EMERTON is Assistant Librarian at California State Polytechnic University, Pomona.